'By focusing on the nature of remembrance at sites located within Germany, *Encountering Nazi Tourism Sites* lends a fresh perspective to the emerging study of tourism that commemorates the victims and exposes the perpetrators of the Holocaust. Derek Dalton recalls both the immense bureaucratic apparatus that made mass murder possible, as well as the considerable challenges facing the institutions charged with presenting this difficult history to subsequent generations. His engaging prose recalls both infamous and more obscure locations on the itinerary of Holocaust tourism, showing how each conveys unique lessons – and runs particular risks – in efforts to educate visitors about the nature of state-sponsored brutality.'

—**Professor Daniel P. Reynolds**, *Grinnell College, Iowa, USA*

'With his incisive new study, *Encountering Nazi Tourism Sites*, Derek Dalton once again pushes the boundaries of dark tourism scholarship, highlighting his unique criminological contributions to an evolving field. In his meticulous and eloquent book, he traverses multiple memorial sites, capturing their diversity, and unpacking their challenges, achievements and limitations with staggering clarity. In doing so, *Encountering Nazi Tourism Sites* eschews simple interpretations of Holocaust tourism and memorialisation, instead offering the reader bold encouragement to think beyond accepted accounts to provide a sweeping scrutiny of complex encounters. This essential book will move the reader with its sensitive analysis of the links between memorials and the foundations of remembrance that at their heart carry the terrible weight of death. Derek Dalton never loses sight of this significance, it drives his inquiry and is an issue carefully balanced throughout the pages of this extraordinary book. This is a searching, compelling and perceptive study of a difficult subject.'

—**Rebecca Scott Bray**, *Associate Professor of Criminology and Socio-Legal Studies, University of Sydney, Australia*

Encountering Nazi Tourism Sites

Encountering Nazi Tourism Sites explores how the terrible legacy of Nazi criminality is experienced by tourists, bridging the gap between cultural criminology and tourism studies to make a significant contribution to our understanding of how Nazi criminality is evoked and invoked in the landscape of modern Germany.

This study is grounded in fieldwork encounters with memorials, museums and perpetrator sites across Germany and the Netherlands, including Berlin Holocaust memorials and museums, the Anne Frank House, the Wannsee House, Wewelsburg Castle and concentration camps. At the core of this research is a respect for each site's unique physical, architectural or curatorial form and how this enables insights into different aspects of the Holocaust. Chapters grapple with themes of authenticity, empathy, voyeurism and vicarious experience to better comprehend the possibilities and limits of affective encounters at these sites.

This will be of great interest to upper level students and researchers of criminology, Holocaust studies, museology, tourism studies, memorialisation studies and the burgeoning field of 'difficult' heritage.

Derek Dalton is an Associate Professor conducting research into gay hate homicide, the representation of homosexuality in popular culture, and crime-themed tourism and memorialisation. He lives in South Australia, loves dogs and going to the cinema to see arthouse films.

Routledge Advances in Tourism
Edited by Stephen Page

For more information about this series, please visit: www.routledge.com/advances-in-tourism/book-series/SE0538

Encountering Nazi Tourism Sites

Derek Dalton

Routledge
Taylor & Francis Group

LONDON AND NEW YORK

First published 2020 by Routledge

2 Park Square, Milton Park, Abingdon, Oxon OX14 4RN

605 Third Avenue, New York, NY 10017

Routledge is an imprint of the Taylor & Francis Group, an informa business

First issued in paperback 2022

Publisher's Note

The publisher has gone to great lengths to ensure the quality of this reprint but points out that some imperfections in the original copies may be apparent.

British Library Cataloguing-in-Publication Data
A catalogue record for this book is available from the British Library

Library of Congress Cataloging-in-Publication Data
A catalog record has been requested for this book

ISBN: 978-1-138-09733-9 (hbk)
ISBN: 978-1-03-233816-3 (pbk)
DOI: 10.4324/9781315104935

Typeset in Times New Roman
by Apex CoVantage, LLC

This book is dedicated to William Cooper.

On a warm summer evening on 6 December 1938, the secretary of the Australian Aborigines League (AAL), William Cooper (a seventy-seven-year-old Yorta Yorta man), led a delegation to protest the murderous violence of Kristallnacht (night of broken glass) which had occurred about a month earlier in Germany.

William and a small group of family and AAL supporters walked ten kilometres from Footscray to the German Consulate in South Melbourne. He intended to deliver a letter that fervently protested the cruel and barbaric persecution of the Jewish people by the Nazi government.

Upon reaching the Consulate, the group was not admitted inside and the Consul General refused to take delivery of the letter. It was surrendered to a guard who, presumedly, disposed of it.

The National Museum of Australia credits William Cooper's actions as the only protest of its kind in the world.

I honour the empathetic vision and courage of this great man who, half a world away, learned of the pogrom and chose to respond by condemning anti-Semitic violence and calling for it to end.

Contents

Figures

Note* All photographs taken by Derek Dalton unless otherwise attributed below:

7.5   Rebecca Scott Bray
7.7–7.10   Official photographs of *Places of Remembrance* as
            supplied by the artists Renata Stih & Frieder Schnock

Photograph permissions

2.2–2.3   Kay-Uwe von Damaros, courtesy of Topography of Terror Foundation
3.2–3.13   Kirsten John-Stucke, courtesy of KriesMuseum, Wewelsburg
5.2–5.8   Stephanie Billib, courtesy of Gedenkstätte Bergen-Belsen
6.2, 6.4–6.8   Valeska Wolfgram, courtesy of Stiftung Jüdisches Museum Berlin
7.7–7.10   Bruno Ferttig, courtesy of Renata Stih & Frieder Schnock

Acknowledgements

After some pestering and initial resistance, my grandmother, Kitty, bought me Martin Gilbert's *Final journey: the fate of the Jews in Nazi Europe* when I was thirteen years old. I thank her for giving in to my persistent requests. Immersing myself in its pages was a confronting awakening to the reality of the genocide that has come to also be known as the Shoah or Holocaust. Over the years, my interest did not wane. Rather, it was rekindled by exposure to new biographies, novels, history books, documentaries and feature films devoted to the Holocaust.

My interest in the Holocaust sometimes feels like an intrusion, despite the fact I have lectured about the Holocaust and its memorialisation for more than ten years. I am not Jewish. I didn't lose any relatives in the camps. I don't claim any inherent right to speak on behalf of those who perished. These caveats aside, I take solace in the reminder that:

> It is . . . important to note that the study of the Holocaust has now passed beyond the confines of Jewish studies or as a sector of German studies and has become a problem of general concern. One need provide no autobiographical or other particular motivation to account for one's interest in it and the important consideration is what results from that interest.
>
> (LaCapra 1998, p. 22)

This book results from *my* interest and I hope it is judged a worthy contribution to our understanding of the ways the Holocaust demands to be remembered in tangible forms: by attracting curious and empathetic tourists willing to learn more and pay respect to the victims of Nazi crime.

Thank you to all my Flinders University colleagues in Criminology for their support and encouragement throughout this journey. I offer particular thanks to Professor Margaret Davies and Dr Heather McRae for soliciting regular progress reports (a process that helped me maintain momentum). Thanks to Associate Professor Rebecca Scott Bray from the University of Sydney. She offered unwavering support and participated in enriching discussions about the memorial landscape in Berlin. Thanks to Associate Professor Greg Martin for sharing tips on staying focused throughout the process. Thanks to my dear friend Matthew Butler for offering encouragement as this project took shape.

Thanks to the Flinders University College of Business, Government and Law for providing a research grant that helped fund field research in Germany and other expenses related to the production of this book.

Many thanks to my brilliant doctoral student Haylie Badman for providing diligent and professional research assistance in relation to securing copyright permissions. I would have been lost without this help.

I offer heartfelt thanks to David Worswick for his amazing photograph editing expertise. Thanks for making the colour photographs suitable for black and white reproduction and for working your Photoshop™ magic.

Thanks to Dr Denise MacLeod for her professional editorial assistance that went well above and beyond the call of duty. I really appreciate your dedication and keen eye for detail.

I offer thanks to the entire 'Advances in Tourism' team at Taylor & Francis for supporting this project from the outset and for patient guidance at all stages of the process. Also, my sincere thanks to Victoria Chow for copy-editing the manuscript with such a deft eye for detail.

Finally, I offer my thanks to the museums and memorial foundations who kindly provided permission to reproduce photographic images for which they possess copyright. In all cases, they kindly waived any fees that may have been payable.

Derek Dalton
April 2019

Reference

LaCapra, D 1998, *History and memory after Auschwitz*, Cornell University Press, New York.

Introduction

Surveying the Holocaust tourism memorial field in Germany

Nazism and tourism: the emergence of a once improbable relationship

My previous book, *Dark tourism and crime* (Dalton 2015), explored the ways that crime has been captured or harnessed by museums and memorials to provide opportunities for an educative and emotional encounter. This book seeks to grapple with arguably the most criminogenic organisation in the history of the world – the National Socialist Nazi Party – whose genocidal crimes were so monumental that they gave rise to the term *Holocaust* as a descriptor for the terror, deportations, torture, medical experimentation, slavery and mass murder committed in the name of the Third Reich. Macdonald fittingly refers to the crimes of the Nazis as 'the appalling and iconic atrocity of modernity – the Holocaust' (2009, p. 1), and Cohen (2008, p. 548) stresses that '[n]othing is more painful to Germans than the mechanized murder of the European Jews, and nothing is more fundamental to its public memory'. Czaplicka observes:

> In post-war Germany, the public acknowledgment of human loss caused by Nazi terror has taken concrete form in works of art, memorials, and monuments as well as in the building of museums and the reclamation and reconfiguration of historical sites.
>
> (1995, p. 155)

It is such forms of the memory of tyranny that constitute the focus of this book. Schulze astutely notes that:

> Until very recently, linking Holocaust memorial sites and tourism was frowned upon in Germany; in the land of the perpetrators, it was regarded as almost unethical to suggest that the two could be mentioned together or could possibly benefit from each other.
>
> (2014, p. 130)

Gross concurs, observing 'Holocaust tourism is, as a rule, treated with more suspicion than Holocaust commemoration' (2006, p. 73). Mindful of these cautions, this book engages with tourism linked to Holocaust memorial sites and museums in Germany with a focus on Berlin by virtue of its sheer saturation with memorials, museums and traces of Nazi crime:

> [B]ecause the city experienced 12 years of Nazi rule, the stock of potential markers is nearly limitless. Theoretically, no part of the city remains untouched by some range of activity from that era, whether bureaucratic complicity, illegal pamphleting or torture and systematic murder.
>
> (Jordan 2006, p. 180)

Indeed, in relation to Berlin, Leshem stresses that 'travellers of all kinds testify to their need to learn about the city's Nazi past' (2013, p. 177). This is in keeping with Stephens' observation that 'Berlin is the capital of National Socialism and the central point from which the Nazi regime's programme of violence was orchestrated' (2010, p. 31). Reynolds (2018, p. 4) concurs, noting that 'Berlin was the administrative hub of the Final Solution' and is accordingly 'the place where tourists confront the fanaticism of the perpetrators'. The city is therefore a fitting focus of this book.

It is my contention that memorial sites and tourism benefit from each other. Tourists exposed to memorial sites garner a more nuanced appreciation of the complexities of the Holocaust and the memorials which, by being *encountered*, collectively fulfil the very purpose of their existence. Memorials provoke memory and, in turn, mourn the absent citizens who were deported and murdered. Some theorists have argued that the modern memorial culture in Germany is partly a commodification of the dead. Berlin and other cities derive a financial benefit from Holocaust tourism, but a concomitant social *cost* operates to quash this somewhat simplistic equation. For, in facing up to its 'difficult heritage' (Macdonald 2009, p. 1) or 'undesirable heritage' (Macdonald 2006, p. 9) and embracing the Nazi past, Germany *accounts* for the dead in ways that render the unsettling crimes visible and tangible for visitors to the country to see and experience for themselves. For Germans, remembering the Nazi past was not merely some sort of therapeutic activity to atone for the past, but rather a process that could 'spread a moral message by educating school groups, tourists, and pedestrians alike about the Nazi past' (Jordan 2006, p. 45).

Adopting a similar methodology to that which informed *Dark tourism and crime* (Dalton 2015), in 2016 I visited various memorial sites in Germany to experience them first-hand in much the same way as any ordinary tourist might encounter them.[1] I sought to experience each site in all its complexity and glean a sense of what it could tell us about the perpetration of Nazi crimes and the terrible legacy of absence produced by crime. Inspired by Jessica Rapson's phenomenological approach to Holocaust tourism, an approach also adopted by Reynolds (2016), I was interested in the way in which 'tourists encounter visual displays of artifacts, photos, and documents or configurations of space as steps towards producing some coherent narrative of the Holocaust' (Rapson 2012, p. 165).

In deference to Kindynis and Garrett (2015), I sought to undertake a 'visceral reading' of the sites, museums and memorials in question, paying attention to the mood evoked by the experience of *encountering* the architecture, exhibits, information or memorial objects. Like Reynolds' recent study of Holocaust tourism (2018, p. 20), I too placed 'more emphasis on exploring the possibilities of knowledge than on a quantitative or statistically verifiable ethnographic account of Holocaust tourists'. I share Reynolds' misgivings about quantitative research in relation to Holocaust tourism: 'Tourists to Holocaust sites come from such a variety of backgrounds and experiences that any effort to make definitive claims about the phenomenon will face enormous challenges in identifying broad trends among different visitors' (2018, p. 20).

Additionally, my approach to analysing tourism sites was informed by my training as a cultural criminologist. This afforded me an appreciation of aspects such as particular curatorial choices employed by museums or techniques employed by memorial artists or architects. Paying very close attention to these attributes was a deliberate strategy utilised to reveal precisely *how* memorial museums or memorials dedicated to the Holocaust invoke and evoke an understanding about the Nazi past. This, of course, is not to say that there is anything remotely equivalent to a 'universal' reaction to a Holocaust memorial. At one end of the spectrum, indifference coexists with ennui; at the other end, sadness, bewilderment and stupefying melancholy can arise when visitors are confronted with reminders of the genocidal crimes of the Nazis. Some tourists I saw at sites looked keen to escape the exhibits; others appeared transfixed and beholden to the moment.

Schulze notes that '[t]he political and social contexts of remembering Nazi crimes and the victims of Nazi persecution and genocide have changed dramatically' (2006, p. 232). As the following section will reveal, before we can explore the physical contours of the Holocaust tourism landscape in contemporary Germany, we must understand something of the collective German consciousness. Uhl employs an apt analogy in this regard: 'Holocaust memorials are seismographs of historical consciousness' (2016, p. 221), in that they measure and give physical form to collective awareness. A burgeoning awareness of the Nazi past gave way to a veritable explosion in memorial culture in the late 1980s onwards. Nowhere was this 'memory boom', as Huyssen (1996, p. 181) has termed it, more self-evident than in Berlin where Jordan notes: 'Memorial work reached a fever pitch throughout the city in the 1980s, in preparation for Berlin's anniversary in 1987' (2006, p. 40).

This book largely focuses on sites where the Holocaust was perpetrated, planned or is memorialised in Germany. Sites where the planning occurred are sometimes referred to as 'perpetrator sites' and are now subject to sustained tourist interest (see Chapters 1 and 2). I make no claim to offer an exhaustive exploration of the phenomenon of difficult heritage as it is tethered to Nazi-themed tourism. Neumann (2000) notes a vast body of literature exists that analyses and critiques German public and social memories of the Nazi past.

Sharon Macdonald's enthralling book *Difficult heritage* (2009) explores stadiums, an infamous Zeppelin field and former Nazi Party rally and marching grounds, with a focus on Nuremberg. Philpott's recent article explores what he terms 'relics of the Reich' with a sustained focus on 'locations associated with the government machine, party apparatus and propaganda of the Nazis' (2015, p. 133). Rosenfeld and Jaskot's *Beyond Berlin: twelve German cities confront the Nazi past* (2010) has made a major contribution to how we understand the representation of Nazi criminality. *Encountering Nazi tourism sites* supplements these other studies by focusing exclusively on tourism rather than heritage management or the preservation of architecture per se. My book also largely excludes any discussion of sites associated with the German war machine; factories, U-boat pens, V2 rocket launch sites and the like. As sites that Philpott decrees as 'less strongly associated with . . . specific crimes and, therefore, less imbued with the Nazis stigma' (2015, p. 141), they largely fall outside the purview of my strict interest in Nazi criminality.

National guilt: Holocaust consciousness as a precursor to memorialisation

Neumann notes that in the 1950s, 'the horror committed in the name of Nazi Germany remained largely nameless' (2000, p. 9). Writing in his brilliant collection of essays, *Guilt about the past*, Bernhard Schlink employs a powerful metaphor in relation to the Holocaust and Nazi past that captures the secrecy and concealment that prevailed in Germany up until the 1960s. He recalled an influential law professor whose approach inspired him to expand his legal education:

> After my exam I started reading the legal literature of the Third Reich that, during my years of study, had been locked away in the so-called *poison closet* and had only become available as a concession to the rebellious students of 1968.
>
> (Schlink 2009, p 130, emphasis added)

The dénouement for delving deeper into his professor's past was shocking for Schlink (2009, p. 130): 'And there they were, his writings on the totalitarian state and its necessary homogeneity and exclusion of the other, the Jew, the enemy.' All over Germany – in a much larger *poison closet* – Germany's Nazi past was locked away, hidden from view. In a sense, the entire nation was unconsciously relieved that the Nazi past was contained in dusty attics, obscure archives and in other largely neglected receptacles of memory. Older generations who lived through the war years were keen to forget, while successive generations occupied a complex position where they could scarcely atone for murderous acts they did not sponsor and yet had to live with the inherited national shame that their parents or grandparents had tacitly or actively contributed to a society that perpetrated genocide.

Oliner notes that the process of an evolving memorialisation culture in Germany 'illustrates the conflict between the wish to commemorate and the need to forget the identification with the crimes committed in the name of Germany' (2006, p. 895). As this book will explore, the need to commemorate has emerged as more important than the need to forget. It is as though the need to commemorate is seen as a fitting penance for the crimes of the past, even though these crimes recede further into the past with each passing year.

Wiedmer notes that Michael Verhoeven's 1988 Silver Bear-winning, and Oscar-nominated film *The nasty girl* 'documents a form of consciousness emerging since the late 1960s, a consciousness characterised by the post-war generations' attention to the Third Reich' (1999, p. 89). Based on a real-life story, the film's protagonist Sonja, digs into the Nazi past of her hometown, Pfilzing, as part of a school project. She uncovers evidence of complicity in mistreating Jews and, in doing so, incurs the wrath of some locals resentful that the dirt of the past has been excavated (Macdonald 2009). The film mirrors other acts of scrutiny that saw people all over Germany dubbed 'barefoot historians' (Koonz 1994, p. 268) investigating the wartime activity of family members or inhabitants of their local area. High school history projects flourished as students probed questions that had been largely quarantined from the syllabus in the 1970s. An interest in local history saw people literally start digging into the soil (see Chapter 2) to reveal archaeological remains of Nazi buildings. Weekend newspaper supplements dredged up the genocidal past, fuelling impassioned debates all over the country. The public questioned long-neglected topics such as the degree of culpability for genocide that should be shouldered by the Wehrmacht.

By the late 1980s, the ambivalence about the Nazi past had gradually been transformed into a fledgling social curiosity, a collective willingness to look into the past and confront the terrible, shameful legacy of Nazism. This was in part aided by the so-called 'Historian's Dispute' (*Historikerstreit*) of the mid-1980s, which primed society to ponder the singularity of the Holocaust and the way it manifested (Blumer 2013). Numerous researchers (Neumann 2000; Quack 2015; Koonz 1994; Niven 2001; Gelbin 2011; Reynolds 2018) credit the screening in West Germany in 1979 of the American television mini-series *Holocaust* – a film so important it made the cover of *Time* magazine in Germany – as awakening a latent preparedness for Germany to face up to its hitherto hidden Nazi past. Koonz notes what while the show was derided by critics as 'kitsch', 'German audiences were riveted' (1994, p. 268). Gelbin elaborates on its importance: 'The programme was broadcast to millions of viewers worldwide, including Germany, where it set off the first large-scale public debates on the destruction of European Jewry' (2011, p. 32). Quack asserts that memory discourse and public debates about 'the role remembrance of the Holocaust should play in Germany's national self-conception' started to proliferate (2015, p. 7). This, in turn, paved the way for such remembrance to be expressed in physical forms.

The return of the repressed: the rise of a Holocaust memorial ethos

Repression is an important theme that underpins any understanding of the emergence of Holocaust memorial culture in modern-day Germany: a culture that, in turn, facilitates tourism. Rita Süssmuth, the then president of the German Parliament, remarked in a speech at the opening of the Wannsee memorial (explored in

Chapter 1): 'Let us not deceive ourselves about what we have done . . . Experience tells us that whatever we repress catches up with us. No one can flee from their history' (cited in Lehrer 2000, p. 135). In a similar observation, Ladd (1997) noted that despite largely repressing its Nazi past by demolishing buildings and attempting to obliterate the memory of past crimes, that very past would not pass away. The German writer, Günter Grass, captures the complex nature of national repression of Holocaust guilt: 'A part of the history of these crimes is naturally the period of 40 years and more during which memories were suppressed, because the manner of suppression helps explain the *cause* of the crimes' (cited in Ladd 1997, p. 166, emphasis added). Here, Grass is alluding to the idea that a certain degree of latent anti-Semitism may have endured after the war to conjoin with a more general social malaise and regret about the war itself. Koonz (1994, p. 262) captures this aspect of social malaise well, writing '[j]olted by the double trauma of devastating defeat and the realisation of their government's wartime crimes, they [Germans] forgot'. This *forgetting* resulted in a type of collective social amnesia, a reluctance to confront the past (see Naumann 2000, p. 22; Koonz 1994). The situation was complicated by the wall dividing Germany. As Koonz notes: 'In the East, as in the West, genocide was forgotten, but unlike the West, the East remembered Nazi crimes. Soviet occupation officials rigorously carried out de-Nazification' (1994, p. 263). Throughout the German Democratic Republic (GDR), Holocaust memorials were erected but they were largely politicised as anti-Fascist monuments (Jordan 2006; Neumann 2000; Morsch 2001). As Niven observes: 'The GDR focused on communist victims of National Socialism, more or less excluding Jews from the picture' (2001, p. 3).

In a society where so many Jews were banished and ultimately murdered, one could argue that there were few tangible reminders around to beckon such an uncomfortable confrontation with the past. If Germans were prepared to look away as the Jews were expelled from their streets during the 1930s and 1940s, why would the next generation seek out a direct encounter with their absence – with what James Smith eloquently describes as 'the footprints they left in the landscape of Germany' (cited in Davies 2007, p. 5)? Yet, these sorts of encounters are precisely what many Germans started to search for in the 1960s and beyond.

An important concept associated with Germany's attempt to deal with the Nazi and Holocaust past is *Vergangenheitsbewältigung* (see Schlink 2009, p. 40; Jordan 2006, p. 43; Macdonald 2009, p. 9; Naumann 2000, p. 20; Quack 2015, p. 7; Neumann 2000, p. 10; Niven 2001, p. 4; Gay 2003, p. 154). It is a challenging concept to define, and is not entirely captured by the various English translations of 'mastering the past', 'working through the past' or 'coming to terms with the past'. The term accounts for how Germans 'struggle with the legacy and actions of their parents' and grandparents' generations and seek inspiration from the small number who did have the courage to stand up to impossible odds and try and rescue their Jewish neighbours' (Smith, in Davies 2007, p. 5).

Brian Ladd's groundbreaking study *Ghosts of Berlin: confronting German history in the urban landscape* (1997) was one of the first texts to explore the conflicting ways that architecture, history and notional identity have both paradoxically enabled and delimited engagement with the Nazi past. For Ladd, the 'removal of above-ground traces of Hitler has made the search for the Third Reich largely an archaeological one' (1997, p. 133). Yet with so many original buildings demolished in the post-war period, a need arose to build new structures that would house artefacts and information to illuminate the Nazi period of German history.

In a similar vein, Jennifer Jordan's meticulously researched monograph *Structures of memory: understanding urban change in Berlin and beyond* (2006) exhaustively documented the ways that places marked by a Nazi past have been both included and occluded from official collective memory. Jordan incisively notes: 'It is, of course, politically, culturally, and physically impossible to mark every site of resistance to or persecution by the Nazis' (2006, p. 10). In her book, she charts the vital role played by moral entrepreneurs who sought to sponsor and promote collective memory about the Holocaust in relation to various sites. Drawing on a discussion of Otto Weidt's *Blind Trust* exhibit of hidden rooms where Weidt sheltered a Jewish family, Jordan explores how authenticity, typified by an 'oppressive expressiveness' (2006, p. 140), is an attribute that draws many people to a particular site. Here, 'authentic floorboards, wallpaper, or cellar walls that were witness to atrocity or heroism' (2006, p. 14) are invested with the power to lure visitors and tourists to a particular place or landscape. In his classic study, *The tourist*, Dean MacCannell was the first theorist to point out an obvious but often overlooked fact: 'Touristic consciousness is motivated by its desire for authentic experience' (1999, p. 101). In keeping with MacCannell's pioneering insight into authenticity, Aschauer et al. stress that '[t]ourists seek out authentic experiences, although they are aware that they stand outside the experienced world in their everyday life, both physically and mentally' (2017, p. 164). Reynolds concurs, noting 'Holocaust tourism is likewise a search for authenticity beyond the pleasure-oriented package tour' (2016, p. 346). In addition, Brown argues that, for many tourists, knowing that visiting sites where atrocities 'not only took place but from where they were orchestrated' accentuates their emotional response (2015, p. 257). The vital but somewhat problematic nature of 'authenticity' will be touched upon in many of this book's chapters. This book proceeds by agreeing with Naumann's observation that one is 'mistaken to suppose that the "authenticity" of a site where unspeakable crimes were committed is somehow of greater value for remembrance that a commissioned memorial' (2000, p. 26).

One of the first Holocaust memorials erected in Berlin was entitled Places of Terror We Must Not Be Allowed to Forget. Referred to in German as a *Denkmal* – a reminder of the past/place to think – this memorial was erected in 1968 outside Germany's then largest department store KaDeWe in Wittenbergplatz (see Neumann 1998; Stein 2005; Koonz 1994; Neumann 2000). The store was picketed by storm troops in 1933 urging Germans not to buy from Jews (Davies 2007). Adventurous for its time, this memorial is a giant sign bearing the names of infamous concentration and extermination camps including Majdanek, Theresienstadt, Dachau and Flossenbürg. The memorial also bears an admonition 'not to forget' (Stein 2005, p. 118). Shoppers could ignore the sign or avert their gaze, but such a memorial moment marked the inception of an insistence that the Holocaust be publically acknowledged in the bustling *here and now* of Berlin's present. Similarly, in 1995, a Holocaust *Denkmal* was erected amid a busy market in the Steglitz district of Berlin. A giant mirrored wall (*die Spiegelwand*) was engraved with the names, dates of birth and addresses of 1,723 local Jewish residents. This memorial acts as an 'unavoidable and uncomfortable reminder of a past that many wished to ignore or forget' (Davies 2007, p. 50). As with the KaDeWe memorial gesture, this wall was placed in a busy civic location that demanded attention.

Counter-monumental turn and the rise of the memorial museum

Crownshaw (2008, p. 213) notes that from the 1990s onwards, German architectural memorisation of the Holocaust took on a 'counter-monumental turn', which he attributes to the foremost scholar of this phenomenon, James E. Young. Young notes that many of the memorial projects throughout Germany in the 1980s took the form of what he termed *counter-monuments*: 'Brazen, painfully self-conscious memorial spaces conceived to challenge the very premise of their being' (1992, p. 271). Unlike the 'barely visible memorial plaques of the past' that tended to recede into the background as inoffensive, almost unnoticeable, reminders of the Holocaust, the counter-monuments announced their presence audaciously and somewhat antagonistically (as will become evident in Chapter 7) (Jordan 2006, p. 57). Most importantly, these counter-monuments 'insist that those who encounter them take a more active role in the act of commemoration' (Smith, in Davies 2007, p. 7). Additionally, as Crownshaw notes, the counter-monument is 'necessarily open-ended' (2008, p. 213). He elaborates: 'the countermonument does not turn the absence of the Holocaust's victims into a presence through their complete memorial (monumental) representation'.

Crownshaw also emphasises that these counter-monuments articulate the notion of 'the rupture or wound as they [Holocaust victims] were torn from the social fabric' (2008, p. 213). Many chapters in this book explore the way these counter-monuments engage tourists and 'provoke remembrance', to borrow Crownshaw's phrase. Indeed, as Reynolds stresses of counter-monuments: 'it is only through their placement within tourism that their multiple and even inherently contradictory meanings come to light' (2018, p. 230). Crownshaw emphasises that the concept of the counter-monument corresponds with the notion of secondary or vicarious witnessing – 'the remembrance of things not witnessed' (2008, p. 213), and it is precisely this type of 'moral witnessing', as Macdonald terms it (2009, p. 170), that draws tourists to Holocaust memorials and museums.

The counter-monumental turn loosely coincides with the rise of the 'memorial' or 'memory' museum: a new type of museum where visitors engage with exhibits related to atrocity (Williams 2007). Arnold-de Simine emphasises: 'A key feature … of memory museums is that they encourage visitors to empathise and identify with individual sufferers and victims, as if "reliving" their experience, in order to thus develop more personal and immediate forms of engagement' (2012, p. 18). The chapters in this book will explore how several German memorial museums afford tourists opportunities to encounter artefacts, narratives, images, and other representations that 'provide a lucid conduit to the event in question' (Williams 2007, p. 22), which, in the case of these chapters, is the Holocaust. Simon (2011) frames the *mise-en-scène* of a museum's exhibition as providing the conditions that might invite the performative act of witnessing. Many of the case studies in this book touch upon the ways that tourists seek to witness the Holocaust through what Simon terms 'the public re-presentation of . . . "difficult" images and artefacts' (2011, p. 197). The hyphen Simon deploys between the terms *re* and *presentation* is no linguistic gimmick, but rather a clever device that reminds us that when *representing* past violence like that of the Nazis, curators have an ethical responsibility to do so very carefully, for the act of *representation* itself is thwarted by the danger of titillation or trivialisation. The case studies in this book demonstrate that German museums are very mindful of their burden to rehearse past Nazi violence in ways that do not render it devoid of its genocidal context.

Some of the most arresting museums in this book are places of former suffering and death. Many former concentration camps have been 'reconstructed as museological sites' (Carden-Coyne 2011, p. 167). Tourists throng to these memorial museums, which play a vital role in memorialising the crimes that took place during the National Socialist era. Carden-Coyne writes '[m]useums [. . .] not only reiterate popular and nationally sponsored memories, but they also have the potential to *create* memories' (2011, p. 169, emphasis in original). This point is more salient when we consider that tourism is a practice of amassing experiences and collecting memories.

Les lieux de mémoire (memory sites), traces and aura

This Introduction would be remiss if it did not note the importance of three concepts that underpin our conceptual understanding of Holocaust tourism in Germany. The first concept is Pierre Nora's influential *lieux de mémoire* (memory places/sites). Memory places relate to 'the embodiment of memory in certain cites where a sense of historical continuity persists' (Nora, 1989, p. 7). Germany abounds in such memory places. Indeed, one might construe the entire city of Berlin as a vast memory place, so saturated is it with spaces, streetscapes and buildings where the memory of past crime is invoked and evoked. At many of these memory spaces tourists can encounter traces of the past trauma, suffering and death associated with the Holocaust. Nora stresses that there is no spontaneous memory. He observes that 'the truth of *lieux de mémoire* [is that] – without commemorative vigilance, history would soon sweep them away' (1989, p. 12). Thus, in relation to the memory sites explored in these chapters, tourists provide a vitally important role by ensuring that Nazi crimes are remembered. They take photographs, post reviews on Facebook and tweet impressions about their experiences at the memory sites. That they do so is profoundly significant, given that Holocaust remembrance has passed through what Reynolds terms a 'critical juncture' (2018, p, 54). He notes with the passing of eyewitnesses to the disaster, Holocaust remembrance 'disperses into every corner of cultural representation' (2018,

p. 54). The emergence of Holocaust tourism is symptomatic of that dispersal. The second concept, traces, are 'indications of something that has disappeared, but has nevertheless left its marks and therefore in some sense still prevails' (Arnold-de Simine 2005, p. 12). This theme of the traces left by violence is particularly potent in relation to the disappearance of Germany's Jews (Schramm 2011). Many of the memorial sites explored in this book attract tourists keen to experience or 'see' these traces for themselves. Indeed, Popescu astutely observes that 'the search for hidden traces that may reveal the truth of history continues to be of relevance for those who visit sites of murder' (2016, p. 274). The third concept, aura, is best described as the mood or emotion evoked by a site, and has been identified as important to the theorisation of Holocaust-themed tourism (Seaton 2009; Dekel 2013; Arnold-de Simine 2013). Many of the chapters in this book explore the aura of sadness and regret evoked by Holocaust memorial sites or memorials. This exploration is in keeping with Lehrer and Milton's observation that: 'Some of the most interesting perspectives on memory work are emerging on the borders where academic and other spheres of cultural practice meet: the museum, the memorial site, the heritage tour' (2011, p. 3).

Dark tourists, regular tourists, accidental tourists and pilgrims

Pearce notes that '[t]he interplay of brutality and bureaucracy is one of the reasons why the crimes of National Socialism continue to fascinate and defy rational explanation' (2011, p. 234). Tourist interest in the Nazi past is partly fed by a world captivated by Nazism. Fuelled by interest in television shows like *Nazi mega structures* which explores 'Nazi gigantomania' (Macdonald 2009, p. 154), documentary films like Lanzmann's groundbreaking *Shoah* (see Koonz 1994), a seemingly endless supply of feature films and what Pollock terms 'kitsch clichés of Nazi insignia, SS uniforms and so forth' (2003, p. 177), Nazi crimes are kept at the forefront of our minds. As Schlink remarks: 'Precisely because the Third Reich and Holocaust have become a universal experience and teach universal lessons they will not fade into obscurity' (2009, p. 40). This universality is not unproblematic. Some aspects that cluster around the allure or fascination with Nazism are troublesome. In deference to Sontag (1975), there can be no doubt that the fetishistic allure of black SS uniforms works to lure some tourists to memorial sites.[2] Other tourists perhaps better educated about the Holocaust are lured by much more venerable motives than the facile veneer of *Nazi-chic* as promulgated by popular culture permeated by a Hollywood standard of aestheticisation that makes Nazism alluring (Gundermann 2015).[3] Other tourists may well come to Germany not planning to seek out Holocaust sites, but rather to shop, eat and drink local food and wine, experience nature and visit attractions like zoos or art galleries. These tourists, whom we might term 'accidental' tourists, may nevertheless encounter Holocaust-themed memorials or museums in the course of their visit. As Reynolds notes, '[t]he point is that tourism, including Holocaust tourism, accommodates both lofty and mundane motivations' (2018, p. 51). This book acknowledges that tourists who encounter Holocaust memorial sites in Germany are not necessarily self-identifying dark tourists. Like Brown (2015, p. 257), I believe dark tourism typologies 'simplify human responses and experiences', and so wish to eschew the assignment of the label 'dark tourist' to all Holocaust memorial and museum tourists in Germany. Indeed, I concur with Aschauer et al.'s observation that determining tourist motives 'remains at a purely speculative level and does not do justice to either the heterogeneous needs of visitors or the various forms of visit to dark tourism sites' (2017, p. 162). Certainly, Berlin's city tourism chief, Burkhard Kieker, thinks the term 'dark tourism' is inadequate to capture the nuances of Holocaust tourism in Berlin (cited in Scally 2015, n.p.). He remarked in 2015: 'We don't use that term at all.' Rather, a complex mix of *dark, regular* and *accidental* tourists merges at each memorial site. The chapters in this book seek to account for this fact through ensuring that I tease out how each site challenges each visitor irrespective of their core motivation for visiting that particular site. Gross notes: 'Visitors are drawn to museums and memorials not only – or even primarily – out of morbid curiosity, but in the same way that pilgrims are drawn to sites of martyrdom . . . *memory* itself has become the ritual' (2006, pp. 77–78, emphasis in original). Some theorists have tried to differentiate pilgrims from tourists and assert that the latter are merely interested in spectacle. However, Gross asserts: 'Thirty years of tourism studies has pointed to the overlaps rather than the divisions between pilgrimage and tourism' (2006, p. 94). Cohen (1979) concurs, arguing that the roles of pilgrim and tourist are often combined in the modern world, and Reynolds (2018) also perceives the dichotomy between tourists and pilgrims as dubious and unhelpful. This book thus collapses pilgrims and tourists together; using the term 'tourist' to capture both types of visitors. It also shares Reynolds' view that '[t]ourists do not arrive as blank slates but as socially and politically situated subjects with different degrees of historical knowledge' (2018, p. 34). Museums and memorials cater to the tourists' desire to remember those who suffered by employing techniques that engender empathy and communicate something tangible about the suffering of Holocaust victims (see Brown 2015; Tucker 2016). Miles (2002, p. 1176) stresses the vital importance of empathy in connection to Holocaust tourism: 'More than evoking historical knowledge, to be successful, any . . . touristic "attraction" must also engender a degree of empathy between the sightseer and the past victim.'

Devices employed at memorial sites to provoke empathy – specifically *voids, synecdoche* and authentic *traces* (so revered by tourists) – are explored in this book. They work as powerful tools to engage tourist curiosity and empathy and, in doing so, perform powerful memorial work, conjuring something meaningful and memorable for each individual tourist in her/his personal moment of encounter.

Reynolds notes that there has been 'a rapid and continual growth in tourist numbers to sites of Holocaust perpetration and remembrance over the past two decades' (2016, p. 335). This book seeks to interrogate how the memorials and museums they encounter offer an opportunity to learn, remember and mourn and, by doing so, depart these spaces with an appreciation of the suffering of those absent people who give meaning to the encounter.

Tourism itinerary: a brief guide to the chapters

Chapter 1

An appropriate case study to begin our vicarious tourism excursion, the notorious Wannsee Villa in Berlin, where senior Nazis held a conference in 1942 to further their genocidal plans, is explored in this first chapter. Now a sombre museum, the villa educates visitors about the so-called Wannsee protocol that underpinned the intensification of mass murder throughout Europe. It is also a site that sponsors human rights education. The chapter touches upon cinema and photography to better grasp the nuances of encountering this confronting museum. Additionally, it explores how the museum manages to coexist with the arresting natural beauty of its surroundings.

Chapter 2

Taking what is known as the *Topography of Terror* in the centre of Berlin as its case study, this chapter investigates the complex ruins of the former epicentre of Nazi rule. Here, tourists encounter a modern documentation centre that exhaustively documents this former perpetrator site that once stretched over an enormous block. The chapter also explores the rich outdoor exhibit that complements the documentation centre. Here, tourists can literally trace the foundations of Nazi bureaucracy as they discover different 'stations' that afford visitors a sobering insight into the crimes of the National Socialists.

Chapter 3

This chapter takes as its case study the seventeenth-century Wewelsburg Castle near Paderborn in north-western Germany; a site where Himmler set up a spiritual home for the Schutzstaffel (SS) in the 1930s. Now a museum whose exhibits are devoted to exploring the ideology and terror of the SS, this chapter addresses how the castle faces the challenge of educating visitors about the crimes of the SS without venerating this murderous organisation. A museum wholly devoted to the SS was always going to be controversial and risk undesirable neo-Nazi inspired tourism. This chapter explores how the museum largely thwarts such a risk with its careful curatorial interventions.

Chapter 4

This chapter which focuses on the *Anne Frank House* in Amsterdam is an anomaly as its case study is not based in Germany. Its inclusion is warranted by the sheer popularity of this famous museum synonymous with Holocaust remembrance and tourism. Lured by her famous diary, hundreds of thousands of tourists a year visit the *Anne Frank House* to vicariously experience her place of sanctuary before she and her fellow hiders were denounced, deported and subsequently murdered. This chapter explores the successes and failures of this most complex site and pauses to consider whether a visitor can commune with Anne in a space brimming over with other tourists.

Chapter 5

Engaging with two infamous locations of Nazi crime, this chapter compares two distinctly different former concentration camps in Germany: Dachau and Bergen-Belsen. Juxtaposing these two former camp museums allows the reader to appreciate that there is no 'typical' concentration camp, and that each camp affords tourists a unique insight into the suffering of its former inmates. The chapter touches upon the relative popularity of Dachau (which attracts mass tourism), with the markedly less-visited site of Bergen-Belsen. It becomes apparent that the reconstructed elements of former are markedly different to the latter: a site where nature intrudes and a quieter, more contemplative experience is offered.

Chapter 6

Taking Daniel Libeskind's avant-garde Jewish Museum Berlin in the Kreuzberg district as its case study, this chapter discusses how, to borrow the museum's promotional blurb, *this really is a museum you need to experience.* For that reason, the trope of experience guides my exploration of this most complex museum that is devoted to both the history of Jews in Germany and the cataclysm we call the Holocaust. However, it is the Holocaust that tends to dominate visitor experiences. Accordingly, this chapter pauses to consider the (in)famous voided architecture and axes of this space, and how specific spaces like the Garden of Exile, the *Fallen Leaves* installation, and the Holocaust Tower make such a profound impact on tourists.

Chapter 7

This chapter examines the diverse array of Holocaust-themed memorials in Berlin that tourists encounter as they traverse the city. Some memorials are well-known and located along the well-trodden tourist trail. Others are obscure and require a tourist to seek them out or perhaps stumble upon them by accident. From the field of stelae of Peter Eisenman's Memorial to the Murdered Jews of Europe, which attracts hordes of tourists, to Christian Boltanski's enigmatic memorial, The Missing House, which only the most curious tourist seeks out, this chapter explores the different scale and form of these memorials and how they coalesce to form a united landscape of memory.

Conclusion

This concluding chapter seeks to unite the disparate chapters to reveal how, taken in their totality, the Holocaust perpetrator sites, memorials, and museums explored in this book form a veritable *mosaic* of national remembrance that attests to the Germany's willingness to confront its Nazi heritage by ensuring that tourists can be exposed to the criminality of the National Socialists and remember its victims. Indeed, tourism facilitates a form of post-witnessing and commemoration that guarantees the memory of Nazi crimes is rehearsed by tourists. So, a legacy to remember, initially borne by Germans, is deftly passed to visitors who leave the country more empathetic to what, before arriving, was a much more abstract concept.

In terms of the curatorial challenges facing museums, Lehrer and Milton argue that 'unique challenges arise in attempts to frame memories and documents of violence for public display, and these have inspired innovations in exhibition, museology, public cultural interventions and the activation of memorial sites' (2011, p. 3). This observation is particularly salient in relation to Germany's burden to commemorate the Nazi crimes and atrocities that emanated on their soil but largely took place in eastern Poland. Accordingly, this book seeks to examine the ways that Germany documents its inherited legacy of Nazi violence and, in doing so, symbolically atones for the monumental crimes perpetuated during such a narrow span of its history.

In pondering the role of the tourism researcher, Reynolds argues: 'It is the job of scholars to offer an account of tourism's motivations and complexities, to take seriously its modalities of signification, to acknowledge both its appeal and its peril, and to put forward questions that prompt deeper reflection' (2018, p. 3). This book shares his vision and strives to contribute to an understanding of tourism's complex relationship with the Holocaust and its remembrance. Like Reynolds, I seek to prompt the reader to eschew simplistic understandings of what is often unfairly maligned and disavowed as a cringe worthy and superficial practice.

Notes

1 Two exceptions apply. I visited the Anne Frank House in 2015 and in the chapter devoted to Dachau I juxtapose my 2016 visit with a previous visit many years earlier in 1992.
2 This allure was recently evinced in Quentin Tarantino's controversial Nazi revenge fantasy, which featured a charmingly menacing SS officer. For a discussion of *Inglourious Basterds* – a film whose central metaphor is 'cinema as a weapon' – see Chapter 10 of Boswell (2012, p. 177).
3 For example, the monstrous wind-up automaton SS officer Karl Kroenen in the Hollywood film *Hellboy* evinces what Florian Evers has termed 'Naziploitation' (see Gundermann 2015) because his SS uniform and facemask are so aestheticised in the film.

References

Arnold-de Simine, S 2005, *Memory traces: 1989 and the question of German cultural identity*, Peter Lang, Bern.
Arnold-de Simine, S 2012, 'Memory museum and museum text: intermediality in Daniel Libeskind's Jewish Museum and WG Sebald's Austerlitz', *Theory, Culture & Society*, vol. 29, no. 1, pp. 14–35.

Arnold-de Simine, S 2013, *Mediating memory in the museum: trauma – empathy – nostalgia*, Palgrave Macmillan, Basingstoke.

Aschauer, W, Weichbold, M, Foidl, M & Drecoll, A 2017, 'Obersalzberg as a realm of experience on the quality of visitors' experiences at National Socialist places of remembrance', *Worldwide Hospitality and Tourism Themes,* vol. 9, no. 2, pp. 158–174.

Blumer, N 2013, 'Disentangling the hierarchy of victimhood: commemorating Sinti and Roma and Jews in Germany's national narrative', in A Weiss-Wendt (ed.), *The Nazi genocide of the Roma: reassessment and commemoration*, Berghahn, New York, pp. 205–228.

Boswell, M 2011, *Holocaust impiety in literature, popular music and film*, Palgrave Macmillan, London.

Brown, L 2015, 'Memorials to the victims of Nazism: the impact on tourists in Berlin', *Journal of Tourism and Cultural Change*, vol. 13, no. 3, pp. 244–260.

Carden-Coyne, A 2011, 'The ethics of representation in Holocaust museums', in JM Dreyfus & D Langton (eds), *Writing the Holocaust*, Bloomsbury, London, pp. 167–256.

Cohen, A 2008, 'Memory and history in Germany', *International Journal*, vol. 63, no. 3, pp. 547–552.

Cohen, E 1979, 'A phenomenology of tourist experiences', *Sociology*, vol. 13, no. 2, pp. 179–201.

Crownshaw, R 2008, 'The German countermonument: conceptual indeterminacies and the retheorisation of the arts of vicarious memory', *Forum for Modern Language Studies, vol.* 44, no. 2, pp. 212–227.

Czaplicka, J 1995 'History, aesthetics, and contemporary commemorative practice in Berlin', *New German Critique*, no. 65, pp. 155–187.

Dalton, D 2015, *Dark tourism and crime*, Routledge, London.

Davies, M 2007, *Absence and loss: Holocaust memorials in Berlin*, David Paul, London.

Dekel, I 2013, *Mediation at the Holocaust memorial in Berlin*, Palgrave Macmillan, London.

Gay, C 2003, 'The politics of cultural remembrance: the Holocaust monument in Berlin' *International Journal of Cultural Policy*, vol. 9, no. 2, pp. 153–166.

Gelbin, C, 2011, 'Cinematic representations of the Holocaust', in JM Dreyfus & D Langton (eds), *Writing the Holocaust*, Bloomsbury, London, pp. 26–40.

Gross, AS 2006, 'Holocaust tourism in Berlin: global memory, trauma and the "negative sublime"', *Journeys*, vol. 7, no. 2, pp. 73–100.

Gundermann, C 2015, 'Real imagination? Holocaust comics in Europe', in D Popescu (ed.), *Revisiting Holocaust representation in the post-witness era*, Palgrave Macmillan, London, pp. 231–250.

Huyssen, A 1996, 'Monumental seduction', *New German Critique*, vol. 69, pp. 181–200.

Jordan, JA 2006, *Structures of memory: understanding urban change in Berlin and beyond*, Stanford University Press, Stanford.

Kindynis, T & Garrett, BL, 2015, 'Entering the maze: space, time and exclusion in an abandoned Northern Ireland prison', *Crime, Media, Culture*, vol. 11, no. 1, pp. 5–20.

Koonz, C 1994, 'Between memory and oblivion: concentration camps in German memory', in A Bakshi (ed.), *Topographies of memories: a new poetics of commemoration*, Palgrave, Cham, Switzerland, pp. 259–280.

Ladd, B 1997, *Ghosts of Berlin: confronting German history in the urban landscape*, University of Chicago Press, London.

Lehrer, S 2000, *Wannsee House and the Holocaust*, McFarland & Company, London.

Lehrer, E & Milton, C 2011, 'Introduction: witnesses to witnessing', in E Lehrer, C Milton & E Patterson (eds), *Curating difficult knowledge*, Palgrave Macmillan, London, pp. 1–19.

Leshem, A 2013, 'Berlin: sustainability and tour guides in a partial dark tourism destination', *Turizam*, vol. 17, no. 4, pp. 177–184.

MacCannell, D 1999, *The tourist: a new theory of the leisure class*, University of California Press, Berkeley, CA.

Macdonald, S 2006, 'Mediating heritage: tour guides at the former Nazi Party rally grounds, Nuremberg', *Tourist Studies*, vol. 6, no, 2, pp. 119–138.

Macdonald, S 2009, *Difficult heritage: negotiating the Nazi past in Nuremberg and beyond*, Routledge, London.

Miles, WFS 2002, 'Auschwitz: museum interpretation and darker tourism', *Annals of Tourism Research*, vol. 29, no. 4, pp. 1175–1178.

Morsch, G 2001, 'Concentration camp memorials in Eastern Germany since 1989', in M Levy (ed.), *Remembering for the future: the Holocaust in the age of genocide*, Palgrave, New York, pp. 367–382.

Naumann, M, 2000, 'Remembrance and political reality: historical consciousness in Germany after the genocide', *New German Critique*, vol. 80, pp. 17–28.

Neumann, K 1998, 'But is it art? Erecting appropriate memorials in Wiesbaden, Germany', *Australian Journal of Art*, vol. 14, no. 1, pp. 91–113.

Neumann, K 2000, *Shifting memories: the Nazi past in the new Germany*, University of Michigan Press, Ann Arbor.

Niven, B, 2001, *Facing the Nazi past: united Germany and the legacy of the Third Reich*, Routledge, London.

Nora, P 1989, 'Between memory and history: les lieux de mémoire', *Representations*, vol. 26, pp. 7–24.

Oliner, MM 2006, 'The externalizing function of memorials', *The Psychoanalytic Review*, vol. 93, no. 6, pp. 883–902.

Pearce, C 2011, 'Visualising "everyday" evil: the representation of Nazi perpetrators in German memorial sites', *Holocaust Studies*, vol. 17, no. 2–3, pp. 233–260.

Philpott, C, 2017 'Relics of the Reich – dark tourism and Nazi sites in Germany', *Worldwide Hospitality and Tourism Themes*, vol. 9, no. 2, pp. 132–145.

Pollock, G 2003, 'Holocaust tourism: being there, looking back and the ethics of spatial memory', in D Crouch & N Lübbren (eds), *Visual culture and tourism*, Berg, Oxford, pp. 175–189.

Popescu, DI 2016, 'Post-witnessing the concentration camps: Paul Auster's and Angela Morgan Cutler's investigative and imaginative encounters with sites of mass murder', *Holocaust Studies*, vol. 22, no. 2–3, pp. 274–288.

Quack, S, 2015 'The Holocaust Memorial in Berlin and its information center: concepts, controversies, reactions', in *The International Handbooks of Museum Studies*, Wiley-Blackwell, Hoboken, NJ, pp. 3–28.

Rapson, J 2012, 'Emotional memory formation at former Nazi concentration camp sites', in D Picard & M Robinson (eds.), *Emotion in motion: tourism, affect and transformation*, Ashgate, Farnham and Burlington, VT, pp. 161–178.

Reynolds, D 2016, 'Consumers or witnesses? Holocaust tourists and the problem of authenticity', *Journal of Consumer Culture*, vol. 16, no. 2, pp. 334–353.

Reynolds, D 2018, *Postcards from Auschwitz: Holocaust tourism and the meaning of remembrance*, New York University Press, New York.

Rosenfeld, GD & Jaskot, PB (eds) 2010, *Beyond Berlin: twelve German cities confront the Nazi past,* University of Michigan Press, Ann Arbor.

Scally, D 2015, 'Site of Hitler's death still a tourist attraction 70 years on', *Irish Times,* 30 April, www.irishtimes.com/news/world/europe/site-of-hitler-s-death-still-a-tourist-attraction-70-years-on-1.2194156, viewed 29 May 2019.

Schlink, B 2009, *Guilt about the past,* University of Queensland Press, St Lucia, Queensland.

Schramm, K, 2011 'Landscapes of violence: memory and sacred space', *History & Memory,* vol. 23, no. 1, pp. 5–22.

Schulze, R 2006, 'Forgetting and remembering: memories and memorialisation of Bergen-Belsen', *Holocaust Studies,* vol. 12, no. 1–2, pp. 217–235.

Schulze, R 2014, 'Resisting Holocaust tourism: the new Gedenkstätte at Bergen-Belsen, Germany', in B Sion (ed.) *Death tourism: disaster sites as recreational landscape,* Seagull Books, London, pp. 121–137.

Seaton, T 2009, 'Purposeful otherness: approaches to the management of thanatourism', in R Sharpley & PR Stone (eds), *The darker side of travel: the theory and practice of dark tourism,* Channel View Publications, Bristol, pp. 75–108.

Simon, RI 2011, 'Afterword: The turn to pedagogy: A needed conversation on the practice of curating difficult knowledge', in E Lehrer, C Milton & E Patterson (eds), *Curating difficult knowledge,* Palgrave Macmillan, London, pp. 193–209.

Sontag, S 1975, 'Fascinating fascism', *The New York Review of Books,* 6 February, www.nybooks.com/articles/1975/02/06/fascinating-fascism, viewed 9 May 2019.

Stein, RA 2005, 'Berlin notes: mostly on a personal scale', *Southwest Review,* vol. 90, no. 1, pp. 112–124.

Stephens, AC 2010, 'Citizenship without community: time, design and the city', *Citizenship Studies,* vol. 14, no. 1, pp. 31–46.

Tucker, H 2016, 'Empathy and tourism: limits and possibilities', *Annals of Tourism Research,* vol. 57, pp. 31–43.

Uhl, H 2016, 'From the periphery to the center of memory: Holocaust memorials in Vienna', *Dapim: Studies on the Holocaust,* vol. 30, no. 3, pp. 221–242.

Wiedmer, C 1999, *The claims of memory: representations of the Holocaust in contemporary Germany and France,* Cornell University Press, Ithaca.

Williams, P 2007, *Memorial museums: The global rush to commemorate atrocities,* Berg Publishers, New York.

Young, JE 1992, 'The counter-monument: memory against itself in Germany today', *Critical Inquiry,* vol. 18, no. 2, pp. 267–296.

1 Profane splendour
The Wannsee House

Introduction

When surveying Holocaust-related tourism sites in Berlin, many people are familiar with Peter Eisenman's Memorial to the Murdered Jews of Europe, the Jewish Museum, or perhaps the Topography of Terror as these places have received saturation media exposure; are located in Berlin's city centre; and draw a steady stream of tourist traffic. The site, and topic, of this chapter is much less familiar and less visited as it is off the central tourist trail, requiring a train ride and a carefully planned walk to encounter.

The site is known as the House of the Wannsee Conference because of its infamous association with a 'single terrible day' in history (Ladd 1997, p. 154). Digan summarises the lure of the house for tourists:

> It is the 'realness' of the place, the feeling of standing in the very room a very symbolic event took place, and the eerie sense of tangible history, that makes the Haus am Grossen Wannsee an attractive place to visit for many people.
>
> (2015, p. 54)

Digan notes of the house that, 'it was not built by the Nazis to serve a National Socialist end, but an existing building taken and abused by the Nazis' (2015, p. 7). To that end, senior Nazi bureaucrats, at the behest of Reinhard Heydrich, met there on a wintry Tuesday on 20 January 1942 to effectively plan aspects of the 'Final Solution' and seek to coordinate their combined ministerial efforts to implement genocide (Lehrer 2000). Eckhoff notes 'today the Wannsee Conference stands as a symbol of the most dreadful plot human beings have themselves perpetrated against civilisation' (2008, n.p.).

Jasch summarises the house and its location well, writing:

> The House of the Wannsee Conference is situated in a picturesque location on a peninsula in south-west Berlin, slightly elevated above the banks of Lake Wannsee. It is set in a large park with pine trees and copper beeches opposite the Wannsee lido, which has been popular with Berliners since the 1920s. The house itself is an imposing three-story villa in an eclectic Italian

Figure 1.1 Entrance view: House of the Wannsee Conference

style featuring a cornice adorned with putti. It is approached via a massive wrought iron gate and an avenue lined with yew hedge, which opens onto a circular driveway in front of the main entrance, a portico pillared with two ionic style columns.

(2017, p. 146)

I visited the House of the Wannsee Conference in 2016 to experience this profoundly important Holocaust site and grapple with its terrible legacy, and to attempt to situate it in the wider scheme of Holocaust memorials in contemporary Germany. Jasch notes that the house receives some 120,000 visitors a year and that its 'pedagogical work' includes classes for professionals and students (2017, p. 149). The centrality of the house is captured by the deputy director of education, Dr Wolf Kaiser, when he states '[o]ur artifact is the house itself. It is a museum, and an artifact, a historical site' (cited in Luxenberg-Eisenberg 2012, p. 58).

The site is under-theorised in general Holocaust tourism literature and my thinking about it owes a debt to three people. Lehrer (2000) provided an exhaustive English-language history of the house and its notorious meeting. Roseman (2003) situated 'the villa, the lake and the meeting' – to borrow the title of his book – in terms of our contemporary understanding of the genealogy of the Holocaust. More recently, Jasch (2017) provided a succinct precis of the contemporary use of the house as a site for transformative education.

Figure 1.2 Front portico: House of the Wannsee Conference

This chapter seeks to accomplish the following objectives. First, it will provide a brief overview of the *Wannsee House* (or villa as it is often called) and explain how it came to be both a guesthouse for the SS and the venue for the infamous meeting of Nazis in 1942 who came to discuss the annihilation of European Jews. To that end, the next section of this chapter will explore what happened on that terrible day in Berlin's history when Heydrich convened the meeting in question. The chapter then explores the post-war history of the house that culminated in the transformation of *Wannsee House* into a memorial and educational site. In turn, the chapter will discuss how visitors might encounter the house by touching on the theme of a quest for aura among the grandeur of the house's interior. Here, cinema is imagined as helping fill the void of the *empty* rooms to help the visitor better envisage the drama of departed Nazi bureaucrats who haunt this space. In the next section, devoted to the exhibits one encounters in the memorial, the chapter dwells on the way in which the memorial explores the legacy of the Wannsee conference by painstakingly documenting the Holocaust and the genocidal actions that can be traced back to the Protocol disseminated after the conference. Here, the chapter explores how, somewhat paradoxically, the facsimile of the Protocol fails to really capture the visitor's imagination and the reasons for this failure. In the following section, the theme of authenticity is addressed. Some visitors come to the house expecting to see an abundance of tangible objects or architectural features linked to the house's Nazi past. This section explores the tensions at play with what one might term *tourist expectations*. The chapter then turns to exploring the vitally important contribution that education makes to the contemporary memorial. In the penultimate section, the chapter explores artistic representation of the *Wannsee House* and argues that photography plays a profoundly important role in how we understand the house and its legacy as a building that played a significant role in the Holocaust. The final section argues that the villa plays a valuable part in the wider Berlin Holocaust tourism landscape despite the challenges that many visitors invariably experience trying to reconcile the dreadful short meeting held so long ago in this house with the unassailable reality that the house and grounds are suffused with beauty. Here, one experiences a kind of emotional dissonance. The Nazi history of the house demands solemnity and sorrow, yet the surrounding beauty of the lake inspires serenity and the elation of feeling close to nature.

A brief history of the house

The building now referred to as the *Wannsee House* has a somewhat chequered history. A prosperous Berlin merchant named Ernest Marlier began building his new Wannsee villa in 1914. The area was then full of members of Berlin's upper middle class who had summer residences by the lake. As Roseman notes: 'ironically, given its later connotations, the name of Wannsee was then associated with cosmopolitanism and a good measure of tolerance' (2003, p. 64). Indeed, before the Nazis confiscated many properties from Jews in the area, Christians and German Jews lived rather comfortably side by side (Roseman 2003). After 1933, the tranquillity of Wannsee attracted a string of leading Nazis including Joseph Goebbels, Walther Funk, Dr Theodor Morell, and Dr Wilhelm Stuckart (one of the conference attendees). Roseman elaborates: 'Like many of them [Nazi leaders], Albert Speer obtained his villa on the cheap at the expense of former Jewish owners' (2003, p. 64).

The Wannsee House was designed by the architect Paul Otto Baumgarten and as Jasch observes: 'Despite its construction date, the villa shows no signs of wartime austerity. Instead, this parvenu historicist building bears witness to the considerable wealth and pretentiousness of its *nouveau riche* owner' (2017, p. 147). The post-war economic downturn, marked by hyperinflation (Webb 1989), forced Marlier to sell his villa to an industrialist named Friedrich Minoux (Lehrer 2000). Lehrer notes that '[a]long with the house, Friedrich Minoux bought many of Marlier's furnishings, including a rare Gobelin tapestry that adorned one of the dining room walls' (2000, p. 5). Minoux was subsequently indicted for defrauding the Berlin Gas company – 'the biggest swindle of the Nazi era' as Lehrer termed it (2000, p. 1). From his jail cell, he sold the Wannsee villa to a foundation called Stiftung Nordhav, which was controlled by the SS (Tuchel 1992) and established by Heydrich in 1939. The express purpose of the foundation was 'the creation and maintenance of refreshment and recreation houses for members of the security service of the SS and their dependents' (Lehrer 2000, p. 55). In what Lehrer termed a cruel irony, 'Heydrich and his henchmen plundered the cash to pay for the Stiftung Nordhav from German Jews being deported east' (2000, p. 2). This process of systematic theft of Jewish property by the German state was called

'Aryanisation' and many historians note that Jews ultimately funded their own transportation and murder. The final purchase price was 1.95 million Reichsmarks, delivered to the preferred bank of the SS: Dresdner Bank (Lehrer 2000; Jasch 2017).

Lehrer, referring to the work of historian Johannes Tuchel, notes that endowing the Nordhav Foundation and the purchase of *Am Großen Wannsee 56–58* a year later, 'were solely for Heydrich's own benefit' (2000, p. 59). Lehrer elaborates:

> As chief of the Reich Security Main Office, Heydrich believed that he was commencing a brilliant political career' and wanted the Villa for official functions. Indeed, Heydrich probably choose this property 'because it was an easy ten-minute drive from his own house at *Augustastraße* in the Berlin suburb of Schlachtensee.
>
> (2000, p. 61)

Having acquired the Wannsee villa, the house was extensively renovated in the summer of 1941 including a new refrigerated kitchen. Heydrich declared that these improvements were intended to turn the building into a guesthouse for the SS. Promoting the benefits of the Wannsee guesthouse over the 'mostly overfilled and exceptionally expensive hotels in Berlin' (Lehrer 2000, p. 62), the SS newsletter *Befehlsblatt* described what was on offer:

> Completely new visitors' rooms, rooms for socializing, a music room, billiard room, a great central hall and conservatory, a lakeside terrace, central heating, running water, and all other comforts. There is a good kitchen serving lunch and dinner. Wine, beer and tobacco products are available. Although the guest house is outside the city centre, accessibility is no problem, since a car is available for transportation to and from the Wannsee train station at any hour, telephone 80 57 60. Overnight stays cost 5 Reichsmarks.
>
> (as reproduced in Lehrer 2000, pp. 62–63)

Conceived as 'the centerpoint: for collegial interaction of SS officials in Berlin' (Lehrer 2000, p. 62), eight weeks after this issue of *Befehlsblatt* was published, the guest villa became the site of the Wannsee conference (Lehrer 2000).

A single day that forever transformed the house: the conference

The Wannsee conference is heralded as a pivotal meeting where the 'collective solution of the Jewish question' (Lehrer 2000, p. 69) was thrashed out by the attending Nazi bureaucrats. However as Lehrer astutely observes, 'the mass murder of Jews had begun well before the conference' (2000, p. 64). Much historical debate has taken place to try and situate the conference in terms of its wider relevance to Holocaust history. The German historian Hans Mommsen casts Hitler as a 'weak dictator' and attributes the Holocaust to the result of a 'horrendous bureaucratic process unfolding with its own momentum' (as summarised by Lehrer 2000, p. 64). More recently, the historian Christian Gerlach has caused renewed debate about the origins of the Holocaust by focusing on a notation by Heinrich Himmler in a document discovered in a secret Soviet archive. The notation is said to indicate Hitler's significance in decreeing it was time to redeem a prophecy he first made in the Reichstag in 1939 that called for the annihilation of all of Europe's Jews (Lehrer 2000). Lehrer elaborates: 'The document supposedly established that Hitler did, indeed, make a personal decision to put to death German and all other European Jews, and that he announced it to his most senior Nazi followers on December 12, 1941' (2000, p. 64). Debate about Hitler's complicity and knowledge aside, Gerlach argues that 'Heydrich called the Wannsee Conference to make clear that German Jews, many of whom had already been deported to concentration camps in Eastern Europe, were to be destroyed' (Lehrer 2000, p. 65). Certainly, historians know that the decision to embark upon the Holocaust was made earlier than December, since Jews from the Soviet territories were being systematically massacred as early as July 1941. Indeed, the building of Bełżec and Chelmno death camps was well underway in October 1941 (Browning 1994). Roseman (2003, p. 29) also notes that the mobile killing squads termed *Einsatzkommandos* assigned so-called 'special tasks' were murdering Jews in Poland as early as 1939.

This begs the question; how do we comprehend the convening of the Wannsee Conference? Lehrer stresses that the best way to understand the conference is to appreciate that it was a *facilitatory* forum. That is, the Nazis used the meeting as a way of facilitating the process of mass murder by dividing up various administrative tasks and seeking to engender coordinated cooperation between a wide range of Reich ministries. Lehrer decrees:

> Mass murder was difficult to arrange and coordinate with the usual German passion for order and precession. The Wannsee Conference was necessary in order to deal with this problem, especially since the situation was bound to get worse, as more territory and more Jews came under Nazi control.
>
> (2000, pp. 68–68)

What is beyond conjecture is that Adolf Eichmann and Heydrich invited fifteen participants to a breakfast meeting that was cancelled and eventually replaced with a luncheon meeting that took place on 20 January 1942. Roseman (2003, p. 57) stresses that the list of attendees comprised two main groups:

> The largest one consisted of representatives of ministries with responsibilities for the Jewish question, including representatives from the Ministries of the Interior, Justice, Economics and Propaganda, the Reich Chancellery, the Foreign Ministry and the Ministry for the Occupied Eastern Territories.

The smaller group consisted of 'Party and SS agencies with special interest in race questions' (Roseman 2003, p. 57). It should be noted that the attendees were, for the most part, well-educated. Roseman notes that '[t]wo thirds had a university degree, and over half bore the title of Doctor, mainly in law' (2003, p. 67).

Lehrer summarises the momentous meeting held in the snow-laden villa:

> Careful examination of the Wannsee Protocol suggests that Heydrich must have been the only speaker for most of the conference. According to Adolf Eichmann's later recollection, the whole gathering lasted an hour and a half, in a very relaxed atmosphere. In contrast to the euphemistic phrases of the protocol, the participants spoke quite openly about mass murder. No one expressed any misgivings or raised any objections.
>
> (2000, p. 70)

Adolf Eichmann compiled the minutes for the Wannsee Conference or protocol as it is sometimes referred to. Thirty copies were made. Most were lost or destroyed but in 1947 a copy was discovered and used in the Ministries or Wilhelmstrasse Trial in Nuremberg between 1947 and 1949 (Jasch 2017). The Protocol is fifteen pages long and is typewritten.[1] Jasch stresses: '[It] became a key document of the Holocaust given that it attests to the authorities' agreement to committing a massive state-sponsored political crime' (2017, p. 148). One cannot underestimate its evidential and historic value; for as Roseman notes, '[t]he Protocol was probably the closest the Nazis ever came to writing down their overall plan of genocide' (2003, p. 103). The process of capturing the sentiment and ideas documented in the Protocol is most accurately described by Eichmann in the transcript of his 1961 trial in Jerusalem:

> The stenographer[2] was sitting next to me and I was to see to it that everything would be taken down; then she deciphered this and then Heydrich gave me his instructions as to what was to be included for the record and what should be excluded. Then I showed it to Heydrich and he polished it up and proofread it and that's how it was kept.
>
> (English transcript of the Eichmann trial from 23 June 1961, as quoted verbatim in Lehrer 2000, p. 177)

The scope of the deportations envisioned was staggering. Heydrich projected: 'Eleven million deportees, with no country escaping the "combing out", even countries not occupied by Germany or under German influence in January 1942. English Jews, Irish Jews, Portuguese Jews, Swedish Jews, and Turkish Jews were all slated for deportation' (Lehrer 2000, p. 71). Much has been made, by historians, of the euphemistic language deployed in the Wannsee Protocol: language that Eckhoff notes was used to camouflage the main theme of the conference (2008, n.p.). Euphemistic language for dealing with the Jews pre-dated the Wannsee Conference. Gerlach notes that Goebbels stated in his diary that: 'As regards to the Jewish question, the Führer has decided to *sweep the floor clean*' (cited in Roseman 2003, p. 60, emphasis added). Roseman notes that in the 1930s, the Nazis decreed that the Jews must leave Germany or be made to disappear (2003,

p. 62). In terms of the actual Wannsee Protocol language: there is the ominous reference in the minutes to the discussion of the various '*forms of solution*' and '*temporary relief*' to the Jewish question (Roseman 2003, pp. 69 and 76 respectively). Arguably, the most sinister euphemism deployed is transportation. Roseman notes: 'Seldom had any German official indicated that transport to the East meant murder' (Roseman 2003, p. 61). Finally, Roseman notes that 'despite the euphemism of *evacuation*, the minutes unmistakably contain a plan for genocide' (2003, p. 1, emphasis added).[3]

Once the conference concluded, the attendees dispersed to their various posts and ministries having forged a colossal bureaucratic plan to cooperate to deport millions of people east where they would be enslaved, worked or starved to death, or exterminated in the various existing or soon to be constructed extermination camps of Bełżec, Sobibór, Treblinka and Birkenau. Eichmann recounted that after the meeting, Heydrich felt relived and that the two men drank cognac and had a pleasant meal (Lehrer 2000). Indeed, Digan asserts that, for the Nazis, this was just another day in the office:

> The eerie symbolism of the Wannsee Conference is only amplified by the stark contrast between the terrible subject of the meeting and the decadent circumstances in which it was held. After discussing the fate of millions of people for a mere two hours, the men famously dined, drank and smoked comfortably in the beautiful house in Wannsee.
>
> (2015, p. 24)

It seems trite to summarise what we know about the legacy of the Wannsee Protocol. Millions perished: their deaths having been partially impelled by the bureaucratic process that unfolded in the lakeside villa. Yet while many other meetings took place to organise the extermination, the existence of the Protocol, itself the product of a few hours of discussion, has forged an association that marks the *Wannsee House* with the imprimatur of genocide. Roseman summarises its importance when he writes: 'The Wannsee Protocol really did capture a decisive transition in German policy, a transition from quasi-genocidal deportations to a clear programme of murder' (2003, p. 106). In any event, Digan astutely sums up the significance of the conference and what it produced when she writes: 'Despite the historical uncertainties surrounding the Wannsee Protocol, the document and the meeting have become a powerful symbol of the Holocaust for the wider public' (2015, p. 23).

Transformation of the villa into an educational/memorial site

After Heydrich's assassination in Prague (Gerwarth 2011), the Nordhav Foundation no longer needed the villa, which was costly to maintain. Consequently, it was sold in 1943 to the Reich Security Main Office (*Reichssicherheitshauptamt* or RSHA)[4] and until the end of the war it continued to be used as a guesthouse (Lehrer 2000). Immediately after the war, Soviet soldiers occupied the villa. They were followed by American troops who used the villa as an Officers Club (Lehrer 2000). The house then underwent a series of transformations. In 1947, the August Bebel Institute established a college to educate functionaries of the Social Democratic Party, but they vacated the house in 1952 due to high maintenance costs (Lehrer 2000; Digan 2015). In 1952, the house was transformed into a youth hostel by the district of Neukölln where local schoolchildren would spend their summer vacations (Lehrer 2000). The historian and Holocaust survivor Joseph Wulf is credited as 'being responsible for reawakening public awareness of the Wannsee Villa's past' (Lehrer 2000, p. 132). In 1965, Wulf advocated for the creation of an International Holocaust Document Centre in the villa, which would house a large library and host research scholars and public seminars. His advocacy met with resistance from politicians who did not want a Holocaust monument (Lehrer 2000). The remarks from Berlin Senator Heinrich Albertz reveal an insight into the thinking of the time around Holocaust memorialisation:

> The Senate's view is that the past will not be overcome by setting aside a house, worth more than a million marks, which is a now a domicile for schoolchildren. One would have to set aside many houses to isolate every house that was a venue for horrors.
>
> (cited in Lehrer 2000, p. 134)

Wulf eventually committed suicide, believing all his efforts had been in vain. Knowledge of his tragic death made it all the more heartening to visit the library that bears his name during my visit. He lamented the reluctance of officials to confront the Nazi past in this era, writing:

> I have published 18 books here about the Third Reich, but this had no impact. You can publish things for the Germans until you are blue in the face, there might be the democratic regime in Bonn, but the mass murderers wander about freely, have their little houses and cultivate flowers.[5]
>
> (cited in Pearce 2011, p. 240)[6]

Wulf's dream to turn the villa into a documentation centre was not thwarted by his death. Digan (2015, p. 30) notes that 'in 1966, the *Haus am Grossen Wannsee 56–58* became a "contested site" [. . .] it sparked discussions about Germany's dealing with its past, what to do with "historically tainted" buildings'. Despite calls to demolish the building, most people recognised the folly of such a response, and so two decades passed with the future of the house in limbo while debate continued about the best course of action. In 1986, the then mayor of Berlin, Eberhard Diepgen, announced an intention to place a memorial at Wannsee (Lehrer 2000). Recalling the occasion he first learned of Nazism as a young student, Diepgen said that 'nothing shocked him more than the Wannsee Protocol' which he described as 'so cool and dispassionate in its form, so immensely evil in its content' (cited in Lehrer 2000, p. 135). In conceiving of the villa as a dedicated memorial space, the Berlin senate stated: 'The danger of murderous bureaucracy must be made clear in this place' (cited in Avidan 1991, p. 26). A local Berlin newspaper, *Der Tagesspiegel*, summarised the situation well: 'The authenticity of the place, the impact of a place where history has taken place, cannot be underestimated. Walls, stones, spaces must speak, when over the years fewer and fewer eyewitnesses are available' (cited in Digan 2015, p. 37). In 1989, the schoolchildren vacated the villa and renovations began. Digan notes that to amplify its 'connection with the past', the house was 'renovated to its old state' (2015, p. 38).[7] Described as a '[m]emorial to an abstract and relatively short moment in history' (Jasch 2017 p. 150) in 1991, fifty years to the day after the Wannsee Conference, the villa was inaugurated as a Holocaust memorial (Lehrer 2000). Digan (2015, p. 38) points out that, 'as a place of perpetrators and because of its history', the house could not be a traditional memorial or museum. Rather, and in keeping with its educational role, she asserts it was 'more a place of warning' (2015, p. 38).

At the dedication ceremony, Auschwitz survivor Heinz Galinski captured the enormity of the house's legacy when he declared: 'In this house, on 20 January, 1942, a barrier of civilisation was broken, and the abyss of barbarism was opened' (cited in Lehrer 2000, p. 135). Galinski's reference to the abyss foreshadowed how architect Daniel Libeskind would use the architectural language of voids and abysses to inform how he conceived of his museum in the coming decade (as discussed in Chapter 6).

Encountering the site

I encountered the *Wannsee House* on a delightfully sunny day in August. Despite being familiar with the house from photographs and through the cinematic depiction in the film *Conspiracy*, like many people who first encounter it, I was struck by its sublime beauty. Strolling to the grand entrance past garden beds in full bloom, the house and its picturesque location exuded an air of tranquillity. Jasch describes the stately interior one discovers upon entering the villa: 'Adjoining the vestibule is a splendid domed and pillared hall with marble fireplace; its tall French windows look out over a stepped terrace and down to the Wannsee lake' (2017, p. 146). He elaborates, explaining how the two wings of the house lead off from the imposing central space:

> On each side, a suite of rooms is arranged in an enfilade with majestic double doors between them: the library and the study on one hand, with a Greek-style bathroom that still retains its original wall decoration, while on the other is the dining room with conservatory and adjoining kitchen, in which a few Delft tiles can still be seen.
>
> (Jasch 2017, p. 146)

With few original traces of the house's original interior remaining, it is hard to imagine that this was 'a place where SS officers, among them death squad henchmen could stay overnight while Jewish forced labourers tended the flowerbeds'

Figure 1.3 Interior view: House of the Wannsee Conference

(Jasch 2017, p. 147). No traces of the SS guesthouse architectural modifications remain. This is hardly surprising given the post-war history of the house.

I stood in the room where the Wannsee Protocol was discussed and found the space paradoxically clinical and, more perplexingly, unmoving.

It did not readily evoke the infamous meeting that took place here. I arrived expecting that the room would convey a charge or aura of doom and terror, as though somehow the terrible deeds planned within its walls could somehow be conjured merely by *being* in the space itself. This is no criticism of the museum (whose excellent exhibits will be subsequently explored) but rather an observation about the realities of a space that is denuded of any period objects.

However, as documented in *Dark tourism and crime* (Dalton 2015), film and other cultural products can help the tourist animate an empty space in her/his mind's eye and bring it to life. Standing in the largely empty space, I recalled the brilliant cinematic montages that re-created the Wannsee Conference in Frank Pierson's sombre film *Conspiracy* (2001). Immediately I recollected: pompous SS officers and municipal officials arguing over the legalities of particular aspects of the plan; raucous table-thumping in praise of various contributors' suggestions to advance the annihilation of the Jews; the general sense of bonhomie that was characterised in the meeting by the clinking of crystal wine glasses. Perhaps German visitors recall other films depicting the Wannsee Conference, such as Heinz Schirk's *Die Wannseekonferenz* (1984) which is a real-time (exactly eighty-five minutes) re-enactment of the conference. This film is said to have inspired the producers of *Conspiracy* to make an English-language adaptation featuring star performers such as Kenneth Branagh (as Heydrich), Stanley Tucci (as Eichmann) and Colin Firth (as Dr Stuckart). Historians might criticise cinematic representations as simulacra or artifice that cannot stand in for the *real* events. However, the rich and nuanced media of cinema is a wonderful conduit that helps us imagine what, for some, is literally *unimaginable*: an eighty-five-minute meeting in which the genocidal logic of the Nazi state was advanced.

Various scenes from *Conspiracy* flooded through my memory and transported me back in time. Standing in the largely empty room, my imagination – aided by the filmic images – filled the space with the requisite horror of the terrible event transacted in 1942. I would urge any visitor to the house to familiarise themselves with the dramatisation of the conference before they visit the villa, as the filmic images help animate the largely empty space and bring it to life in all its abject horror.

The villa's exhibits

Jasch notes that one of the challenges of introducing this historic site

[r]elates to the administrative nature of the Wannsee Conference, which many visitors who are not familiar with the workings of public administration find a decidedly abstract occurrence, and which needs to be set in correlation with the widely known and rather more vivid images of exclusion and persecution.

(2017, p. 150)

To that end, one of the displays features photographs and biographies of the attendees of the Wannsee Conference, including Heydrich and Eichmann. Norbert Kampe, director of the House of the Wannsee Conference, describes the house as a 'site of perpetrators' (cited in Pearce 2011, p. 239), and so it is fitting that we encounter these photographs and biographies *in situ*. This exhibit certainly helps the visitor situate themselves in the space where the conference took place. Many other exhibits capture the different stages of the Nazis' genocidal activities: 'the exhibition covers the fate of the victims in detail, with sections on deportation, ghettos, forced labour and the concentration and extermination camps' (Pearce 2011, p. 240). This overview provides the necessary wider context to the Holocaust and is a fitting inclusion given the crimes that were planned in this room. Indeed, the title of the permanent exhibition, *The Wannsee Conference and the Genocide of European Jews*, makes it absolutely explicit that this site is linked to genocide. Indeed, Reynolds notes that 'each room of the first floor [exhibition space] documents a particular point on the way to the Final Solution' (2018, p. 159).

Jasch states that the memorial strives to make it clear that '[t]he history of the perpetrators' physical comforts is one of the key characteristics of the site: it was here where they drank alcohol to excess, for example, and went on summer picnics' (2017, p. 150). While not wishing to launch a strident criticism of the memorial here, I nevertheless wish to flag that this aspect of the physical comforts of the SS is not well evoked in the space. It is a great shame that the archive has not yielded photographs of the house's use when it was an SS guesthouse. There are too few objects present to help the visitor conjure the presence of the SS in the site as it exists. There are no doubt museological and curatorial challenges at play. I kept wondering whether excerpts from the German-language dramatisation of the conference might be played on large screens to help *fill* the space with some sense of the past presence of the SS.

To my mind, the most enigmatic aspect of the space was the display in a glass-topped long table of a facsimile of the minutes/Protocol.

Figure 1.4 Long table with Wannsee Protocol on display

It is wholly fitting that the Protocol takes centre-stage, as most visitors come to see the house because of its association with the Protocol. And yet, as I stood contemplating the various pages, they failed to really move or disturb me. Perhaps this is not so much a failure of curatorial practice, but rather a failure of the artefact itself. Despite their profound evidential importance, the pages seem too ordinary in their form. They certainly capture the homicidal intentions of the Nazi bureaucracy, but they cannot capture the sheer weight of trauma, despair, suffering, anguish and death that was unleashed by the directives and policies they convey. Indeed, the Protocol does not capture details of the murder process including the nascent technology for mass gassing and cremation. Eichmann admitted during his interrogation by the Israelis that such a discussion 'had indeed taken place [at Wannsee] but he had deleted it from the official summary' (Steinweis 2002, p. 676).

This is not to say that the Protocol is wholly inscrutable. As Jasch stresses: 'The Wannsee Conference is thus a prime example of the barely imaginable, yet utterly banal bureaucratic co-ordination process that went hand-in-hand with the collaborative, state organised and efficiently administered genocide of European Jews' (2017, p. 151). In that sense we must understand the Protocol in terms of its evidential form: a typewritten document that outlines genocidal intent.

Remnants of the house: a thwarted desire for authenticity

Ruminating on the concept of authenticity, Digan remarks that: 'When it comes to historical memory sites, the authenticity of the site is seen as the defining factor of the site, its most important characteristic, or – if you will – its selling point' (2105, p. 54). Furthermore, Jasch notes that: 'Memorial sites connected with Nazi crimes tend to be also sites attracting "dark tourism", as they are often visited with the aim of seeing and experiencing "the way it really was" and thus experiencing the dark side of history' (2017, p. 149). Notwithstanding the fact that motives for dark tourism can vary from genuine curiosity to inappropriate veneration (e.g., neo-Nazi sympathisers visiting to fantasise about the SS while in the house), Jasch (2017, p. 149) remarks that due to the villa's reconstruction and conservation, 'it is hard to identity elements that are truly authentic remnants of its period as the RSHA guesthouse of 20 January 1942'. He elaborates: 'Many visitors are also influenced by the film *Conspiracy* . . . and tend to be disappointed with the lack of authenticity, which they experience at the Memorial with its sober scientific exhibition on the Holocaust' (Jasch 2017, p. 149). He explains that visitors often express regret that a 'supposedly historic table was removed' since the exhibition was remodelled in 2006 (Jasch 2017, p. 149). Staff at the memorial go to great lengths to explain that the table was only an 'artistic installation' and that it is far from clear whether there was indeed a table present on the day of the conference. Some historians speculate that the participants present may have sat around several tables (Jasch 2017, p. 149). To that end, the memorial should be congratulated for removing an inauthentic item. Furthermore, the Wannsee site has 'refrained from using furniture to represent the dining room as it was as the time of the conference (Pearce 2011, p. 243). Pearce continues, explaining that this decision 'avoids encouraging identification with the perpetrators or normalising the site by likening it to any historical house' (2011, p. 243).

Still, the lack of tangible authenticity of a *single* relic from the day of the conference, or indeed the period that the villa was an SS guesthouse, seems to confound and trouble some visitors. On the day of my visit, an elderly male American tourist I spoke to in the garden lamented that there was 'nothing to see at the house' (his words). I thought that his sentiments were misplaced, as though the superb exhibits documenting the Holocaust had escaped his attention. Yet Digan reminds us: 'tourists have certain expectations of a place and having their expectations met during their visit makes the visit an authentic experience to them' (2015, p. 62).

It occurred to me that if an authentic object could be traced to the day of the conference and displayed at the memorial, it could not bear the weight of visitor scrutiny. To provide a hypothetical, even if it were somehow possible to posit that a particular Montblanc fountain pen had been used by a participant at the conference, the display of such an object would detract from the *only* item of real historic importance – the Protocol itself. So, in the villa, the *authentic* must make way for the *duplicate*: the original Protocol being too important to exhibit in the space of the memorial. The memorial trustees should be commended in this regard. Any attempt to recreate the period of the SS guesthouse with props or accoutrements from the era would sound a ghastly false note. Those who misguidedly come to the villa expecting to see tableau of Nazi bureaucracy – a table replete with SS china and place-cards – must understand that such items may, in fact, never have existed on the day of the conference and are a product of their imagination.

The villa as school: the vital role of education

Ruminating on the role of education at this site, Jasch declares that 'one of the founding aims of the board of trustees of the House of the Wannsee Conference Memorial and Education site is to provide education in democracy and in defence of human rights' (2017, p. 151). To that end, the 'Memorial has developed from the outset an innovative programme that attempts to set the authentic location of this abstract event at its heart' (Jasch 2017, p. 151). The house functions as a place where German civil servants and students can come to learn a little about the bureaucratisation of mass murder, which has relevance in contemporary times. Jasch elaborates on this important mission:

> By focusing on the dark side of German professional history in the twentieth century, and particularly with professional groups in sensitive or responsible fields such as medicine and healthcare, justice and the police . . . we can prompt a process of reflection and raise awareness of specific procedures and courses of action.
>
> (2017, p. 152)

That lesson for attendees at these professional courses, as it were, is that the Wannsee Conference represents a process of coordinated decision-making within a tiered administrative structure 'that is still typical of modern management organisation to this day' (Jasch 2017, p. 152). Here the spectre of diffused responsibility and the excuse of 'only following orders' haunt the present and remind participants that vigilance is still required to stave off the threat of human rights abuses in the modern era. Indeed, this is in keeping with Simon's (2011, p. 198) argument that exhibitions of difficult knowledge that inform citizens about historically significant events 'serve as a stimulus to actions that would otherwise guard against the re-currence of violence'.

The memorial exhibits also 'promote empathy with the victims on the receiving end of this logic' (Jasch 2017, p. 152), that effectively saw fifteen representatives of the government and the SS enshrine homicidal intent in every layer of civic authority. Jasch stresses the importance of this empathetic imperative:

> Only in doing this can we break the spell of such a 'dark site' and commemorate and honour the victims while still acknowledging and explaining the motivations and perspectives of the perpetrators and the great majority of those who stood by and choose to look the other way while these heinous crimes were committed.
>
> (2017, p. 153)

Of course, tourists who visit on a quiet day might leave oblivious to the important role education plays at the villa unless they happen to encounter a group of professionals participating in an educational program that seeks to combat xenophobia and racism (Luxenberg-Eisenberg 2012).

Imagining the villa: the value of photography

The photographer Werner Zellien described his impetus to photograph the then deserted Wannsee Villa in the summer of 1988: 'No one needs an introduction to this subject. We have all seen and heard it before. Yet nevertheless it is important to tell everything one more time, and to tell it over and over again' (2008, n.p.). In 2008, a lavish book was published that featured forty of Zellien's photographs of the Wannsee house when it was abandoned and in a state of architectural stasis awaiting transformation into a memorial. Zellien said: 'These images provoke very specific associations with the horrors of war and the thorough preparations for genocide' (2008, n.p.). The book's title *Villa Wannsee: melancholy grandeur* borrows the term that the chief prosecutor for the USA at the Nuremberg Trials, Robert H. Jackson, used to describe the villa. In an essay entitled 'A maximum melancholy', which accompanies the photographs, Iain MacKenzie summarises them: 'Werner Zellien's series from 1988 – three years after Lanzmann's film [*Shoah*] – is documentary evidence of both its medium, photography, and its motif, the Villa outside Berlin' (2008, n.p.).

Commenting on the photographs, Eckhoff notes: 'Zellien shows us simply an abandoned house with empty rooms' (2008, n.p.). In interior and exterior photographs, we behold empty rooms and neglected grounds charged with an aura that is both disquieting and meditative. Eckhoff observes 'the partial lighting throughout Zellien's interiors makes our inspection of the Villa seem furtive' (2008, n.p.). Zellien's photographs have a hidden menace that evokes comparisons with the aesthetics of crime scene photography. Eckhoff elaborates on the power of the images:

> The Villa takes on the character of a ruin – out of use, without an element of social milieu, a place where time has stopped. The twilight and effects of the light, which mark Zellien's pictures, underscore all these fatal aspects and contribute to the impression of a great melancholy.
>
> (2008, n.p.)

The grandeur of the villa's façade dominates most of the exterior photographs. In a particularly beautiful image, a window envelops the grand staircase in dappled light. However, the images are far from neutral as Eckhoff (2008, n.p.) asserts:

> The certainty of the Villa's wartime use and above all the notorious meeting on January 20, 1942, however, imbue the photographs with a particular horizon of meaning from which they can never be disassociated. Thus these photographs become a kind of projection screen for the atrocities the pictures do not depict.

Eckhoff's point about projection is profound. As I contemplated the book of photographs in the Wulf Mediothek, it occurred to me that the images are a powerful imaginative conduit to ponder both the history of the house, and – more particularly – the millions of lives obliterated in part by actions set in train by the Protocol that was formulated within the villa. If we look very carefully at these photographs, they transport us to other places: the extermination camps of Poland with their terror-inducing names: Sobibór, Treblinka, Bełżec and Auschwitz. Indeed, MacKenzie notes that photographs are imaginative conduits that summon the horrors of the Holocaust: 'Yet for all the photographs evoke the whiff of celebratory cognacs, these rooms must also be superimposed, in the mind's eye, with stark images of the medical examination huts and gas chambers of the Nazi concentration camps' (2008, n.p.). Zellien's photographs have been exhibited in Oslo, but I wonder if a few photographs could be purchased by the Wannsee Trust to be exhibited at the villa. They are very arresting images. When I looked at them, I was struck by the accuracy of Eckhoff's (2008, n.p.) description of them: 'The pictures of this uninhabited villa with its vacant rooms are charged with transcendent emptiness, as the ruins of atrocity, and as an imprint of an infinite absence.'

The motif of absence is a powerful Holocaust trope that informs many memorial objects, representations and spaces, and how we respond to them (as will subsequently be explored in Chapters 6 and 7). With so much explanatory text jostling for our attention in the space of the museum, I think Zellien's photographs might assist visitors perform the sort of imaginative feats that this villa warrants: remembering the absence of the murdered that can, in part, be traced back to this house. The images speak so powerfully of that one day in the life of this villa that transformed it into a planning site for genocide. As MacKenzie observes: 'there is a sadness that emanates from each image, a sense of loss within each frame' (2008, n.p.). They are haunted images and are, fittingly, haunting to view. To my mind, these photographs provide a partial key to understanding the villa and warrant some sort of formal inclusion in the memorial space.

Strolling in the garden: a moment of contemplation

Many visitors comment on the contrast as they see it between the beautiful place and the terrible events that transpired there (Jasch 2017, p. 149). Reconciling the two is challenging as Reynolds attests:

> The contrast between the horrors the villa documents and its romantic lakeside setting are among the more jarring experiences that tourists take away, leaving them to ponder how plans for mass murder on an industrial scale could coincide with such a picturesque scene.
>
> (2018, p. 160)

Standing in the garden on a glorious day with the garden in full bloom, it is hard to reconcile these two facts. The grounds on which the villa is situated are magnificent.

The chestnut, oak and maple trees provide a canopy of shade and a sense of communing with nature, yet nature is no refuge from some of the associations we make with the Holocaust. I recalled a grove of beautiful birch trees at Auschwitz Birkenau (Dalton 2015) and how incongruous they looked so close to the gas chambers: as though nature should not intrude on a place of extermination.

Balakian observes: 'We know that years of foreground preceded the Wannsee meeting. But perhaps one comes here not only to learn the narrative of history, but to experience the place and understand the relationship between the place and deed' (2014, p. 2). Balakian is right to suggest that many people come here to fathom the relationship between this house and its significant role in the unfolding of a complicated genocidal event that we now call the Holocaust. He captures his exit from the house in the following manner:

> I left the center [museum] after an hour of trying to juggle the colliding sensations of wood panels, photographs, and tape recordings of survivors amid coffered ceilings, high arched windows, the patina of wood mouldings. I tried to imagine the chandeliers, the stuffed chairs, the marble colonnades and wall tapestries of the High German décor of the house in 1942.
>
> (2014, p. 2)

Figure 1.5 The beauty of the Wannsee House grounds

It is no criticism of the museum's detailed explanatory exhibits to agree with Balakian that a visit evokes an array of colliding sensations that are not easily reconciled. The passage of time has left the house largely denuded of authentic traces of the day the Nazis met. So, a great deal of imaginative labour must be performed by a visitor who wishes, out of deference to the victims, to try and visualise what took place here. Additionally, Fein makes a profound observation:

> Each of the villa's 15 ground-floor rooms is crowded with documents and photographs, not enough, not even with all the documents and all the

photographs and all the testimonies in all the museums and all the libraries in the world, to make sense of this dreadful stain.

(2008, p. 10)

Following his logic, it is not perhaps surprising that, despite the best intentions of this museum, many visitors will leave as powerless to properly comprehend the Holocaust as they were upon their arrival.

Indeed, the beauty of the site makes the task of comprehending the crimes planned here extremely challenging, particularly when one exits the interior of the house, which is so controlled in its 1940s focus, and enters the outside with its vista of the lake. The seasons and nature cannot help but capture one's thoughts. As Luxenberg-Eisenberg noted during her visit, '[t]he beautifully kept gardens, the roses, all take one's breath away' (2012, p. 56). Indeed, the view of the shimmering Wannsee Lake from the terrace was the loveliest sight I beheld during my time in Berlin.

The *site* of the conference and its Nazi horrors seem to dissipate as one takes in the beautiful *sights* of nature that envelops the grounds. Try as I could, I found it hard to meditate on the Holocaust surrounded by such beauty. Perhaps the task would be easier on a cold, snowy day in winter, and yet even then I imagine the view is still alluring.

So, to my mind, the experience of visiting the *Wannsee House* cannot be one where the horrors of Holocaust completely govern our emotional reaction

Figure 1.6 The view of Wannsee Lake from the terrace

to the space. Despite my reverential intention (primed by an awareness of the house's history) I could not help but feel overwhelmed by the sheer beauty of the house as a piece of architecture and by its sublime location. This disturbed me, as though somehow I was betraying those who perished in connection to the house's monstrous history. Contemplating the lake, I noticed a restaurant, Haus Sanssouci,[8] teeming with luncheon customers. Balakian described it on the day that he encountered it: 'Its red awnings and big windows evoked Central European charm, and inside people were buzzing over drinks and lunch. Why anyone would set a restaurant here and name it *Sanssouci* (Without a Care)?' (2014, p. 2). Balakian elaborates:

> Germany has engaged in an unusually impressive task of self-scrutiny and soul searching about its Nazi past . . . Few, if any, nations have been as exemplary in their confrontation with a criminal past. So it's all the more bewildering to walk out of Haus de Wannsee and find House *Sanssouci*.
>
> (2014, p. 2)

I wonder if the choice of name for the restaurant Sanssouci (Without a Care) is the chief form of antagonism at play here. Some seventy-five years after the infamous meeting in this house, is it so unforgivable that *Wannsee House* shares its vista with an adjoining restaurant? The very existence of the memorial house attests to Germany's confrontation with its Nazi past. Given the commercial imperatives in the contemporary word, it is hardly surprising to find a restaurant next-door. It is not a stretch to argue that memory work (Nora 1989) might take place in this restaurant. Perhaps visitors depart from the museum to honour their booking and partake in a lunch while discussing their visit to the memorial. Being so close to the Wannsee House, tourists might naturally gravitate to this place for refreshment. Whilst the thought of wining and dining so close to the memorial might leave some aghast, we should recall the reality that Holocaust memorialisation takes place in a contemporary world where life goes on in all its richness. While I eschewed the opportunity to dine at Sanssouci, I could not quite bring myself to judge its existence or its nonchalant name as harshly as Balakian. I would also refute any suggestion that the restaurant's existence somehow negates the powerful memorial work performed at the villa next-door.

Leaving the villa on foot and walking back to the Wannsee train station, it struck me that the *Wannsee House* is something of an enigma in the Holocaust memorial landscape. Unlike some of the German concentration camps that operated for years with their grotesque exhibits that document torture and imprisonment, its brief life as a site where genocide was planned presents some real challenges. Architecturally grandiose and with imposing gardens, the villa's natural beauty cannot be wholly overshadowed by the deeds planned here. Perhaps that unassailable truth should not be shied away from when encountering the house. In any event, the beauty of the site and the existence of the house where genocide was partly conceived are not mutually exclusive. The memorial work performed *in* the house strengthens democracy and human rights and that is also a *beautiful* thing.

Notes

1 The original Wannsee Protocol is held in Koblenz in the *Bundesarchiv* (Federal Archives) in the Foreign Office section (Lehrer 2000).
2 It is interesting to note that in the depiction of the Wannsee Conference in the film *Conspiracy*, the stenographer is played by a male SS officer. Perhaps the director of this film was unaware that the stenographer was historically credited as being a woman; this would be surprising given the attempt at the cinematic verisimilitude pervading other aspects of the film.
3 Technically, the exact minutes of the Wannsee have been lost to history (see Digan 2015), but many historians use the term 'minutes' to refer to ideas that can be adduced from reading the actual protocol.
4 The *Reichssicherheitshauptamt* was 'the body combining the Gestapo, the criminal police and the SD for the whole of Germany' (Roseman 2003, p. 55)
5 The allusion to cultivating flowers is not merely a metaphoric flourish of language. At the Topography of Terror Documentation Centre, a photograph is exhibited of Karl Wolff (the former chief of Heinrich Himmler's personal staff and his liaison officer in the Führer's headquarters) watering the garden of his house in Lake Starnberg. Wulf's point is that having murdered millions, some Nazis were able to pursue everyday pleasures in peacetime.
6 This is a famous remark by Wulf and many different versions exist that suggest it has often been refashioned when translated into English by different translators.
7 In something of a paradox, the house was renovated according to its 1914 original architectural plans, rather than in deference to its original state when the Nazis met in 1942 (see Digan 2015).
8 The restaurant Sanssouci derives its name from the opulent Rococo-styled summer palace of Frederick the Great, located in Potsdam, near Berlin.

References

Avidan, I 1991, *The Jerusalem Report*, May 2, p. 26.

Balakian, P, 2014, 'Wannsee: place and the deed', *Chronicle of Higher Education*, 20 January, www.chronicle.com/article/Wannsee-The-Placethe/144023, viewed 29 May 2019.

Browning, CR, 1994, 'The Nazi decision to commit mass murder: three interpretations: the euphoria of victory and the Final Solution: summer – fall 1941', *German Studies Review*, vol. 17, no. 3, pp. 437–481.

Dalton, D, 2015, *Dark tourism and crime*, Routledge, London.

Digan, K. (2015) *Places of memory: the case of the house of the Wannsee Conference*, Palgrave Macmillan, New York.

Eckhoff, A 2008, 'Pictures of absence', in W Zellien (ed.), *Villa Wannsee: melancholy grandeur*, Bergen Kunstmuseum, Oslo.

Fein, L 2008, 'In Berlin, where the past is present', *Forward Forum*, October 24, p. 10.

Gerwarth, R 2011, *Hitler's hangman: the life of Heydrich*. Yale University Press, New Haven.

Jasch, HC 2017, 'The House of the Wannsee Conference: tourism and Holocaust education at a perpetrator site', *Worldwide Hospitality and Tourism Themes*, vol. 9, no. 2, pp. 146–157.

Ladd, B 1997, *Ghosts of Berlin: confronting German history in the urban landscape*, University of Chicago Press, London.

Lehrer, S 2000, *Wannsee House and the Holocaust*, McFarland & Company, London.

Luxenberg-Eisenberg, F 2012, 'Set in motion: the final plan to terminate the Jews', *Holocaust Studii Si Cercetari*, vol. 4, no. 1, pp. 48–60.

MacKenzie, I 2008, 'A maximum melancholy', in W Zellien (ed.), *Villa Wannsee: melancholy grandeur*, Bergen Kunstmuseum, Oslo.

Nora, P 1989, 'Between memory and history: les lieux de mémoire', *Representations*, vol. 26, pp. 7–24.

Pearce, C 2011, 'Visualising "everyday" evil: the representation of Nazi perpetrators in German memorial sites', *Holocaust Studies*, vol. 17, no. 2–3, pp. 233–260.

Pierson, F (dir.) 2011, *Conspiracy*, motion picture, HBO, BBC.

Reynolds, D 2018, *Postcards from Auschwitz: Holocaust tourism and the meaning of remembrance*, New York University Press, New York.

Roseman, M 2003, *The villa, the lake, the meeting: Wannsee and the Final Solution*, Penguin, London.

Schirk, H (dir.) 1984, *Die Wannseekonferenz*, television film, Bayerischer Rundfunk.

Simon, RI 2011, 'Afterword: the turn to pedagogy: a needed conversation on the practice of curating difficult knowledge', in E Lehrer, C Milton & E Patterson (eds), *Curating difficult knowledge*, Palgrave Macmillan, London, pp. 193–209.

Steinweis, A 2002, 'Review of Conspiracy (BBC/HBO Films), directed by Frank Pierson from a script by Loring Mandel', *American Historical Review*, vol. 107, no. 2, pp. 674–675.

Tuchel, J 1992, *Am Grossen Wannsee 56–58: von der Villa Minoux zum Haus der Wannsee-Konferenz*, Edition Hentrich, Leipzig.

Webb, SB 1989, *Hyperinflation and stabilization in Weimar Germany*, Oxford University Press, New York.

Zellien, W 2008, 'Background', in W Zellien (ed.), *Villa Wannsee: melancholy grandeur*, Bergen Kunstmuseum, Oslo.

2 The *Topography of Terror*
The foundations of Nazi rule

Introduction

The former Prinz-Albrecht-Straße,[1] next to the Martin-Gropius-Bau exhibition centre, was arguably the most notorious address in Nazi-era Berlin. On this enormous block sat the headquarters of almost all the most significant Reich ministries and organisations. Johnston-Weiss (2019, p. 96) sums up the importance of this location, noting: 'the *Topography of Terror* stands at the intersection of some of the most iconic spaces of Nazism'. Furthermore, as Ladd (1997, p. 156) astutely puts it: 'From this location, then, Himmler and Heydrich laid plans for terror and mass murder that had their consequences elsewhere'. In so far as Berlin was the centre of Nazi rule, this location was its epicentre. It was an address that, in the 1930s and 1940s, instilled fear and dread in any non-Party member summoned there. Leoni summarises precisely how complex the site is in terms of its geography and wider importance in German history:

> The story told by the *Topography of Terror* . . . is complex. It is about Germany during the Second World War, the Nazi institutions that once existed on this site and the horror that originated there. It is also a story about post-war Germany, the possible forgetting or repressing of the past, the site's rediscovery, and the struggle to find an appropriate form of remembrance.
>
> (2014, p. 111)

This chapter engages with this story by exploring the product of this history, a Documentation Centre that now occupies the site amid a gravel-strewn terrain that gestures to the traces of the buildings that once stood there. In that sense, as Nachama writes: 'what had been a partial wasteland in the shadow of the Berlin Wall was ultimately transformed into a Centre for the documentation of Nazi crimes' attracting thousands of visitors every year (2014, p. 6).

To eliminate any potential confusion for the reader, it is important to stress that visitors to the site can encounter two specific exhibits: a Documentation Centre (an *indoor* exhibition space), and a much smaller *outdoor* exhibition space that contains traces of Nazi building foundations. Both exhibits are united by the descriptive title *Topography of Terror*. Such a title is fitting as it attempts to approach 'the connections between Nazi repressions and German society by examining the terror's geographical embeddedness in Berlin' (Ladd 1997, p. 163). The open-air presentation 'provides a frame narrative' as the executive director, Professor Andreas Nachama puts it: 'The consequences of what was planned and coordinated on this site – the Nazi crimes of violence committed throughout Europe – are documented in the indoor exhibition' (2016, p. 7).

The indoor and the outdoor elements work to complement each other's powerful history as the following sections will reveal. However, they are not mutually exclusive. Some people, perhaps rushed for time, seek to encounter the terrain and do not visit the indoor exhibit. Other visitors, perhaps satiated by the indoor exhibit's exhaustive coverage of Nazi criminality, do not seek to dwell on the smaller outdoor exhibit. Many, of course, wish to experience both and are certainly afforded a more nuanced appreciation of the entire site for doing so. As a 'site of the perpetrators' (Bucholtz 2016, p. 97), visitors come to learn about the Nazi bureaucracy and reflect on the ripples of violence and genocide that emanated from this centre of Nazi terror, spreading out as far as Eastern Europe. Leoni notes: 'It is . . . a unique site where the victims are absent, and the perpetrators cannot be commemorated' (2014, p. 111). This chapter explores the unique attributes of the site and how it ensures that the former Nazis who worked there are not commemorated, but rather posited as agents of genocidal violence.

This chapter is divided into distinct sections. Having introduced what precisely the *Topography of Terror* is in the introduction, the first section provides a brief overview of the post-war history of the space leading up to its recent transformation into a joint memorial and educational site. This section explores two contentious city of Berlin competitions to develop the site. The first competition saw winning architect Peter Zumthor's ambitious vision for the site ultimately fail in controversy and acrimony. A second competition – even though construction had already started (Herz 2005) – led to the building of the extant Documentation Centre, a building many commentators have criticised as being too neutral and timid a response to the brief. The next section explores what visitors encounter when they tour the Documentation Centre. Johnston-Weiss (2019, p. 93) observes that '[o]ne of the hallmarks of museal Holocaust representation is the use of photographs'. Accordingly, my discussion explores how photographs aid the visitor to better imagine the enormity of the Nazi bureaucracy and its reach into the daily life of every German citizen. As a prelude to exploring the open-air aspects of the *Topography of Terror*, the following section briefly explores the important history of relics and ruins in Berlin as they relate to the post-war era. This section touches upon the tensions at play with the imperative to demolish and 'forget' dominating the times. This is a helpful segue to discuss how visitors encounter the traces of Nazi rule that exist on the site. Here the chapter explores how the foundations of Nazi rule were uncovered among the rubble. These traces, in the form of the excavated ruins of the Gestapo basement torture cells, can now be observed at one of the 'stations' of the open-air tour that permit visitors to expose themselves to these moving and provoking remnants of Nazism. In the penultimate section, the chapter pauses to ruminate on two aspects of architect Peter Zumthor's thwarted vision for the site. The conclusion gestures to the success of the site as an 'open wound', which provokes an encounter that allows tourists to appreciate the enormity of the crimes that were orchestrated from this site during the Nazi reign of tyranny.

The post-war life of the site and its recent transformation into the *Topography of Terror*

Dawson notes 'by 1956, the west Berlin authorities had cleared away the bombed ruins in which all the Nazi concentration camps were planned and organised' (2010, p. 29). Ladd continues, '[t]his once feared address became one of many stretches of neglected ruins' (1997, p. 157). By 1970, the site was put to various eclectic uses including a recycling ground, a car park, a dodgem car entertainment attraction, a place for cars to race and for learners to practise driving (Leoni 2014), and a heliport (Irwin-Zarecka 1995). Leoni observes 'no reminders of the site's history remained above the ground' (2014, p. 111). Irwin-Zarecka concurs with this view, noting that '[t]he absence of any reminders of the once all-powerful Nazi apparatus of destruction suited the prevalent sentiments: the physical void did not stand out enough to provoke questioning' (1995, p. 21). Indeed, Ladd asserts that 'after the site faded into obscurity, a new generation of scholars and activists began to accuse the city and its people of denying their roots in the Third Reich' (1997, p. 158). That accusation was remedied over time.

It took more than forty years for the site to be deployed as an open-air museum, coinciding with Berlin's 750th anniversary celebration in 1987 (Dawson 2010; Leoni 2014). This exhibition was curated by the Verein Aktives Museum (Active Museum Association), which had the following aim as described by Leoni: 'Facts and sober documentation should provide an active reprocessing of history rather than an artistic interpretation' (2014, p. 112). The exhibition was very popular and attracted many thousands of visitors. Eventually, however, the need to deal with the rest of the site – a vast rubble-strewn terrain – gave rise to a competition to develop the site. In 1992, twelve architects were invited to take part in a limited competition to design a treatment for the site (Dawson 2010, p. 29). Galilee remarks:

> The Swiss architect Peter Zumthor was declared the winner and he set about designing a new educational building; befitting the Nazi history of the site. Zumthor's designs proved controversial and despite site work commencing in 1997, work ground to a halt in 1999 due, in part, to spiralling costs, but also arguably because the political will to build it had moved on.
>
> (2010, n.p.)

In 2005, a second competition was staged with a €26 million budget. Dawson notes: 'Competitors had to work with landscape architects and design a documentation centre, with exhibition and conference rooms, library and offices' (2010, p. 29). Of the 309 architectural teams that participated and from a shortlist of twenty-three, the winner was announced as Ursula Wilms (from the firm Heinle,

Figure 2.1 Exterior view, *Topography of Terror* Documentation Centre

Wischer & Partners), who worked with the landscape architect Heinz W. Hall-mann from Aachen. The resulting building – a 'still grey metal box' (to use Gali-lee's term) opened in 2010. Folkerts describes it as 'a rather neutral matter-of-fact building' (2015, p. 74). At the opening, the architect was unwilling to talk about her concept, saying that the building 'spoke for itself'. When asked why every-thing was grey, the landscape architect replied, 'what else could it be?' (Dawson 2010, p. 29).

In *The Architectural Review*, Dawson describes the building in relationship to the site: '[a]t its centre sits the low, square new building. Clad in a double metal skin, it is a grey horizontal gash in the landscape, obscuring one side of the Martin Gropius building' (2010, p. 29). It is difficult to tell if Dawson's term 'gash' is deployed as a compliment to the new building, or whether she is using the term to denote that it sits unsympathetically in the landscape: an aesthetically ugly blight. This ambiguity aside, many other memorial structures like the Parque de la Memoria in Argentina – which memorialises the dead of the 'Dirty War' – are described in metaphoric terms as 'wounds' or 'gashes' because they success-fully invoke something tangible about human trauma and suffering (Dalton 2015, p. 91). Galilee describes the building in the following terms:

> The metal mesh skin of the centre shrinks tightly to the sides of its rigid walls. The mesh allowing a degree of lightness and softness to its frame. Although

its perimeter is flanked by low concrete walls it stands amid a dusty unkept landscape overgrown with shrubs and trees, deliberately left untended.

(2010, n.p.)

The metaphor of the gash (sympathetic or unsympathetic) seems inappropriate to me. I liken the building to a giant box that appears isolated by the crushed granite surrounding it. It seems a suitable container to house the documents it holds. Free from nostalgia, the building offers no obvious symbolism save for the fact that when viewed from the left side, it appears to *sink* into its foundations with a cantilever effect. Bucholtz describes the perspective of being inside the building and looking out: 'From the building's exhibition space, one looks east across an "abrasion" and the barren surface of the terrain to a new plantation of trees along the building traces on Willhelmstraße' (2016, p. 100). The design of the new Documentation Centre is itself a statement on the representation of Nazi perpetrators. The plain, one-storey white and grey building is consciously non-commemorative and the grounds are devoid of greenery to avoid any 'heroic' or 'idyllic' features (Pearce 2011, p. 242). A courtyard at the centre of the building has a large, paved square of shallow water. Dawson says of this feature: 'Anyone who has studied the architecture of concentration camps might be reminded of the ash swamps at the edge of Auschwitz' (2010, p. 29). Her comments are profound, for the pool is certainly evocative of the murky grey pond of ashes one encounters at Birkenau (see Dalton 2015). Reflecting pools play a vital role in memorial culture, but this pool struck me as far too implicit an architectural feature, relying on the visitor to make some sort of connection between this feature and the thing it resembles so far away in Poland. Is the pool meant to evoke a comparison with Auschwitz? The failure of the architect to elaborate on her intentions leaves one guessing.

Encountering the site: the Documentation Centre's exhibition space

Visitors enter the Documentation Centre by walking up some rather non-descript steel stairs. One immediately encounters banks of enormous white display boards that are suspended from the ceiling by steel cables. The effect is surprisingly powerful. From a distance, the cables are not visible to the eye and the boards appear to float as though disconnected from the building. As Pearce observes, the museum 'has opted for a defined emphasis on perpetrators from the start, as demonstrated by the exhibition's full title: "Topography of Terror: Gestapo, SS and Reich Security Main Office on Wilhelm-and Prinz-Albrecht-Straße"' (2011, p. 241). Nachama stresses: 'The permanent exhibition is not an orchestrated presentation with original objects, but rather a historical documentation built mainly on photographic and written sources' (2014, p. 8). He elaborates on its evolution:

The permanent exhibition has evolved on the basis of its tried and tested previous versions, but in a restructured and thematically expanded form. It continues to convey, in a concise presentation with carefully chosen examples, fundamental information on the headquarters of the SS and the Gestapo located on this site between 1933 and 1945 and the crimes initiated by these institutions, their leaders and personnel.

(2014, p. 7)

While it is possible to move through the exhibition space and encounter the displays somewhat randomly, many visitors seem to favour a sequential encounter that details the gradual rise of Nazism to its eventual genocidal actions. Accordingly, the exhibition boards are divided into five distinct themes:

1   The National Socialist Takeover of Power
2   Institutions of Terror
3   Terror, Persecution and Extermination on Reich Territory
4   The SS and Reich Security Main Office in the Occupied Countries
5   The End of the War and the Post-War Era

While the need for brevity will preclude a detailed discussion of all five thematic sections, I nevertheless wish to help evoke something tangible about the experience of encountering the exhibits. The exhibition starts with the National Socialists' rise to power in 1933. As Pearce observes: 'It explains how institutions like the Gestapo and the SS functioned from 1933 and how they evolved from instruments of securing power to coordinators of mass terror and persecution' (2011, p. 252).

The executive director, Professor Nachama, describes the concept of the exhibition areas in the new Documentation Centre as

based on the idea of portraying the terror exercised by the Gestapo beginning in 1933 and the Reich Security Main office beginning in 1939 from various perspectives, which – much like an adjustable magnifying glass – brings the visitor even closer to the crimes conceived and coordinated from this place.

(cited in Bucholtz 2016, p. 100)

This metaphor of an adjustable magnifying glass affording different perspectives is quite apt, and it is texts and images that afford us a unique insight into Nazi rule and criminality. The array of textual artefacts is vast and eclectic and includes: newspaper excerpts; official Nazi ministry notices; advertising posters; public notices affixed to billboards; maps; letters; Führer decrees; cardboard punchcards used by the SS Racial Office to process data; schematic drawings; extracts from police files; propaganda posters and internal memorandums (e.g., a 1942 document informing members of the SS that homosexual acts are punishable by death). It should be stressed that none of the items is authentic. Rather, the items are reproduced as facsimiles.

This is not a museum suited to a rushed visit. To appreciate all five main thematic exhibitions, one must be prepared to spend a good few hours slowly navigating the space and pausing often to read the detailed boards. The task is laborious, but the centre has placed many large white square benches on which to sit and rest. To my mind, the most powerful exhibits in the space are the period photographs, reproduced in enlarged format to aid the visitor's ability to take in their detail. Many visitors, perhaps rushed for time, seemed to skip reading the voluminous textual accounts and stood transfixed staring at the images. This may not be such a bad way to experience the exhibition, as several excellent books are for sale that painstakingly capture the text on the boards.

Some of the most powerful images are those that capture the *lost* architecture of the site: those buildings levelled by bombs and bulldozers. One enormous photograph depicts an aerial view of the area in 1934. Prinz-Albrecht-Straße and Willhelmstraße and several other streets are laid out with a huge central park. The photograph speaks to the sheer size of the Nazi bureaucratic apparatus that dominated the area. Public features are visible like the Hotel Excelsior and a giant Allianz$_{TM}$ neon sign, but the images still feel loaded with menace.

Other architectural images feature in the exhibition. The Reich Main Security Office is depicted circa 1941/1942, as is the Secret State Police Office circa 1933. Both images capture the full panorama of the buildings' façades. In another photograph, the entrance to the Secret State Police Office is depicted with a close-up of its grand baroque entrance. In an interior shot of the same building circa 1933, Nazi flags and busts of Hermann Göring and Adolf Hitler are visible. The bureaucratic tasks performed in the various Nazi buildings are outlined along with photographs of key Nazi officials from the SS, SD or Reich Main Security Office.[2] Much in the same way that images of *real* Nazis are profoundly important at Wewelsburg (as documented in Chapter 3 of this book), Nachama captures the importance of these photographs, writing:

> The theme of delving into the 'site of the perpetrators' is addressed in leitmotif form in the contemporary individual and group photos of SS and police perpetrators that make up part of the photographic source material on the ribbon of panels.
>
> (2014, p. 8)

By adopting Nachama's metaphor of the adjustable magnifying glass, one can appreciate how the exhibition photographs, in their totality, help the visitor literally calibrate their understanding of Nazi bureaucracy by providing perspectives that take in both the *macro* (the buildings that housed Nazis) and the *micro* (the individual Nazis who worked in specific buildings). Yet, it is not just the site's photographs of the lost architecture and inhabitants of these buildings that captivate the visitor. Some of the most powerful photographs in the exhibition attest to the manner in which Nazi rule saturated every aspect of life between 1933 and the end of the war. Photographs of children and teenage girls co-opted into Nazi youth pursuits 'suggest an absence of choice for some citizens in belonging to the criminal regime' (Pearce 2011, p. 253). Pearce discusses some of the images that captured her attention during a visit:

> The 'normal abnormality' under National Socialism is additionally demonstrated by photographs of a young couple embracing on a beach surrounded by swastika flags, by people dancing at a café terrace just 100 metres from a Gestapo prison, or a couple giving a Nazi salute as they walk past a war memorial.
>
> (2011, p. 252)

As Pearce emphasises, *The Topography of Terror* exhibition 'also affords a rare glimpse into the role of women as perpetrators with a photograph of grim-faced female concentration camp guards after capture, and in court' (2011, p. 247). The section 'Pursued, spared and integrated: SS and police perpetrators after 1945' contains a series of photographs of smiling relaxed former Nazis at leisure and at a SS veterans' reunion. As Pearce perceptively observes: 'In the early post-war decades, many perpetrators were not viewed as such, which makes this section all the more shocking when viewed through the lens of the present' (2011, p. 247). The exhibition draws to a close by depicting 'Nazi perpetrators in the context of post-war German society, with sobering evidence of how many simply returned to their normal lives' (Pearce 2011, p. 247).

In concluding this section about the Documentation Centre exhibits, I wish to dwell on one aspect that is not very successful. In the entrance, one encounters a large-scale model of the buildings that constituted the Nazi bureaucracy on Prinz-Albrecht-Straße, Willhelmstraße, and adjoining streets. The model is approximately two by four metres and the miniature buildings are modelled to scale. They do not feature individual period details, but rather are square edged and uniform. A legend describes the address and function of the various Nazi offices that once occupied each specific site. While the model certainly helps the visitor envisage how extensive and sprawling the Nazi bureaucracy was, it fails to really evoke the topographical features of the site. I recalled a smaller model of a clandestine detention centre in Santiago, Chile (see Dalton 2015, Chapter 5) and how that model, albeit on a radically smaller scale as it depicted a much smaller landscape, helped the visitor better imagine the site they were visiting. Few people stood looking at the *Topography* model in the exhibit space. Its clinical white properties seemed too sanitised and ordered to help it really evoke a long-flattened block that held modernist, art deco and baroque architecture with distinct aesthetic styles. I think the problem with the model was its very modern form. The models on display in the *Anne Frank House* (see Chapter 4) work so well because they employ the period details that help us locate their form in the past. I wonder if a more lifelike and realistic *Topography of Terror* model might aid the visitor? Perhaps such a model would be technically too expensive to produce. Indeed, perhaps the architectural form of many of the buildings have been lost in time with no archive existing that could attest to the form of the buildings. Notwithstanding these musings, the model *in situ* fails to adequately engage the visitor or animate his/her curiosity about the site.

A long history of relics/ruins in Berlin

Before exploring the how the ruins at the *Topography of Terror* site have been transformed, it is helpful to provide a context that situates why ruins are so important to the contemporary landscape of Holocaust memory in Berlin. A good starting point is Sandler's observation: 'Ruination is not a rare sight in Berlin. The bombings and street battles of the Second World War destroyed a large portion of the city' (2011, p. 688). Prior to the advent of an economic boom and its concomitant gentrification, Berlin was represented as desolate and damaged: 'Photographic essays, films and memoirs from the 1980s depict a city pervaded by empty lots, grey facades and ramshackle structures' (Sandler 2011, p. 689).

How these ruins have been perceived within Germany has evolved. In the 1950s, Berlin's ruins were associated with 'defeat and the trauma of war'; later they came to be associated with 'political division' and 'a lack of investment'. In contemporary times, ruins are now invested with the 'feel good token of cultural consciousness' (Sandler 2011, p. 691). Sandler expands: 'ruins are transformed by changing social contexts – and therefore must be understood not simply as isolated architectural signifiers but also as an integral part of these contexts' (2011, p. 689). Writing about a ruin in Berlin, Haus Schwarzenberg, which has intentionally been kept in a dilapidated state sponsored by the notion of counter-preservation, Sandler ruminates on its romantic qualities:

> The spaces are haunted by the signs of the past even when the memory of events has faded. This gap between physical sign and faded memory contains the seduction, the fog of mystery that invites visitors to guess, to imagine possible histories, to fill in the missing parts, or simply dwell in the murky corners.

> (2011, p. 696)

This notion that ruins can be seductive is very important. As the next section will explore, many visitors are transfixed by the remains of the Gestapo basement cellars that they encounter when visiting the *Topography of Terror*. Sandler's metaphor of *dwelling in the murky corners* seems apt. The cellars are haunted spaces that were the staging ground for torture, horrific suffering and murderous violence. James-Chakraborty asserts 'the ruined cellars [were] put to such horrific purposes during the Third Reich' (2018, p. 168). As this next section will document, many people stare at these ruins lost in thought, dwelling on their unassailable history as sites of violence. As we contemplate these brick walls, we *imagine possible histories*, to borrow Sandler's phrase. These histories, as documented in the Documentation Centre, are harrowing. Czaplicka stresses that whilst 'the ruin may conjure up an image of melancholy or even nostalgia' (1995, p. 185), he reassures us that in the context of the *Topography of Terror*, 'this "romantic" tendency is compensated for by the factual historical presence in the form of documentation' that annuls any sense that these ruins are romantic.

Encountering the foundations of the site: rubble, ruins and stations

One part of the *Topography of Terror* site that attracts a great deal of attention from local German visitors and tourists alike is the uncovered foundations of the Gestapo detention cells. This is not surprising as Clark states that 'many trauma memorials explicitly embrace ruins as a core element of their exhibition strategy' (2015, p. 84). The history of this site is well worth documenting before I explore the contemporary aspects of the exhibit that one encounters in its current manifestation.

Moshenska documents: 'In the cells below the office buildings political prisoners and other enemies of the state were imprisoned, interrogated and tortured by the Gestapo' (2010, p. 42). We learn in the Documentation Centre that the Gestapo set up what was termed a 'house prison' in the summer of 1933. Political prisoners were held in the one communal and thirty-eight individual cells of the basement at Prinz-Albrecht-Straße 8, and were sometimes tortured in these cells. What was termed 'enhanced' interrogation took place on the building's upper floors. As Steinbach notes: 'Prisoners were beaten, tortured, or intimidated with threats that their family members would be subjected to the same methods. Many prisoners attempted suicide. Some succeeded' (2014, p. 193).

Many prisoners were turned over to the Nazi-run judicial system. Men and women were sentenced to imprisonment in German prisons or transported directly to concentration camps. Some were sentenced to death (Bucholtz 2016). The Documentation Centre has myriad eyewitness accounts of the violence perpetrated in the basement cells and upper floors of Prinz-Albrecht-Straße 8. It also features galleries of Gestapo mug-shots once used to capture the criminality of prisoners but now rendered powerful photographic evidence that incriminates the Nazi state apparatus that imprisoned them. One particularly powerful account of the basement cells comes from Christabel Bielenberg, who voluntarily visited Gestapo headquarters in January 1945 to provide a statement to exonerate her husband who was imprisoned in connection with conspiracy. She was taken downstairs to the cellar to be shown what would happen if she persisted in being obstinate:

> He [Herr Kriminalrat Lange] led me down the corridor from cell to cell past these windows with completely beaten up faces. No . . . you never forget those images, ever . . . to look into those faces, completely beaten up, faces that were no longer faces at all, and then go upstairs again, and then the man said to me 'if you persist in your obdurate behaviour the same thing will happen to you. We can do it.'
>
> (cited in Bucholtz 2016, p. 84)

A combination of Allied bombing, Red Army shells and the passage of time saw many of the buildings on Prinz-Albrecht-Straße, including the infamous Gestapo headquarters, standing empty, abandoned and so badly damaged that they were neglected throughout the 1950s. Many buildings were demolished. Till has questioned the motivation for destruction by pointing out that many other nearby dilapidated buildings without such 'dark histories' were left standing (2005, p. 76). As Moshenska notes: 'These demolitions marked the first inscriptions of the dominant historical narrative of amnesia onto the landscape of West Berlin. By 1963, the Prinz Albrecht Strasse terrain had become a rubble processing area and an auto drome for learner drivers' (2010, p. 42). Of course, so much was irretrievably lost during the quest to purge the German landscape of these antagonistic architectural reminders of Nazism:

> It was we – not others – who demolished the stone witnesses to Nazi dictatorship after 1945. In any event, we did not protest oddly enough. They were in the way because we wished to erase them from memory, because we could not bear to see them. Today, we regret the almost complete disappearance of the victims' cells, the torture rooms, and the perpetrators' offices. The *architectural evidence* is gone.
>
> (Dr Franz Freiherr von Hammerstein, survivor of Buchenwald and Dachau concentration camp, cited in Bucholtz 2016, p. 92, emphasis added)

As will be explored later in this chapter, perhaps that is why the traces of the Gestapo cells in Prinz-Albrecht-Straße so enthral visitors; they are a trace of *architectural evidence* of an enormous building now lost to history.

The first proposals to redevelop the site came in 1957 but the plan collapsed due to the construction of the Berlin Wall in 1961. In 1982, the Social Democratic party proposed a competition to design a permanent memorial to fascism on the site (Moshenska 2010). In 1993, winners were announced but a change of local government saw the cancellation of the commemorative project due to lack of political will. In 1995, the future of the site was still uncertain when something unpredicted happened. A citizens' group consisting of an alliance of former anti-Nazi activists, architects, artists and historians conducted a guerrilla operation sponsored by the organisation, Active Museum, which came to be known as operation Let's Dig. This excavation removed grass, topsoil and rubble from the site of the Gestapo prison buildings (Moshenska 2010). Conceived as a symbolic act, slogans were deployed to attract the attention of the public: 'GRASS MUST NEVER BE ALLOWED TO GROW OVER IT' and 'THE WOUND MUST STAY OPEN' (Baker 1990, p. 58).

Based on this unlawful project, official excavations of the site were carried out a year later. Moshenska notes: 'This project uncovered the foundations of the Gestapo detention cells, whereupon proposals for a memorial were shelved in favour of an interpretation centre on the site' (2010, p. 42). That original interpretive exhibition was entitled *Topography of Terror*. While the exhibition was initially intended to be temporary, it captured the public's imagination and endured both as a feature of the site and a moniker that would later describe the entire site and the new Documentation Centre (Moshenska 2010).

Having explored how the foundations of the Gestapo cells came to be uncovered, I wish to explore the site from the perspective of a visitor. One literally descends from the Documentation Centre to experience the outdoor aspect of the museum, which is accessed by stairs and a ramp. As Fein describes: 'The long outdoor walkway – just below one of the only remaining sections of the infamous Berlin Wall – . . . takes the visitor from the earliest days of the Nazi villainy through the war's end and beyond' (2008, p. 10). Steep gravel-strewn embankments help add to the sense that one is in an excavated site. Indeed, Nachama (2014, p. 7) describes the exhibition as being situated in a 'trench'.

Visitors are commandeered between fifteen stations. As Nachama adds, '[t]hese stations contain information panels commenting on the history of the terrain' (2014, p. 7).

A flat glass canopy roof affords some protection from the rain and the visitor encounters glass suspended panels that feature photographs, texts and biographies from the 1930s onwards. As one walks from right to left, the years progress and one eventually encounters the genocidal logic that underpinned Nazism. Pearce argues that 'representing crimes as part of "everyday" society can help break stereotypes about Nazi perpetrators' (2011, p. 256). The walking history is certainly powerful because it explores how anti-Semitism shaped everyday life in 1930s Germany. Concrete seats allow opportunities to rest and one can walk the stations at one's own pace. Much like the indoor museum exhibits, photographs make up

Figure 2.2 Outdoor *Topography of Terror* exhibition space situated in trench

Figure 2.3 Information 'station' depicting persecution of homosexuals

a significant portion of the outdoor displays. Fein remarked on his experience of walking the circuit:

> My disposition is to stop before each of the photographs of those who resisted, and were therefore murdered, and to read, word by word, the all too brief paragraph that conveys their story. Not, mind you, because the stories are either all that interesting or informative, but out of humble respect: these are the ones who dared. But one can't, there being so many of them.
>
> (2008, p. 10)

During my visit, it was apparent that most tourists were not reading the detailed accounts of life in Berlin during the cabaret era or many of the other specific stations. As interesting as the stations are and, despite being thematically different to the internal museum, it is the exposed ruins of the site that appear to transfix most visitors. It is impossible to tell if they are recalling the photographic images and narratives of individual prisoners as presented in the Documentation Centre, or whether they are just ruminating on the general sense of trauma and suffering associated with a site of torture and death. The distinction seems unimportant. Clark eloquently argues that 'ruins are palimpsests, texts that have been overwritten' (2015, p. 92). These ruins are overwritten with the narratives of trauma that are so powerfully presented in the Documentation Centre. As Clark astutely asserts: 'In some ways, ruins are the most ideal architecture for a trauma memorial to inherit . . . They evoke the "right" emotions, the kind of longing, sorrow, wistfulness that we believe to be the appropriate emotions for memorial sites' (2014, p. 22).

Two attributes of the site's ruins struck me as particularly interesting. One long section of the Gestapo basement cellars featured a colonnade of arched red bricks. Aesthetically speaking, the effect is one of symmetry and beauty. This pleasing attribute is thankfully augmented by larger sections of the former basement walls that are much less aesthetically pleasing and gesture more successfully to the claustrophobic nature of the former cells. The display has received some strident criticism. Souto notes: 'there is no room for seeing the ruins without engaging

Figure 2.4 Ruins of Gestapo basement cellars: colonnade of arched red bricks

with the permanent exhibition: there is literally no space to follow the path without paying attention to the exhibition' (2013, p. 84). Indeed, it is the tidiness of the exhibition that disturbs Souto:

> The Topography of Terror has been transformed into topography of control, of tidiness that does not connect with the site, with the authenticity of the location, with the weight that the past and collective memory should have in that particular space.
>
> (2013, p. 84)

While I share Souto's misgivings concerning the tidiness of the exhibit, I think that, it its totality, it still performs powerful memorial work. As Reynolds notes, 'the presentation of these exposed basements speaks a traditional language of musealized structures that enshrine memory as permanent' (2018, p. 166). A paved pathway gives way to anthracite-coloured gravel, and many people venture over the threshold to look more closely and, in a few instances that I witnessed, reach out to touch the bricks. It is by no means clear whether such touching is permitted or forbidden: the usual prohibition about touching museum exhibits being disrupted or perhaps suspended in the minds of some visitors. In her review of the Documentation Centre, Dawson poses the question: 'How could a few excavated bricks and walls compete with a major new building?' (2010, p. 29).

Dawson's criticism of the site goes further: 'The imprisoned, tortured and murdered, once held in the cellars, have been relegated to minor roles' (2010, p. 29). Her misgivings about how this 'dirty site' has been 'cleansed' seem somewhat unfair to my mind. First, a city that desired to cleanse or hide its Nazi past would not have given rise to a grassroots movement that dug up the site in 1985, paving the way for this intervention. The few excavated bricks and walls one does encounter walking the stations of the *Topography of Terror* are a profoundly powerful architectural synecdoche of the type one encounters at dark tourism sites (Dalton 2015). While being only *part* of one building – the basement of the Gestapo cells – these red brick walls speak to the countless other walls that featured in buildings on Prinz-Albrecht-Straße. They are the *foundations* for our imagination to imagine the sheer variety of buildings that comprised the *whole* Nazi bureaucracy that, we know from visiting the Documentation Centre, once existed on the site. As Czaplicka notes of the brick colonnade; 'its aesthetic entices the beholder to engage his or her own imagination in a process of *reconstruction*' (1995, p. 185, emphasis added). We imagine the entire edifice and the terrible deeds performed within it. Modern museology teaches us that visitors crave exposure to authentic traces of the past. So, in response to Dawson's question: *How could a few excavated bricks and walls compete with a major new building?*, I would posit that the few excavated bricks that make up the walls captivate visitors as compellingly as the totality of the displays inside the Documentation Centre. Furthermore, while most visitors seemed underwhelmed by the replica model of the site presenting Nazi buildings that featured inside the Documentation Centre; in contrast, many were transfixed by the authentic traces encountered on the walk outside.

Lament: mourning Zumthor's lost vision for the *Topography of Terror* site

In the section of this chapter devoted to the architectural vision for the site, it was noted that the Swiss architect Peter Zumthor's vision for the site did not come to fruition due to 'spiralling costs, technical problems and acrimonious disagreements' (Leoni 2014). Leoni (2014, p. 111) suggests that the principal reason the project failed was connected to the grandiose vision Zumthor had for the site; a vision the world was not ready to accommodate. In this section, I wish to dwell on two aspects of Zumthor's failed (indeed demolished) project since it provided a unique opportunity to interrogate the limits of memorial practice in contemporary Germany. The first aspect relates to the external site and the second concerns the way that Zumthor hoped the exhibits would be curated within the Documentation Centre.

Leoni describes how the building Zumthor intended would be 'positioned in the site according to the shape of the excavations and the gap between two rubble heaps' (2014, p. 112), and that it would sit tentatively on thin needle-like foundations 'as if the building does not want to touch it [the ground] at all'. Zumthor described his vision in his own words as 'a building which would be close to the ground, close to the earth, a building which would almost be a bit uncomfortable' (Spier 2001, p. 31). The key attribute of Zumthor's vision was that 'the surrounding environment is then left as found' (Leoni 2014, p. 112). Leoni captures the intended effect: 'The building was to sit awkwardly on the site, marking the "open wound" in the urban context' (2014, pp. 111–112).

As hitherto discussed, the building that eventually replaced Zumthor's vision was criticised in architectural magazines and newspapers as being dreary and backward-looking and for 'washing away traces of the past rather than preserving them' (Leoni 2014, p. 118). Leoni elaborates on this problematic washing away of the past: 'The physical remnants of the site's history are less visible because the rubble mounds have been removed and the area covered with crushed aggregate. Thus, post-war traces of the site, the signs of *repression* of history, are almost gone' (2014, p. 118, emphasis added). As one stares at the flat aggregate surrounding the site, one cannot help but agree that the erasure of the rubble, and its replacement with trucked-in gravel, has distorted the site and divested it of its expressive authenticity. Zumthor characterised the importance of the rubble on the site as 'these hills, these mounds, mementos from the war' which would create 'shadows' when observed from inside his intended building (cited in Spier 2001, p. 32). The flat crushed aggregate strikes a false note at the site. It is a real shame that such an irreversible intervention took place, as the gravel is uniform and has sanitised the site. If one imagines the demolition of the former Nazi office structures as an attempt to eradicate the past, surely the removal of the last traces of rubble on the site can be conceived as an act that sits on the continuum of trace removal.

The second aspect of Zumthor's failed vision I wish to dwell on relates to how he envisaged the history of the site would be presented. Zumthor disliked the idea of a themed, mediated presentation of the key documents. He elaborates in an interview with Spier:

> I'm for the original. I'm not for mock ups . . . If someone puts one of these letters of former prisoners in Gestapo headquarters there on site in front of me, and just says what is written and so on, I get the information . . . It doesn't need to be reduced or blown up . . . I don't want to deal with something didactically prepared.
>
> (2001, p. 36)

To that end, Zumthor's thwarted vision for the Documentation Centre was that some 500 glass tables 'lit up like glowing table tops', would be deployed to contain documents 'in their original size'. The visitor's encounter would thus be 'an intimate one' (Spier 2001, p. 36). Zumthor described his vision for the exhibition of original documents in the following terms:

> I picture the exhibition being like a big book lying there, lying in space. The didactic element should be reduced to pure necessity, and, like in a good newspaper, the comments should be made in a way that the comments of the historians are clearly separate from the original documents.
>
> (as cited in Spier 2001, p. 35)

There was a beautiful economy to Zumthor's unrealised vision:

> What I like about my idea is that you can go down one of these aisles, or two of them, or another one, and look at documents. You don't have to go and look at all of them. But having this overview of how many there are gives you a consciousness of what they did there.
>
> (cited in Spier 2001, p. 36)

This vision of displaying the documents in their original size with minimal supplementary or explanatory text was certainly radical. Eschewing a thematic approach would have required the visitor to perform much more hard work to make sense of the exhibits, and yet one is left to ponder whether, paradoxically, the light-box tables might have proved more *enlightening*. During my visit to the Documentation Centre I saw many people looking overwhelmed and daunted by the sheer volume of massive enlarged boards to read. I observed several young people enter the space and walk out almost immediately as if the prospect of reading so many boards was unappealing or too time-consuming. Many tourist blogs linked to the Documentation Centre bemoan the fact there is too much to read and take in. One wonders if Zumthor's proposed intimate encounter with the key documents of Nazi terror might have been powerful enough to negate the need for a laborious thematic encounter: an encounter that could be conveyed by reading a book. Certainly, the Wewelsburg museum exhibits (see Chapter 3) are more powerful for being less saturated with text. Leoni certainly has misgivings about the current exhibition: 'There is no doubt that the information provided by the current institution is of great importance. But the endless repetition of information becomes a disturbing mode of education which fills you with consternation' (2014, p. 119). Unlike the authentic rubble that has been removed from the site and can never be returned, one must acknowledge that curatorial interventions can take place within museum walls. Perhaps, sometime soon, the Documentation Centre might revise its heavy, textual approach and adopt one where the original documents might be permitted to speak more powerfully on their own behalf. Such a change would certainly fulfil the vision of the commissioning authorities: 'It was generally agreed that the site could not speak for itself and that its authenticity "must be given a voice" through documentation' (Leoni 2014, p. 112).

Conclusion: an open wound

Moshenska poses a very intriguing question: 'To what extent . . . can an archaeological site such as the Prinz-Albrecht-Strasse, constitute or contribute to the creation of a memory arena?' (2010, p. 43). The *Topography of Terror* site was a challenging site to assimilate in contemporary Berlin because, as Irwin-Zarecka notes, it is 'one of the most haunted places of our time' (1995, p. 18). Once a largely disused and infrequently visited site, the *foundations* of Nazism were largely hidden by years of demolition, abandonment and civic neglect. In a time when the undesirable heritage of the Nazi past in Germany presented multiple challenges and no clear solutions, the site's past lay hidden beneath the ground awaiting its re-discovery. The Let's Dig initiative coincided with an era where the past, however confronting and undesirable, was beckoning to be unearthed. The impetus to *dig into the past*, itself such a powerful metaphor of history, paved the way for the Gestapo basement to be revealed. This, in turn, led to the *Topography of Terror* outdoor exhibit that fuelled further debate about the future of the site. That future culminated in a Documentation Centre eventually appearing on the site to supplement the excavated ruins.

The resulting building's permanent exhibition conveys a powerful lesson, as Pearce notes: 'The Topography of Terror shows how quickly democracy and the rule of law can be overturned'. She elaborates: 'The sobering message is that anyone is capable of committing such crimes' (2011, p. 255). And yet, the ways the site was transformed has led to some harsh criticism. Dawson says of the transformation: 'However well meaning, this architecture projects an obsession with order, control and, ultimately, a lack of humanity' (2010, p. 29). Souto concurs, writing 'the original topography of the site has been silenced, erased' (2013, p. 86). To her mind, 'the most staggering characteristic of the site was the powerful simplicity of the void left in the city', and a few traceable remains of buildings, a characteristic now gone from the site along with the 'strong presence of authenticity' that was part of the void (Souto 2013, p. 86). She laments that '[t]he attention has been shifted from the overwhelming scale of an immense void in the city centre of Berlin to a tidy organization that simply aims to inform' (Souto 2013, p. 88).

Whilst sharing some of Dawson's concerns regarding the ordered nature of the architecture (which disturbingly accord with the Nazis' desire for symmetry and order in their desired architecture), in its totality, the *Topography of Terror* is something of a triumph. As a site that combines *inside* and *outside* activities, it is a very social space. Moshenska warns us that 'on sites of contested or traumatic memory, popular engagement cannot be guaranteed' (2010 p. 44). Whatever misgivings people might have about the architecture, the space lures hundreds of thousands of German and foreign tourists annually who are keen to imaginatively excavate the site in the same spirit of those who literally dug into the soil in 1985. The site is not just one of *excavation* (where the Gestapo cells are revealed) but of *exhumation*. The full horror of the Nazism is unearthed in exhaustive and confronting detail in the Documentation Centre. It is here that visitors come face-to-face with the crimes the Nazis planned and implemented on the site in the 1930s and 1940s. Johnston-Weiss (2019, p. 103) lauds the collective power of the photographs and facsimile documents marshalled at the site: 'Topography is an extremely effective documentation center, because its location on the grounds of the SS and Gestapo headquarters can collapse the historical distance between the past and the visitors [sic] present.' Furthermore, James-Chakraborty is right when she asserts '[t]he somber characters of this place is evident to all who come upon it' (2018, p. 168). Moshenska stresses that: 'archaeological approaches to contested heritage are a mechanism whereby sites, artefacts and bodies can be made public, powerful and resonant' (2010, p. 46). Her comments endorse the successful way that the *Topography of Terror* site works to actively engage visitors with the Nazi past. It matters not that the sole artefact that resonates at the site is an expanse of red brick wall with a notorious past linked to detention and torture. The *foundations* of Nazi rule are, somewhat paradoxically, supported by this relic and by the accompanying museum that painstakingly accounts for the terror that was planned from this site when it was the bureaucratic epicentre of Nazi rule. To the extent that the 1980s activists asserted that 'THE WOUND MUST STAY OPEN' when conceiving of how the site must be handled, one can conclude that the architectural, landscape and curatorial responses at the site we encounter today do not seek to suture the wound. Rather, they lay bare the trauma that National Socialism unleased on its initial victims and, ultimately, the entire German population who were left devastated by the war years. In closing, it should be stressed that exhibition space is conceived of as a 'work in progress', and that 'new special and challenging exhibitions' are envisaged for the future (Nachama 2014, p. 8). In that sense, the different aspects of the trauma associated with the Nazi years might be elucidated by future exhibits. In any event, I concur with Irwin-Zarecka's observation that the *Topography of Terror* offers tourists and visitors alike 'the means to better understand complex layers of history and memory' (1995, p. 25).

Notes

1 The thoroughfare Niederkirchnerstraße was known as Prinz-Albrecht-Straße until 1951, when its name was changed by the post-war German government due to its connotation with Nazi Germany.

2 The full title *Sicherheitsdienst des Reichsführers*-SS, or abbreviated form, *Sicherheitsdienst*-SD, was the intelligence agency of the SS and the Nazi Party in Nazi Germany.

References

Baker, F 1990, 'Archaeology, Habermas and the pathologies of modernity', in F Baker & J Thomas (eds), *Writing the past in the present*, St David's University College, Lampeter, pp. 54–62

Bucholtz, E 2016, 'The site of memory: *Topography of Terror*' in *Site tour: Topography of Terror*, Stiftung Topographies des Terrors, Berlin.

Clark, LB 2014, 'Ethical spaces: ethics and propriety', in B Sion (ed.), *Trauma tourism: death tourism: disaster sites as recreational landscape*, Seagull Books, London, pp. 9–35.

Clark, LB 2015, 'Ruined landscapes and residual architecture: affect and palimpsest in trauma tourism', *Performance Research*, vol. 20, no. pp. 83–93.

Czaplicka, J 1995, 'History, aesthetics, and contemporary commemorative practice in Berlin', *New German Critique*, no. 65, pp. 155–187.

Dalton, D, 2015, *Dark tourism and crime*, Routledge, London.

Dawson, L 2010, '*Topography of Terror* has washed away too much dirt in presenting its Nazi history', *The Architectural Review*, July, p. 29.

Fein, L 2008, 'In Berlin, where the past is present', *Forward Forum*, October 24, p. 10.

Folkerts, T 2015, 'Landscape as memory', *Journal of Landscape Architecture*, vol. 10, no. 1, pp. 68–77.

Galilee, B 2010, 'Wilms (Heinle, Wischer & Partner): *Topography of Terror*', *Domus* www.domusweb.it/en/architecture/2010/05/12/wilms-heinle-wischer – partner – topography-of-terror.html, viewed 29 May 2019.

Herz, M 2005, 'Institutionalized experiment: the politics of "Jewish Architecture" in Germany', *Jewish Social Studies*, vol. 11, no. 3, pp. 58–66.

Irwin-Zarecka, I. 1995 '"Topography of Terror" in Berlin: is remembrance of forgetting possible?', *The Journal of Arts Management, Law, and Society*, vol. 25, no. 3, pp. 17–26.

James-Chakraborty, K 2018, *Modernism as memory: building identity in the Federal Republic of Germany*, University of Minnesota Press, Minneapolis.

Johnston-Weiss, E 2019, 'In the eye of the beholder: gaze and distance through photographic collage in the *Topography of Terror* and the Canadian Museum for Human Rights', in J Echternkamp and S Jaeger (eds), *View of violence: representing the Second World War in German and European museums and memorials*, Berghahn Books, New York, pp. 92–108.

Ladd, A 1997, *The ghosts of Berlin: confronting German history in the urban landscape*, Chicago University Press, Chicago.

Leoni, C 2014, 'Peter Zumthor's "Topography of Terror"', *Architectural Research Quarterly*, vol. 18, no. 2, pp. 110–122.

Moshenska, G 2010, 'Working with memory in the archaeology of modern conflict', *Cambridge Archaeological Journal*, vol. 20, no. 1, pp. 33–48.

Nachama, A 2014, 'Introduction', in *Topography of Terror – Gestapo, SS, and Reich Security Main Office on Wilhelm and Prinz-Albrecht-Straße: a documentation*, Stiftung Topographies des Terrors Berlin, pp. 6–9.

Nachama, A 2016, 'Foreword', in *Site tour: Topography of Terror*, Stiftung Topographies des Terrors, Berlin, pp. 6–7.

Pearce, C 2011, 'Visualising "everyday" evil: the representation of Nazi perpetrators in German memorial sites', *Holocaust Studies*, vol. 17, no. 2–3, pp. 233–260.

Reynolds, D 2018, *Postcards from Auschwitz: Holocaust tourism and the meaning of remembrance*, New York University Press, New York.

Sandler, D 2011, 'Counterpreservation: decrepitude and memory in post-unification Berlin', *Third Text*, vol. 25, no. 6, pp. 687–697.

Souto, A 2013, 'Architecture and memory: Berlin, a phenomenological approach', in S Bandyopadhyay & G Garma Montiel (eds), *The territories of identity: architecture in the age of evolving globalization*, Routledge, London, pp. 77–90.

Spier, S 2001, 'Place, authorship and the concrete: three conversations with Peter Zumthor', *Architectural Research Quarterly*, vol. 5, vol. 1, pp. 15–36.

Steinbach, P 2014 'Terror, persecution and extermination on Reich territory', in *Topography of Terror – Gestapo, SS, and Reich Security Main Office on Wilhelm and Prinz-Albrecht-Straße: a documentation*, Stiftung Topographies des Terrors, Berlin, pp. 190–254.

Till, K 2005, *The new Berlin: Memory, politics, place*, University of Minnesota Press, Minneapolis.

3 Wewelsburg Castle

Against an SS phantasia

Introducing the castle: the problem of mythology

The seventeenth-century Wewelsburg Castle near Paderborn in north-western Germany recently received sustained international media attention when a new permanent exhibition entitled *Ideology and Terror of the SS* opened in 2010. As John-Stucke notes: 'The exhibition documents numerous aspects of the SS, including its organization and structure, its ideological origins, its concept of art and culture, and its notions of religion and history' (2015, p. 21).

Crossland captures the aura of fascination around the castle well, writing:

> Wewelsburg Castle, once a pseudo-religious sanctum for Hitler's SS, has been shrouded in mystery since 1945. Its echoing crypt and mysterious occult symbols have spawned fantasies of pagan, torch-lit ceremonies held by the murderous brotherhood. A new exhibition aims to dispel such myths – and reflects Germany's new approach towards explaining its darkest places.
>
> (2010, n.p.)

Since the 1960s, the castle has attracted unwanted attention from Far Right and neo-Nazi groups who made pilgrimages to the site. It has featured in fantasy genre novels as a place for battles. Lured by the pagan symbols associated with the castle, Satanists have been recorded as breaking into the crypt to celebrate black masses in the 1970s (Crossland 2010; Boyes 2010). Described variously as: a Nazi Camelot (Cook & Russell 1999); a gothic nightmare (Klimczuk & Warner 1999); a Nazi Grail castle (Coppens n.d.); and a spiritual castle home of the infamous SS (Hall 2010), Wewelsburg Castle is steeped in mythology and folklore, much of which is based on supposition and historically unsustainable falsehoods. The precise nature, scale and frequency of SS rituals at Wewelsburg remain obscure (Klimczuk & Warner 1999). There were pagan celebrations of the winter and summer solstices. Marriages of SS officers were celebrated with pagan rites, and other significant anniversaries in Nazi lore are said to have been celebrated with torchlit processions (Klimczuk & Warner 1999). Lost sums up the importance of Wewelsburg to the SS: 'The castle became an almost religious place where esotericism, runes, pagan lore, and racial theories were studied by a handful of high-ranking SS' (2013, p. 95). Klimczuk and Warner describe Wewelsburg as a kind of 'Black Vatican', the headquarters of a theology of death that brought grotesque suffering and extermination to millions (1999, p. 62). They elaborate:

> There, with the help of ancient Nordic pagan mythology and the extravagant theories of twentieth-century esoteric theories and downright cranks, Himmler manufactured a pseudo-religion designed to take the place of Christian morality, to give his SS units an alternative 'spirituality' that would steel them to commit mass murder under the banner of a German mysticism at once old and new.
>
> (1999, p. 63)

As Crossland (2010, n.p.) asserts: 'There can be no doubt that the place lends itself to fantasy.' This chapter, grounded in a field visit made to Wewelsburg in September 2016, aims to explore the site from the perspective of a visitor encountering both the restored castle (as an architectural entity) and a carefully curated memorial space to explore precisely what one can learn from a place that already carries a heavy burden of signification. Indeed, so controversial has the castle been that some critics have dubbed it 'Naziland'. Such a criticism seems provocative and facile, evoking an association with the most corporate and marketed tourism spaces on the planet: Disneyland. However, if the semiotics of Disneyland include Mickey Mouse, Pluto and the ensemble of lovable characters that have inhabited our childhood *dreams* as evoked by the enchanted Disneyland castle, then perhaps it is no stretch of the imagination to invoke the comparative term 'Naziland' for a sinister castle full of SS officers that is the stuff of *nightmares*. In any event, this chapter seeks to explore what an encounter with Wewelsburg Castle yields for a visitor exposed to its traces of SS occupation. As Hall notes 'the new museum feeds a growing hunger in Germany for knowledge of the Third Reich' (2010), and a steady procession of tourists come to this museum to learn more about its subject: the SS.

Overview of Wewelsburg: Himmler's quest for an ideological and spiritual SS sanctuary

The head of the Schutzstaffel, Heinrich Himmler, had been looking for a castle that he could convert into a symbolic SS site throughout the 1930s (Cook & Russell 1999). After plans to secure Schwalenberg Castle broke down, the triangular Wewelsburg was identified as a castle that could be converted into a Reich Leaders School (*Reichesführerschule* SS) by the SS architect Hermann Bartels (Cook & Russell 1999). Cook and Russell sum up the appeal of the castle to Himmler: 'Desiring this virtuous symmetry as an exemplary framework for the SS, the Reichsführer had now found the special place where Germanic ideology and tradition could be effectively reinstated through archaeology, objective research and education' (1999, p. 22). In 1934, Himmler signed a 100-year lease with the Paderborn district to renovate the castle. Coppens (n.d.) notes that 'the Wewelsburg was to be the place for preserving the rings [*Totenkopfringe*] of those officers who had fallen'. The central focus of the Nazis' redesign was the North Tower. Two key renovations were the creation of a circular crypt with a gas pipe embedded in the floor to create an eternal flame, and a circular ceremonial hall directly above the crypt with a mysterious cult symbol *Schwarze Sonne* (Black Sun) set into the floor. Reproduced in the form of a mosaic inlaid in green and black on the grey marble floor, this crooked spoked sun emblem (which is now banned in Germany) has long fascinated neo-Nazis and partly explains the lure of the castle to right-wing extremists. Klimczuk and Warner note that the twelve-prong design: 'was perfect for his [Himmler's] purpose, since the cult celebrated within the castle was to be presided over by the "Twelve Knights" (SS officers of Gruppenführer status) appointed by Himmler' (1999, p. 67).

Bartels' grandiose vision, which was never completed, was to displace the existing village and build an exclusive residential suburb for high-ranking SS officers. Architectural drawings showed that the conceived design of the estate was that of a giant spear. Historians have speculated that the Nazis planned to acquire the *Spear of Destiny* from a museum in Vienna because 'Hitler was convinced that whoever possessed it controlled the fate of the world' (Coppens n.d.). From 1941 onwards, the architects called the complex the 'Centre of the World'. While Bartels conceived of the castle transformation as vitally important, competing war demands saw scant funds provided for what was essentially a private restoration project. Himmler financed the project from party grants, public subsidies and private donations (Coppens n.d.). Niederhagen concentration camp – the smallest camp in the Nazi KZ universe – supplied the slave labour, which included a variety of prisoners including so-called 'green triangle prisoners (professional criminals), Jehovah's Witnesses, Sinti and Roma' (Klimczuk & Warner 1999, p. 62). It is estimated that 1,341 prisoners died at Niederhagen of starvation, overwork or beatings. Some fifty-six prisoners were executed. As Klimczuk and Warner remind us, these deaths 'invest Wewelsburg with a particular horror' (1999, p. 62). By 1943, all work on the project had stopped with the concentration camp closing in 1943.

Transforming the castle into a memorial/museological space

In 2000, a museological workshop concluded that Wewelsburg Castle was '*the* historic site for an exemplary . . . unique exhibition on the subject of the SS' (John-Stucke 2015, p. 21, emphasis in original). 'The exhibition charts the origins and the exponential growth of the SS' (Crossland 2010, n.p.) and is 'the first museum presentation of the history of the SS' (Brebeck et al. 2015, p. 9).[1] The museum exhibits encompass: the history of the SS and its association with the castle, as well as documenting the organisational structure of the SS; the persecutory and murderous history of the SS; the use of slave labour from Sachsenhausen and Niederhagen concentration camps at Wewelsburg; the end of SS rule in Germany and Wewelsburg; and the fate of victims and perpetrators after 1945. The Kreismuseum Wewelsburg employs original artefacts, photographs, printed and

Figure 3.1 Wewelsburg Castle/Kreismuseum

audio-visual media to both educate visitors and memorialise the camp victims who suffered to modify the castle for the SS.

Like most museums the world over, artefacts are a great draw card for visitors. Accordingly, at Wewelsburg, 'objects from the lifeworld of the SS', as John-Stucke (2015, p. 21) terms, act as a real lure for potential visitors. The array of objects on display in the museum is eclectic and includes uniforms, caps, uniform insignia, ceremonial swords, documents, photographs, diary pages, furniture, lamps, glass *Julfest* ornaments,[2] dinnerware, silver cutlery, ceremonial goblets and 'everyday objects from life under National Socialism' (John-Stucke 2015, p. 22) such as flags and 'people's radios'.

Figure 3.2 Black service cap of General (*Allgemeine*) SS, circa 1934

Figure 3.3 Carved oak bench end decorated with heraldic lion's head and skull

Figure 3.4 Julfest ornaments with carved oak furniture in background

Many of these original objects are from the 'perpetrators' living environment' and were procured from SS members' personal estates (John-Stucke 2015, p. 22). Other significant exhibits supplement these items: 'The museum collection also comprises ideologically significant art, such as drawings, paintings, and SS jewellery, as well as porcelain and ceramics from the SS owned Allach Porcelain Manufactory, from which Himmler had a collection of samples created at Wewelsburg' (John-Stucke 2015, p. 22). Most of these SS artefacts are ideologically charged, 'affirmative' objects. In this context, the term is used to denote 'original objects that affirm and endorse National Socialism, specifically, the world view of the SS' (John-Stucke 2015, p. 23). It is important to stress that these items are displayed with information that link the SS to their criminality. As Pfeifer notes: 'We want to show that you can't divorce the ideology from the crimes that resulted from it, so we display SS artefacts alongside information on the Holocaust and the victims' (cited in Crossland 2010).

John-Stucke emphasises: 'The new Wewelsburg exhibition forgoes replicas and presents original objects, to avoid creating distorted or fictional impressions' (2015, p. 23). Dalton (2015) has documented that replica objects are quite problematic at tourism sites and that people crave exposure to authentic objects. In conceiving this new exhibition, John-Stucke stated that 'the importance of originality and authenticity of objects has long been a point of discussion in museums' (2015, p. 23). Fittingly then, a *replica* flogging table which proved somewhat controversial in an earlier exhibition has been replaced with a photograph that substitutes for the former three-dimensional reproduction. *Original* prisoner index cards (listing reasons and details of punishment) are a better way of helping visitors imagine the violence perpetrated at Wewelsburg and correspond with the visitors' quest to encounter authentic items.

A faux castle

Given Himmler's desire to convert Wewelsburg into an edifice that suited his aesthetic taste, slave labourers toiled to radically alter the architectural features of the castle. As Crossland notes, renaissance plaster from the castle walls was replaced with stone and cladding 'to give it a medieval appearance totally out of keeping with its 17th century design' (2010, n.p.). The faux aura of the castle is captured well by Crossland who elaborates:

> The overriding impression is that everything about this castle is fake. The crypt resembles the set of a 1940s Hollywood movie about King Arthur and his knights. The arches in the 'Hall of Generals' may be covered in medieval-looking stone, but are made of concrete.
>
> (2010, n.p.)

Commenting on the artifice employed, Jan Eric Schulte (an expert on the SS who helped devise the Wewelsburg exhibition) observes: 'It's an impressive example of how the SS and its architects tried to falsify and recreate history to justify their own ideology . . . when you strip off the façade, there's nothing behind it' (as cited in Crossland 2010, n.p.). It is fitting that the exhibition takes great pains to explain to the visitor that the castle was substantially modified in the 1930s and 1940s. It helps the visitor appreciate that castle was envisioned as a fantasy space where the SS could indulge their grandiose vision as the ruling elite of the Nazi party.

Supplementing the artefacts: the importance of SS biographies in the exhibition

The social and organisational structure of the SS is offered using biographical material. John-Stucke stresses: 'the diverse views and career paths of the SS men highlight the heterogeneity of the SS' (2015, p. 27). Some twenty-odd SS officers (with accompanying official portrait photographs) both of low and high rank and from all the different SS divisions, including *Waffen* SS, are presented to the visitor in rich and detailed biographical detail. Exposure to these biographies helps the visitor better comprehend some of the physical exhibits encountered in the museum. For example, SS officer Oswald Pohl is showcased as a man whose 'unconditional loyalty secured his meteoric rise within the organisation' (Brebeck et al. 2015, p. 97). We learn that Pohl, a former Navy purser, joined the SS in 1934. Aligning himself as an ally of Himmler, he rose to power as an Obergruppenführer and a general of the Armed SS. Pohl controlled the administration and finances of the SS as well as concentration camps and various other SS enterprises, and 'sponsored a patronage system with strong personal ties, which was designed to guarantee unity within his organisation' (Brebeck et al. 2015, p. 97). Pohl also helped convert the Wewelsburg Renaissance castle into a SS centre suggestive of a medieval knight's castle (Brebeck et al. 2015, p. 155). He was tried in Nuremberg in 1947 for war crimes, was sentenced to death that same year, and was executed at Landsberg Prison in 1951.

Pohl's biographical vignette helps the visitor better comprehend an exhibit encountered later in the museum. An oil painting, circa 1940, depicts Pohl in splendid blue knight's armour. The museum signage informs the visitor: 'Pohl underscored his importance in the National Socialist political and ideological system by having himself pictured as a knight from the heroic past' (Brebeck et al. 2015, p. 155). If the folklore associated with this museum promised a pageant of SS chivalry; this painting of Pohl clutching a swastika-embellished sword *almost* delivers on this promise; yet the biographical information neutralises the potential effect. Rather than observe the painting (and its subject) as an appealing medieval hero, the visitor now perceives Pohl as a vainglorious, narcissistic planner of Nazi finance and administration. What allure the painting might have held is banished as one contemplates a ruthless, egotistical Nazi – the man behind the armour as it were. This is more important when we note Carden-Coyne's warning that 'the dangerous allure of imagining perpetrators' carries a threat to the 'solemn memorial to victims' (2011, p. 170).

A lower-ranked SS officer can be juxtaposed with Pohl. Richard Walther Darré is photographed in an SS Gruppenführer uniform in 1934. Visitors learn that his power base was the 'Race and Settlement Main Office' which he founded and led until 1938. Furthermore, '[t]he main tasks of this office consisted of assessing the "racial" reliability of SS men and their wives, as well as to provide their ideological training' (Brebeck et al. 2015, p. 100). Displayed alongside Darré's photograph and biography is a copy of his 1929 book *The peasantry as life source of the Nordic race*. This book laid the foundations of his racist beliefs. Darré 'harboured a deep aversion to the modern city, liberalism, capitalism and the Jew' (Brebeck et al. 2015, p. 100). The book, published by an esteemed Munich publisher, helps the visitor behold that the SS was deeply entrenched in pseudo-scientific beliefs propagated by well-educated men, many of whom held doctorates. Many genocidal policies can be traced back to tracts like Darré's which helped the SS justify their homicidal actions in the east.

The problem of the fetishisation of Nazi artefacts and iconography

Susan Sontag's classic essay 'Fascinating fascism' was first published in *The New York Review of Books* in 1975. The obscure book she reviewed, Jack Pia's *SS Regalia*, is long since forgotten, but Sontag's tiny review still looms large in cultural theory and semiotics. It was the first text to point out that which became obvious once articulated: that the SS uniform was charged (post-war) with a sexual aura. As Sontag (1975, n.p.) wrote: 'Though *SS Regalia* is a respectable British-made compilation (with a three-page historical preface and detailed notes in the back), one knows that its appeal is not scholarly but sexual.' She elaborates: 'Uniforms suggest fantasies of community, order, identity (through ranks, badges, medals which "say" who the wearer is and what he has done: his worth is recognized), competence, legitimate authority, the legitimate exercise of violence' (1975, n.p.). Her thesis on the erotic allure of the SS uniform makes the argument that:

> [T]he SS seems to be the most perfect incarnation of fascism in its overt assertion of the righteousness of violence, the right to have total power over others and to treat them as absolutely inferior. It was in the SS that this assertion seemed the most complete, because they acted it out in a singularly brutal and efficient manner; and because they dramatized it by linking it to certain aesthetic standards.
>
> (Sontag 1975, n.p.)

This notion of aesthetic importance is not accidental. Sontag (1975, n.p.) notes that '[t]he SS was designed as an elite military community that would not only be supremely violent but also supremely beautiful'. Indeed, as the book jacket of *SS Regalia* proclaims: 'The SS wore a vast variety of decorations, symbols, badges to distinguish rank, from collar runes to the death's head. The appearance was both dramatic and menacing' (Sontag 1975, n.p.). Sontag (1975, n.p.) writes: 'If the message of fascism has been neutralized by an aesthetic view of life, its trappings have been sexualised.' A black SS uniform is now profoundly over-coded with meanings that transcend its wartime symbolism. To employ Roland Barthes' concept of the *sign* (1972), if the combined death's head insignia and colour black synonymous with the SS is the *signifier*, then the *signified* in our modern world is eroticism and a fascistic power over life and death. That this is the case is due to the fact that since the war, the SS uniform and the death's head insignia has been heavily embedded in popular culture in Hollywood and arthouse cinema (see Rohr 2010).[3] This is not to say that the uniform does not still bear the connotations of wartime use, but rather that these connotations coexist with other associations that have been layered upon as a sort of semiotic baggage that could never have been predicted in the 1930s and 1940s. Sadomasochistic culture, for example, is often invested with a sartorial eroticism redolent of the SS: black leather peaked caps and black leather coats. As Sontag (1975, n.p.) proclaims 'the SS has become a reference for sexual adventurism'. The shock that such associations first provoked seems to have dissipated as 'Nazi material enters the vast repository of popular iconography', to borrow Sontag's term (1975, n.p.). In 1975, Sontag proclaimed: 'The definitely sexual lure of fascism, which *SS Regalia* testifies to with unabashed plainness, seems impervious to deflation by irony or overfamiliarity' (1975, n.p.). Some forty-odd years since she wrote these words, and confronted with a seemingly never-ending array of SS *signs*, Sontag's implicit suggestion that the sexual lure of fascism invested in the SS would not abate seems to ring true.

Countering the problem of potential fetishisation at Wewelsburg

Confronted with these cultural associations and the aura that is invested in SS uniforms and objects presented the museum with a profound challenge. The museum understood from the outset that many of the exhibits function as devotional objects in the eyes of some potential visitors, especially Far Right and neo-Nazi sympathisers.[4] The paradox at play, however, is that since the 1990s, there has been a 'general trend towards the "auratic" at memorial sites' (John-Stucke 2015, p. 20). In part, this trend can be traced back to Walter Benjamin's highly influential book *Illuminations* in which he writes that an object is 'auratic' if it has a capacity to convey its historical authenticity. Its unique existence is based on its 'historical testimony' (Benjamin 1968, p. 215). It is imbued with the magic of having 'been there' (Benjamin 1968, p. 215). Visitors wish to see original objects and artefacts *in situ* in places where they have 'been', and this adds to the viewers' sense that their encounter with the past has been authentic.

The museum developed presentation strategies at a workshop to manage the fact that castle visitors crave exposure to authentic objects. This was perceived as both just and appropriate while at the same time keeping in mind 'the possible effect and appeal of these artefacts, which were very important for community building within the SS' (John-Stucke 2015, p. 23). A balance of sorts was struck with the museum determining that SS objects should be exhibited 'in a bid to inform the public about the ideology of the SS and to demystify the objects' (John-Stucke 2015, p. 23). However, it was decided that 'the affirmative objects should not be shown without comment', and that 'a responsible contextualization would be needed to help prevent fetishization, but also a naïve dehistoricization of the objects' (John-Stucke 2015, pp. 23–24).

In terms of responsible presentation strategies, the museum established five principles that underpinned the exhibition of the SS objects (John-Stucke 2015):

- The Principle of Storage Facility Arrangement
- The Principle of Obscuring but not Concealing
- The Principle of Massification
- The Principle of Contrast
- The Principle of Responsible Contextualization

In the following section I will discuss each principle, and will comment on its efficacy with reference to specific exhibited items and in connection to a wider memorialisation and museological context.

The Principle of Storage Facility Arrangement

As John-Stucke observes:

> The showcases are integrated into plain exhibition display units, which are designed to resemble storeroom cabinets and are covered with panels

in different shades of white. The functional, neutral storage in the display cases is intended to strip the objects of any hint of a supposed 'magic of the mysterious'.

(2015, p. 24)

This tactic works well. Unlike some museums that deploy larger and more elaborate cabinets to display particularly important pieces, the uniformity of cabinetry confounds attempts of the eye to quickly discover anything that might be perceived of as a main attraction. There is what one might term a *democracy of display* at play. Everything is important and nothing is afforded any special status. I peered into one cabinet and beheld a death's head fabric collar patch (accompanied by shoulder boards) embroidered in silver thread.

This is the *sign* synonymous with the SS and one that Sontag alluded to as being charged with a particularly potent aura. Yet, in the cabinet – bathed in muted light on a white cardboard matt board – the item resisted any charge of glamour or fascistic appeal. Without any accent lighting, the item looked modest: unspectacular. Its menacing connotations were not for a moment diminished, for we associate this sign with death: all those subsumed during the Shoah. However, the item resisted easy fetishisation. In part, this is due to the unembellished, locker-like cabinets. The technique of unfussy presentation is also typified by the display of a white sports singlet emblazoned with a black SS logo in a circle.

Figure 3.5 Death's head fabric collar patch in silver thread (accompanied by shoulder boards)

Figure 3.6 Athletic sports singlet emblazoned with a black SS logo

The SS symbol is overloaded with connotations of power and authority, and nevertheless the item looked innocuous in such a rudimentary display. It is just a sports garment that resists the imposition of any narrative that might fetishise its use. While it would be impossible for the museum to employ presentation tactics that wholly thwart Nazi fantasies in the minds of some beholders, these plain display cabinets certainly do not inspire such flights of imagination.

The Principle of Obscuring but not Concealing

John-Stucke outlines the principle of obscurement and concealment at play in the museum:

> The SS uniforms or pieces of Wewelsburg furniture with swastika emblems shown in the display cases are partially obscured by frosted screens in order to disrupt any potential fascination they might possess. The partial covering of display cases hinders an unobstructed view of the artifacts.
>
> (2015, p. 24)

This technique is perhaps best illustrated by reference to the display of an SS Untersturmführer officer's tunic adorned with a 'K' and a death's head on the collar patch which, we are instructed, was worn at a KZ (concentration camp). In that case, an Oberführer's black cap with white piping is also displayed, along with a ceremonial dagger, dagger sheath, belt buckle and assorted SS pamphlets.

Writing about curatorial strategies in museums, Feldman asserts: 'The metonymic contact point . . . retains nothing of the body, but is an object associated with one part of the body that stands symbolically for the whole' (2006, p. 256). Adhering to this logic as we contemplate this empty uniform, we fill it with the missing body of an SS officer and it becomes more menacing as an artefact.

In terms of our viewing perspective, a large frosted glass panel impedes our view. The placement of the cap is very low and does not have the same dramatic effect that would be achieved by placing it on a mannequin with a head. Upon

Figure 3.7 SS Untersturmführer officer's tunic and Oberführer's black cap, ceremonial dagger, sheath, belt buckle and assorted SS pamphlets

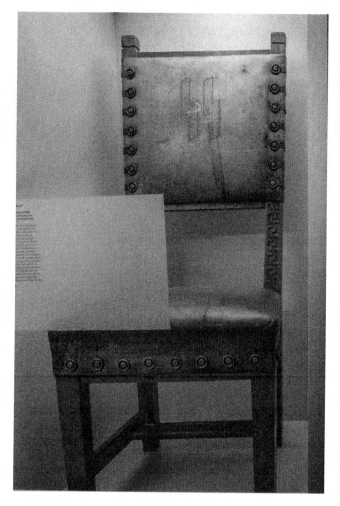

Figure 3.8 Oak chair with brass fittings and double sig rune impressed into leather backrest

leaving the museum, if one were to pose the question: *Which museum exhibit might most appeal to neo-Nazi sympathisers?*, one might well answer that it is this tableau of SS regalia and accoutrements. Yet the large frosted glass screen serves its intended purpose well. It intrudes in the spectator's frame of sight and obscures the tunic. The visual foil is ingenious in its simplicity. During my visit I witnessed several visitors moving their heads to try and peer at the left side of the jacket. The frosted screen functions as an *imaginative* barrier – aiding to block the imposition of any fantasies that the spectator might project onto the objects. The objects are not concealed, so the museological imperative of permitting scrutiny is not thwarted. Similarly, a large oak chair with brass fittings, leather upholstery, and the double sig rune impressed into the backrest is displayed with a similar obscuring frosted panel.

Here, perhaps the obscuring effect is less successful; however, the principle of concealment still blocks an unhindered view. Additionally, the text printed on the frosted glass panels serves an additional purpose for it is educative as to the 'ideological and political meaning' (John-Stucke 2015, p. 24) of the objects on display for the SS.

The Principle of Massification

The third technique at play is that of the principle of massification. John-Stucke provides the example of mass-produced National Socialist everyday items such as the badges of the Winter Relief Agency, which are exhibited in large quantities in acid-free archival boxes (2015, p. 24). She elaborates: 'They do not appear as individual objects of value but in the way they are conceived under National Socialism – as mass-produced propaganda materials, which now are in storage, as if in a depot' (2015, p. 24). To my mind, the best illustration of massification was a pile of seven or eight cheaply manufactured paper Nazi flags emblazoned with a black swastika in a white circle on a red background; and affixed to wooden sticks. This flag, synonymous with Nazism, functions as a powerful synecdoche for the murderous National Socialist State.

Figure 3.9 Nazi swastika flags, assorted badges and photographs depicting mass Nazi public gatherings

In a clever curatorial intervention, several photographs depict mass Nazi rallies and the badges produced to celebrate such occasions are exhibited alongside the flags. One depicts a throng of cheering people at the Harvest Festival Day near Hameln behind an SS cordon.

Museum exhibits never function in a vacuum. The true power of the massification themed exhibits at Wewelsburg is that they gesture to more potent and confronting mass exhibits: those associated with the Auschwitz-Birkenau concentration camp. Contemplating the massification themed displays at Wewelsburg, I recalled the disturbing mass displays at Auschwitz I had seen in 2007: an enormous pile of empty Zyklon B canisters; an assortment of artificial limbs and crutches piled together in an entangled jumble; leather suitcases of all shapes and sizes; thousands of shoes of all shapes, types and sizes; and the horrific spectacle of piles of human hair so decayed it was scarcely recognisable (Dalton 2015). As 'trauma icons' (Stier 2003; Williams 2007), these objects testify to the detritus produced by genocide and, once observed *in situ* at Auschwitz, can never be forgotten.

The Principle of Contrast

The fourth responsible presentation strategy employed is characterised by John-Stucke (2015, p. 24) as ensuring that portrayals of the SS worldview did not merely present the 'organizations' self-promoted claims, but also the everyday reality'. While John-Stucke cites the example of the intended role of women as mothers within the SS community, I found the display of Allach™ figurines to be quite instructive of the concept of contrast. Two white porcelain dogs, a dachshund puppy and a German shepherd are displayed in a locker-style cabinet.

At first they seem somewhat incongruous items, but the instructive text explains that the Nazis believed 'nature should be the taskmaster of art' and that 'Germans were thought to possess an innate love of nature that was compatible only with "true" representation' (Brebeck et al. 2015, p. 186). Furthermore, the visitor is instructed: 'To speak of the German soul, animals – including those made from porcelain – should always be presented as naturalistically as possible. Moreover, (human) character traits were ascribed to animals, such as loyalty and obedience to shepherd dogs' (Brebeck et al, 2015, p. 186). Allusions to loyalty aside, the everyday reality of SS life was the use of German shepherds as 'watchdogs among the SS concentration camp guards' (Brebeck et al. 2015, p. 186). The daily reality was that dogs savaged concentration camp inmates and were used as instruments of terror by the SS in the camps.

The Principle of Responsible Contextualisation

John-Stucke (2015, p. 25) outlines this fifth responsible presentation strategy employed in the museum: 'The Principle of Responsible Contextualization . . . requires that objects be displayed with documents and photos to prevent a glorification of ideologically charged objects.' A good example of this approach is the

Figure 3.10 Two Allach™ porcelain dogs and other statuettes

display of two large photographs that depict Nazi racial profiling practices. In one photograph, a swatch of glass eyes is being held up against a women's face for an unseen officer to determine her eye colour. In a corresponding image, measuring callipers are being applied to a boy's face by an officer engaged in some sort of phrenological process.

When one contemplates the ironstone crockery in a nearby cabinet – an egg-cup, teacup and small teapot – the quaint rune patterns look suitably medieval and mundane. Confronted with the photographs, the visitor casts aside the image of civility and decorum, as conjured by the breakfast set, and recalls immediately that the SS were engaged in acts of racial profiling and categorising that effectively paved the ways for Jews, Slavic people and Roma to be sent east

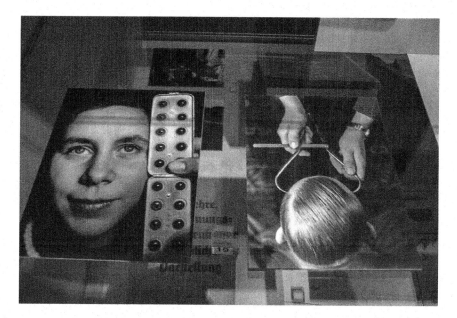

Figure 3.11 Two photographs depicting Nazi eugenic and phrenological processes

to the extermination camps. These documents and photographs are profoundly important at Wewelsburg. They help anchor so many of the seemingly innocuous items that might otherwise civilise the SS (e.g., quality hallmarked silver and fine porcelain) by explicitly linking them to acts of persecution, discrimination and, ultimately, genocide. Indeed, as John-Stucke argues: 'The presentation of all topics and objects considers the genuinely criminal character of the SS' (2015, p. 25). Perhaps the most potent example of such anchors in the museum is the display of four large glass photographic plates taken covertly by a prisoner in the *Sonderkommando* in Auschwitz-Birkenau in 1944. They depict an area near Crematorium V where bodies were being burned in the open air. Looking at these (in)famous photographs, I recalled Heinrich Heine's prophetic statement: 'Where books are burned, in the end, people will also be burned.'[5] On 10 May 1933, in the name of Nazi ideology, books by many so-called 'un-German' authors were thrown onto huge pyres by Nazis, including the works of Thomas Mann, Karl Marx and Erich Kästner. In homage to this terrible event, the art deco cover of Erich Kästner's *Emil and the detectives* – so redolent of the 1920s – is displayed at Wewelsburg and at the Wannsee House (see Chapter 1).[6]

Encountering concentration camp victims

One of the most important functions of the Wewelsburg museum is to represent the experiences of the many victims who suffered from being used as slave labour to modify the castle. Various artefacts are displayed in warm accent lights that humanise these objects. For example, a prisoner's ubiquitous striped prison jacket and cap, in stark contrast to the SS officer's tunic, is displayed without frosted glass obscuring the two objects. Fittingly, the storage style cabinets used for the display of SS objects are 'consciously abandoned' for objects associated with prisoners (John-Stucke 2015, p. 25). The jacket and cap are framed in a manner that signifies their importance as original garments that testify to the provision of concentration camp labour at the castle. Placed more prominently than that SS tunic, they are afforded a respect not afforded to the SS garments.

Softly lit document drawers, which slide out in a gentle inviting gesture, allow visitors to behold and read original letters from the concentration camp inmates at Niederhagen. The museum anticipated that 'what today is living memory . . . will be communicated tomorrow through media' (John-Stucke 2015, p. 25), and so visitors can listen to interviews with twenty-one concentration camp survivors. Under the title *The survivors tell their stories*, these filmed conversations with survivors from Germany, Poland, Russia, Ukraine, Austria, Belgium and the USA are augmented with translated subtitles. Their testimony, significantly, does not present the perspective of victims, but rather of 'human beings who . . . regained their freedom and dignity' (John-Stucke 2015, p. 26). At audio stations, visitors can listen to statements by survivors that evoke the terror and deprivations of camp life. Hunger and starvation are common survivor themes. Strategically, we never hear from former SS officers stationed at Wewelsburg: 'Audio documents of remarks by SS men are not included in the exhibition. The domain of the spoken word is withheld from them' (John-Stucke 2015, p. 26). The museum curators stress that 'neither relics nor documents of the camp administration can represent the personal view of the victims' (John-Stucke 2015, p. 26). Therefore, testimony in both written and audio-visual forms is a profoundly important device to account for Nazi criminality in the space of this castle. One particularly disquieting piece of testimony justifies the death of a fifteen-year-old Jewish boy who was hanged as punishment for a 'racial crime'. His offence was to accidentally hit the daughter of an SS officer with a snowball (Boyes 2010). Such testimony reminds the museum visitor that life was precarious for prisoners who inhabited the SS universe.

Encountering the Obergruppenführer Hall and crypt

As John-Stucke notes: 'Passing the moat on their way to the Northern tower, visitors are able to grasp the transformation of the SS of the former secondary residence of the prince-bishops into what the organization held to be a "German Castle"' (2015, p. 28). Having left the main exhibition space, as one heads to the tower, the faux architectural interventions become apparent. Along the way one encounters a very powerful memorial to the Niederhagen concentration camp slave labourers. Against the walls that they helped render, a selection of aluminium square poles is clustered. Capped with translucent coloured triangles, the poles conjure memories of the nameless and faceless prisoners who were exploited at this site.

Figure 3.12 Memorial to the Niederhagen concentration camp slave labourers

Anyone familiar with KZ uniform markings would recognise that the different coloured triangles were used to identify different classes of prisoners (e.g., political prisoners were assigned red; criminals, green; Sinti and Roma, assigned brown; homosexuals, pink; and Jehovah's Witnesses were allocated purple). Glinting in the light, the memorial is aesthetically very beautiful against the austere stone backdrop. It serves its purpose well, interrupting the stroll and inviting the visitor to reflect on their suffering.

Depending on whether ascending or descending the North Tower, one either encounters the Obergruppenführer Hall[7] (Generals' Hall) at the very top of the tower or the architectural space referred to as the *crypt*. The two historical chambers are subject to closed-circuit television (CCTV) surveillance and the museum has the right to evict Far Right sympathisers who misbehave (Boyes 2010). Germany has a strict criminal code, so few people would be foolish enough to attempt to perform a Hitler salute and risk prosecution. Despite all the mythology and supposition alluded to earlier in this chapter, Brebeck and John-Stucke (2015, p. 13) note:

> There is no information about their [the chamber's] intended use – at most, it can be inferred from Himmler's ideas for Wewelsburg Castle. In all likelihood, they would have played a major role in the overall function of the castle, serving as a central venue for meetings and oath-taking ceremonies for the Gruppenführer corps.

The Obergruppenführer Hall now has orange and grey bean bags scattered over the floor to encourage groups to sit and reflect. There is little to see here and even the imagination struggles to animate the space given that very little is known about its use. The hall is denuded of objects. Klimczuk and Warner (1999, p. 67) speculate that:

> A great circular table made of oak was installed there in Himmler's time, with a dozen chairs set round it, each with its owners' names inscribed on a silver plate. Around the walls were hung shields bearing the coats of arms of the twelve senior SS officers, invented for them by the *Ahnenerbe*,[8] the arm of the SS created to deal with mystical matters.

Some museums, where a fitting context exists, recreate the interior fittings and fixtures of a bygone period to help visitors imagine how a space once functioned. To even contemplate such a recreation of the Nazi Knights of the Round Table fantasy in the Obergruppenführer Hall – as propagated through popular culture (namely the fantasy novel, *The spear of destiny* by Trevor Ravenscroft)[9] – would seem a travesty in this space. There is little to see save for a subtle feature that, as hitherto outlined in this chapter, once drew neo-Nazis to the site. The *Schwarze Sonne* is inlaid in the floor. It is smaller in scale than one would imagine and is somewhat unremarkable despite the weight of popular culture that accounts for its existence, ensuring that a paradox exists. Familiarity with the black sun can be traced back not so much to Wewelsburg itself, but rather to the publication of various books, such as the occult Nazi-thriller *The black sun of Tashi Lhunpo* which was published under the pen name of Russell McCloud in 1991 (Lost 2013, p. 101). Brebeck and John-Stucke stress that the novel 'marked the apex of this type of Wewelsburg castle mythologization. It contains all the elements of extreme right-wing crypto-historiography' (2015, p. 15). In terms of the narrative: 'The story . . . mentions – and this is a novelty – the sun wheel intarsia in the Northern Tower's Obergruppenführer Hall as the central symbol of a secret association of former SS members: the "Black Sun"' (Brebeck & John-Stucke 2015, p. 15). As Brebeck and John-Stucke (2015, p. 15) observe of the sun wheel symbol: 'The novel became a best seller throughout the right-wing scene . . . A full-fledged market for "black sun" devotional objects" emerged: T-shirts, scarfs, flags, table cloths, lamps among other things, have been decorated with this sign ever since [its publication].' The black sun symbol always posed as risk to the museum given its symbolic lure to neo-Nazis and right-wing sympathisers. Fortunately, CCTV surveillance cameras have 'successfully prevented expressions of right-wing views and sentiments on the exhibition premises' (Brebeck & John-Stucke 2015, p. 16). Indeed, the website promoting the castle advises potential visitors that pro-Nazi language and gestures are prohibited.

If the Obergruppenführer Hall threatens to be a space that might attract undesirable displays by visitors with inappropriate motives, the crypt is arguably an even more potently charged space. The crypt is a dark, dank space which is enveloped in a soft light afforded by four large overhead shafts. It has a cupola roof and 'was probably designed to serve as a hall for the dead' (Brebeck & John-Stucke 2015, p. 14). The dome shell was made of concrete and, in keeping with the faux aesthetic employed by the SS architect, was faced with limestone by concentration camp labourers. Brebeck and John-Stucke describe the central aesthetic feature of the domed hall: 'At the apex of the dome, a swastika is embedded in a meander ornament; the openings of shafts are visible between its arms' (2015, p. 14). According to oral accounts, a central sunken basin in the middle of the crypt was apparently equipped with an eternal flame. To the extent that Wewelsburg has been likened to a Black Vatican, this space where the SS might venerate their dead is perhaps the most loaded room in the castle. The challenge to the museum was how to best intervene in this space to counter the aura of veneration of the SS engendered by the architecture and the swastika-embellished roof.

The solution to this problem had its roots in the past. In the 1950s, a memorial was commissioned for the crypt: '[T]he young Büren painter Josef Glahé was commissioned with the creation of ten large-format paintings addressing the destructive effects of National Socialism, including prison labour at Wewelsburg Castle' (Brebeck & John-Stucke 2015, p. 14). These expressionistic paintings met with general disapproval. A defensive attitude towards the paintings was manifested from a public that had been confronted by the graphic nature of the art at a time where *forgetting* rather than *remembering* the trauma of the war prevailed in most parts of Germany. One painting, entitled *Displaced, Gassed, Extinguished* was removed from display following a complaint that it 'offended public decency' (Brebeck & John-Stucke 2015, p. 14). By 1973, the damp climate of the crypt had caused the remaining paintings to deteriorate and they were also removed from public display. In conceiving of the contemporary use of Wewelsburg as a museum space, it was debated 'whether a reinterpretation of the room [the crypt] or a "refraction" of its alleged impact could be achieved by a reconstruction of the Glahé cycle' (Brebeck & John-Stucke 2015, p. 16). The original paintings are not displayed, but identically sized format prints are hung in the crypt, accentuated by new lighting. The effect is very powerful. These paintings, individually and as a suite, speak to the horrors of Nazism. These powerful images – suffused with pain and suffering – disinhibit the formation of Nazi fantasies, unless one wilfully blocks out their presence in the crypt. The reinstallation (albeit of facsimile paintings) is a real triumph of intervention. Without the paintings, the space may well have been too loaded with a pseudo-religious Nazi aura. The paintings disrupt any such potential aura. To the extent that the crypt space now encourages any solemn refection, it is not on the glories of the SS; but rather on the legacies of its homicidal actions.

Conclusion

Wewelsburg does not offer the typical tourist a medieval castle 'experience' where one is confronted with ghoulish and grisly torture exhibits. In such places, the victims of medieval torture must be imagined and are situated too far back in time for visitors to develop any real empathy for them. The museum at Wewelsburg is a remarkably sensitive place and accomplishes a feat that few people could have predicted would 'work' in such an ideologically charged environment. It presents visitors with an opportunity to contemplate a vast array of SS objects and paraphernalia in a carefully curated manner that delimits opportunities to venerate or fetishise these items. Heralded by some critics in the media as a veritable Naziland, it is factually true that this castle possesses the most concentrated holding of SS artefacts in the world. The imposing castle itself is evocative of SS mythology and ceremony, and yet the experience of visiting it puts paid to any clichéd accusations that this is Naziland. To my mind, the castle museum is *anti*-Naziland. It offers no Disneyland-esque experience for the visitor. There are, of course, no rides, amusements or immersion experiences. Nor are there any themed restaurants serving fare favoured by the SS. Instead, there is a multi-tiered series of exhibits and documents that cover every facet of the SS from its inception, mindset and crimes to its use of concentration camp labour to renovate the Castle into a medieval Nazi phantasia. From the mid-1930s until the closing years of World War II, this castle's heavy oak furniture, rune-adorned objects and faux medieval architecture may well have underwritten many SS fantasies of Germanic superiority and purity. Encountered today as a museum, the space is not one that speaks to fantasy but rather to the brutal reality of criminality associated with every aspect of the SS.

The idea that the SS was simply an organisation run by monsters is countered by Kirsten John-Stucke, the deputy head of the exhibition:

> It's important to deal with the perpetrators and explore how people behaved the way they did, and what type of men they were. The SS weren't all monsters. Saying they were all sick in the head would make it too easy. A lot of them were normal men who wanted to advance their careers.
>
> (cited in Crossland 2010, n.p.)

We are faced with this painful and unassailable truth as we encounter the numerous biographies of SS officers encountered in the earlier parts of the exhibition. While the castle may well lure Nazi sympathisers enlivened by a popular culture diet that has done much to invigorate SS iconography as alluring in recent decades,[10] the castle does not allow for pro-Nazi fantasies to be easily staged in the mind's eye within its walls. Every carefully curated object is surrounded by a wealth of photographic and documentary evidence that disrupts any process of potential veneration of the SS. The potent mythology and folklore attached to the space (itself largely as faux as the stone and concrete cladding affixed to the castle walls), peels away like a thin veneer and one is confronted with an overwhelming sense of criminality and genocidal logic.

Simon argues that 'curating an exhibition of difficult knowledge clearly involves *much more* than devising an iconic display of images and artefacts whose significance is rendered through emotionally underwritten moral injunctions and admonitions' (2011, p. 201, emphasis added). The *much more* to which he alludes relates to the *mise-en-scène* of an exhibition and its capacity to invite an act of witnessing. The triumph of the Wewelsburg museum is that we are invited to witness the SS as architects of misery, suffering and genocide. The exhibition space is fraught with tension, and this is productive. Glancing at a wrought iron lamp with a vellum lampshade displayed alongside art deco-styled silverware embossed with the personalised 'Wewelsburg SS' stamp, one is struck by the realisation that the SS sought decorative beauty in their daily life while they routinely engaged in murder.

The frivolity of interior design coexisting with the perpetration of genocide: civility and barbarity coexisting. Similarly, the SS uniforms and objects are divested of any cachet they may have been invested with by popular culture

Figure 3.13 Metal fabricated SS and swastika decorations, wrought iron and vellum lamp, assorted silver cutlery and bowls

and are *re-invested* with more befitting connotations: exploitation, suffering and death. That such a process occurs is supported by Crownshaw's observation that: 'The meaning of an artefact is dependent upon its narrativization. It is the visitor's gaze, then, that might reinterpret artefactual meaning, loosening artefacts from their exhibitionary anchor and metaphysics of presence' (2007, p. 179).

Coda: a flight of butterflies to counter Nazi flights of fantasy

The district administrator of Paderborn Manfred Müller writes that: 'the exhibition intends, among other things, that visitors learn from the racist, and unjust behaviour of the National Socialists . . . that they engage for themselves peace, human rights, and integration' (2015, p. 7). As I prepared to depart the museum, I came across a temporary art exhibition inspired by a visit to the museum by schoolchildren. One work among the naïve art, which I will describe for the reader, indeed stood out. On a matt black background, two silver foil cut-out effigies of the infamous SS Death's head were affixed. Seventeen colourful butterflies encircled the skulls – a vivid pageant of colour contrasting with the black background. This is a brave and audacious work of art: clearly the work of a young person unencumbered by any direct link to the past. Some may have found the artwork disrespectful, as though nature – as symbolised by the butterflies – should not be allowed to intrude on an image bearing such a notorious *sign* (Barthes 1972): the *Totenkopf* (skull and crossbones and death's head symbol). To my mind, it was a beautiful and heartfelt response to the powerful exhibition sponsored by the castle. The allegorical properties of this artwork suggested to me that the artist had heeded the message to which Administrator Müller alluded. The castle was very much a moribund space. All of the events it depicts concern people long dead or soon to pass on. Life ensues, and with it the hope that a young person could engage with peace and populate her/his canvas with a flight of butterflies rather than a Nazi *flight of fantasy* (as underwritten by popular culture). Similarly – adjacent to the art exhibition – a collage of local newspaper articles depicted local senior students engaged in archaeological digs around the castle environs. This reminded me that serious pursuits to learn about the past are enacted regularly at this site.

Notes

1 It should be stressed that a smaller exhibition devoted to the SS was established in the 1980s and was expanded in the 1990s before being reconceived into the current exhibition.
2 These *Julfest* ornaments reflect how the National Socialists tried to transform a Christian celebration in a way that responded to the ideology of Germanic heritage. Adorned with runic symbols such as the sun, tree of life (a symbol of fertility), and man-rune (a symbol of power for the Germanic people); they were designed as "meaningful tree decorations" (Tegethoff 2018, n.p.)
3 Most recently, Quentin Tarantino's *Inglourious basterds* has attracted criticism for investing the SS uniform with allure. In terms of arthouse cinema, Liliana Cavani's *The night porter* (see Gelbin 2011) hypersexualised the SS uniform, as did Luchino Visconti's *The damned*. The most notorious film to sexualise the SS uniform was

Salon kitty, a soft-porn depiction of an exclusive brothel in Berlin catering to the Nazi elite.

4 Rosenfeld (2010) explores how Nazi objects are primed to court controversy when exhibited. He documents that the Munich Stadtmuseum had to cancel an exhibition entitled *Munich 1933–1945* after the then Mayor Christian Ude became incensed that the artefacts on display – including SA (Sturmabteilung-Stormtroopers/Brownshirts) uniforms and Nazi kitsch – could be construed as Nazi devotional objects. A local newspaper noted the intended exhibition 'perilously flirted with the sacralization of the items and their elevation into cultic objects' (cited in Rosenfeld 2010, p. 176).

5 *Almansor: a tragedy* (1823), as translated in *True religion* (2003) by Graham Ward, p. 142.

6 It should be noted that this illustrated children's book was the only one of Kästner's pre-1945 works to escape Nazi censorship.

7 Lost (2013) notes that the hall was used only once as a meeting space when the SS generals gathered prior to the 'Operation Barbarossa' invasion of Russia.

8 Lost (2013, p. 98) describes the *Ahnenerbe* as the 'Heritage of the Ancestors Department of the SS in charge of pseudo-science and esoteric researches'.

9 More recently, Phillip Kerr's *The pale criminal* (1990) – the second historical detective novel in the Berlin Noir trilogy of Bernhard Günther novels – featured Wewelsburg as a key site in its plot.

10 For example, the character of Dr Elsa Schneider is an undercover blonde female SS officer in the blockbuster film *Indiana Jones and the last crusade*. Playing a duplicitous *femme fatale*, she beguiles both Henry and Indiana Jones before meeting her end in the Grail Temple.

References

Barthes, R 1972, *Mythologies*, trans. A Lavers, Hill and Wang, New York.

Benjamin, W 1968, *Illuminations,* ed. H Arendt, Schocken Books, New York.

Boyes, R 2010, 'Museum lays bare the black heart of Himmler's SS', *Times*, 1 May, www. thetimes.co.uk/article/wewelsburg-museum-lays-bare-the-black-heart-of-himmlers-ss-nz3fnh93gfh, viewed 29 May 2019.

Brebeck, WE & John-Stucke, K 2015, 'Wewelsbug – about the historical site', in WE Brebeck, F Huismann, K John-Stucke & J Piron (eds), *Endtime warriors: ideology and terror of the SS*, Deutscher Kunstverlag, Berlin, pp. 10–19.

Brebeck, WE, Huismann, F, John-Stucke, K & Piron, J (eds) 2015, *Endtime warriors: ideology and terror of the SS*, Deutscher Kunstverlag, Berlin.

Carden-Coyne, A 2011, 'The ethics of representation in Holocaust museums', in JM Dreyfus & D Langton (eds), *Writing the Holocaust*, Bloomsbury, London, pp. 167–256.

Cook, S & Russell, S 1999, *Heinrich Himmler's Camelot*, Kressmann-Backmeyer, North Carolina.

Coppens, P (n.d.) 'The Wewelsburg: the Nazi Grail Castle', www.philipcoppens.com/wewelsburg.html, viewed 29 May 2019.

Crossland, D 2010, 'New exhibition explodes myth of SS Castle Wewelsburg', *Spiegel online*, 6 April, www.spiegel.de/international/germany/confronting-the-nazi-perpetrators-new-exhibition-explodes-myth-of-ss-castle-wewelsburg-a-687435.html, viewed 29 May 2019.

Crownshaw, R 2007, 'Photography and memory in Holocaust museums', *Mortality*, vol. 12, no. 2, pp. 176–192.

Dalton, D 2015, *Dark tourism and crime*, Routledge, London.

Feldman, JD 2006, 'Contact points: museums and the lost body problem', in E Edwards, C Gosden & R Phillip (eds), *Sensible objects: colonialism, museums and material culture*, Berg, Oxford, pp. 245–268.

Gelbin, C 2011, 'Cinematic representations of the Holocaust', in JM Dreyfus & D Langton (eds), *Writing the Holocaust*, Bloomsbury, London, pp. 26–40.

Hall, A 2010, 'Spiritual castle home of infamous SS opens to public with £8m exhibition', *Daily Mail Australia*, 24 March, www.dailymail.co.uk/news/article-1259803/SS-castle-Nazi-murderer-Himmler-round-table-knights-open-public.html, viewed 29 May 2019.

John-Stucke, K 2015, 'Origins, conceptual principles, and structure of the exhibition "Ideology and Terror of the SS"', in WE Brebeck, F Huismann, K John-Stucke & J Piron (eds), *Endtime warriors: ideology and terror of the SS*, Deutscher Kunstverlag, Berlin, pp. 20–30.

Klimczuk, S & Warner, G 1999, *Secret places, hidden sanctuaries*, Routledge, London.

Lost, F 2013, *Nazi secrets: an occult breach in the fabric of history*, Kindle Edition, Createspace-Independent-Publishing-Platform, Amazon Digital Services LLC.

Müller, M 2015, 'Preface', in WE Brebeck, F Huismann, K John-Stucke & J Piron (eds), *Endtime warriors: ideology and terror of the SS*, Deutscher Kunstverlag, Berlin.

Rohr, S 2010, '"Genocide pop": the Holocaust as media event', in S Komor & S Rohr (eds), *The Holocaust, art, and taboo*, Universitätsverlag, Heidelberg, pp. 155–178.

Rosenfeld, GD, 2010, 'Memory and the museum: Munich's struggle to create a documentation center for the history of National Socialism', in GD Rosenfeld & PB Jaskot (eds), *Beyond Berlin: twelve German cities confront the Nazi past*, University of Michigan Press, Ann Arbor, pp. 163–184.

Simon, RI 2011, 'Afterword: the turn to pedagogy: a needed conversation on the practice of curating difficult knowledge', in E Lehrer, C Milton & E Patterson (eds), *Curating difficult knowledge*, Palgrave Macmillan, London, pp. 193–209.

Sontag, S 1975, 'Fascinating fascism', *The New York Review of Books*, 6 February, www.nybooks.com/articles/1975/02/06/fascinating-fascism, viewed 29 May 2019.

Stier, OB 2003, *Committed to memory: cultural mediations of the Holocaust*, University of Massachusetts Press, Amherst.

Tegethoff, C 2018, 'Email correspondence re: clarification of use of Nazi Christmas ornaments', *Kreismuseum Wewelsburg*, October 12 (on file with author).

Ward, G 2003, *True religion*, Blackwell, Oxford.

Williams, P 2007, *Memorial museums: the global rush to commemorate atrocities*, Berg Publishers, New York.

4   The Anne Frank House/ Museum

Introduction: the cultural saturation of Anne Frank

If ever a museum came pre-loaded with an overbearing weight of cultural expectation carried by visitors to its space, it is surely the Anne Frank Museum in Amsterdam. Consider the following:

> The list is daunting. Dozens of musical compositions, ranging from oratorio to indie rock. A dramatization given hundreds of productions annually. Thousands of *YouTube* videos. A museum visited by millions. To these add a growing number of works of fine art, biography, fiction, poetry, and dance, as well as films, radio and television broadcasts, and websites. Plus, tributes in the form of commemorative coins, stamps, and other collectibles, memorial sites and organizations around the world, eponymous streets, schools, and institutions, to say nothing of a day, a week, a tulip, countless trees, a whole forest . . . and a village.[1]
>
> (Kirshenblatt-Gimblett & Shandler 2012, p. 1)

Kirshenblatt-Gimblett and Shandler remind us that all these things are 'inspired by a book that has been translated into scores of languages, published in hundreds of editions, printed in tens of millions of copies, and ranked as one of the most widely read books on the planet' (2012, p. 1). Her diary is mediated, sung, filmed and rendered in various dramatic and textual treatments, but it is her clandestine home that will bear the focus of this chapter. Bidden by my memories of having read the diary as a teenager – and long having imagined the space in my mind's eye – I came to the museum in April 2015 accompanied by my twin brother Sean, to experience arguably the most famous hidden space in the world. Before entering the museum, I beheld giant bollards and a bus bearing huge posters advertising a play entitled *Anne*. I also stumbled upon a large statue of the diarist overlooking a canal. The presence of this long-dead girl seems ubiquitous. She haunts Amsterdam.

Throughout the course of this chapter, I seek to do four things. First, I wish to provide a personal account of what an encounter with that which the museum terms *Anne's world* feels like. Emotion and affect are critical concepts here. While traditional museums tend to eschew emotion, memorial museums unapologetically seek to evoke emotional responses in visitors and engender empathy in the process (Williams 2007). This is perhaps fitting in relation to the Anne Frank House. Tourists feel as though they *know* Anne (having read her diary or been exposed to her story at school). People react to the museum in ways that are emotive and highly personal; partly because Anne's tragic life story is so familiar to them. Second, this chapter will engage with the architecture, exhibits and displays in the museum in an effort to fathom precisely what one learns from exposure to this most famous museum. In doing so, I will touch upon the sheer volume of bodies that flow through the museum space and how the crowded space delimits our engagement with it, since there is no going back in this museum. One must follow a pre-assigned route. This is because 'planners have developed a rigid tour structure that essentially forces the patron to adhere to a pre-determined path through the building. She or he cannot but feel forced through a relentlessly linear maze of passages, stairs, rooms' (Sanbonmatsu 2009, p. 118).

Third, this chapter will draw on various debates about the problematic nature of Anne's status as an archetypal or universal Holocaust victim – a problem that is, of course, inextricably linked to her fame and the fact that an entire museum carries her name. In doing so, it will question the extent to which the museum disrupts this problem. Fourth, this chapter will make a thematic detour (from the space of the *actual* museum to the space of the museum as *imagined in film*). To achieve this aim, I will touch upon a recent depiction of the Anne Frank museum in the phenomenally popular film (based on the novel by John Green) *The fault in our stars*. The relationship between the *real* (Anne and her former home) and the *fictive* (a key scene set in the Anne Frank museum) is instructive of how sites of Holocaust pilgrimage, like museums, do not exist in some sort of vacuum. They inspire acts of imagination that lay claim to space and use it as a *mise-en-scène* upon which life's dramas might be projected.

Overview of Anne's life and flight into hiding

Anne and her family went into hiding on 6 July 1942, 'secreted in abandoned rooms in the rear of 263 Prinsengracht, where Opekta and Pectaron, two businesses run by her father, Otto, had their offices' (Shandler 2012, p. 27). The Franks were a middle-class family who fled to Amsterdam in 1933 so that they could escape the growing menace of an openly anti-Semitic social climate in Germany. Otto moved to Amsterdam and set up a franchise selling pectin, a gelling agent used in preparing jam. His wife, Edith, and their two daughters, Anne and Margot, followed him months later. The family assimilated quickly, learning Dutch within a year. To make his business less seasonally dependant, Otto offered a man named Hermann van Pels a job due to his knowledge of spices and the preparation of sausages. Hermann's wife and son, Peter, were also Jews who had fled Nazi Germany. In May 1940, the war began in the West and the Netherlands was occupied. The registration of Jews and the decree that they must wear the yellow Star of David were ominous signs of the segregation and persecution to follow. In September 1941, Margot and Anne started attending a special Jewish High School. Jews were no longer permitted to own their own businesses, so Otto had to appoint a non-Jewish director of his company Opekta. In the spring of 1942 – sensing a more oppressive future – Otto and Edith furnished the empty annex behind Otto's company at 263 Prinsengracht as a hiding place. The perilous situation for the Frank family worsened when, on 5 July 1942, sixteen-year-old Margot received a call-up notice to report for work. Complying with this command would have seen Margot separated from her family. On a cold Monday on 6 July, Anne and Margot gathered a few essential items and walked through the pouring rain to the hiding place. The cold weather enabled them to wear many layers of clothing on their covert journey to hiding (Lee 1999). They left the house in a state of disarray to add to the subterfuge that they had fled the city in haste. One week later, the van Pels family joined them in hiding in what came to be known as the Secret Annex. On 16 November 1942, Fritz Pfeffer became the eighth person to seek sanctuary in the hiding place. The inhabitants of the Secret Annex would spend more than two years in hiding aided by four of Otto Frank's most trusted and loyal employees. Their fates are recorded later in this chapter. Otto Frank survived Auschwitz and, in 1945, Miep Gies, an employee who rescued the diary from oblivion, handed him Anne's notebook with the words 'Here is your daughter Anne's legacy to you' (Metselaar et al. 2013, p. 230). The act triggered a series of events that could not have been predicted. Otto read the diary, realised its powerful potential and published it. In 1960, the former hiding place was spared demolition, donated by its owner, restored and opened as a museum.

The diary: the textual key to the entire museum

Anne began her journal in a plaid diary with an ornamental lock that she was given for her thirteenth birthday shortly before she went into hiding. Miep Gies, Anne's father's employee, gave Anne an ordinary exercise book to continue her diary. Anne also wrote entries in her sister's chemistry exercise book and later, as writing space became scarce, went back and used blank unwritten sections to continue writing. Anne continued writing her diary, 'framed as addresses to her imaginary friend Kitty' until August 1944, several days before her arrest by the SD (Shandler 2012, pp. 29, 27). Returned to her father after the war, the diary underwent various revisions, edits and alterations. These facts aside, the *essence* of the diary extracts – the daily musings, fears, fantasies (of outings she could no longer pursue; e.g., shopping and ice skating), and aspirations of a young woman in hiding – have long captured the imagination of readers the world over. Privy to the inner thoughts of this precocious young girl, it is the inner monologues captured as diary entries that allow each reader to come to know Anne (or at least a semblance of who she was) that seem wholly authentic because of the cumulative nature of the diary. More powerful that any second-person narrative, the written entries act as conduits of empathy. We, the readers, are devastated by Anne's fate, which, of course, is recounted at the end of the published diary and is given greater pathos because we miss the narrative voice of the writer to which we have become so accustomed. This pathos is all-the-more acute since we appreciate that Anne 'implicitly imagined that she would live to complete this work as a validation of surviving Nazi persecution' (Shandler 2012, p. 30). Published as *The diary of Anne Frank*, the narrative is so compelling because Anne captures for us an intrinsically unusual experience: what it is like to live a furtive life.

The Dutch government in exile had appealed over Radio Orange for Dutch people to keep diaries and other documents 'as evidence of their resistance to Nazi occupation' (Shandler 2012, p. 28). A fact often overlooked when reflecting on this publication is that Anne 'envisioned the diary as a literary project on a larger scale' (Shandler 2012, p. 28), as a book that would one day be published and bear the title, *Secret Annex*. Ilya Ehrenburg stresses that through the diary, Anne endures: 'One pure, young voice lives – as evidence of these violent deaths' (cited in Shandler 2012, p. 39). The diary underpins the entire museum experience. Visitors imagine Anne's life in the annex: her daydreaming; awakening desire for Peter; fights with her mother; the need to be very quiet and avoid peering out or doing anything that might jeopardise the sanctuary of their hiding space. Most visitors will recall that the diary is an open text – unfinished – the life of its author cut short by murder (Kirshenblatt-Gimblett & Shandler 2012, p. 5).

Introducing the museum: vicariously experiencing Anne's world

Having been refurbished several times since opening in 1960, the Anne Frank House/Museum has attracted a staggering thirty-three million visitors as of 2017.

Recently, with yet more renovations required, the sheer flood of tourists keen to visit the museum necessitated the introduction of an internet ticket purchasing system with a predetermined date and time slot for visits between October 2017 and January 2018. To proclaim that this is one of the most visited Holocaust-themed sites is an understatement.

One might question why Anne's former house is so popular. The answer is elusive but is linked to the fame of its former occupant and saturation exposure of her diary to the world. Additionally, the Anne Frank story seems to be constantly replenished, keeping her name and image in the public's imagination. Recent developments such as contemporary discussion about the precise month of her death and renewed debate over who denounced the family to the Nazis fuel news stories and reinvigorate interest in her life.

The Anne Frank Museum presents visitors from all over the world with an opportunity, albeit briefly, to inhabit the space where Anne and her family sheltered from the Nazis before they were denounced. To characterise the space as mythical is no exaggeration. Readers imagined the fabled space of the Secret Annex having immersed themselves in Anne's world by reading the diary. Whilst their memories of all that transpired in the diary may well be clouded – save for the basic elements of a life spent hiding – most readers vividly recall the *essence* of the diary: the precocious voice of Anne as conveyed to Kitty.

Figure 4.1 The Anne Frank House on Prinsengracht

As one enters the museum to begin the tour, one is confronted with a suite of four enlarged black and white photographs of Anne that are juxtaposed – two to each side of the wall – meeting at a right angle. The photographs conjure our memory of Anne and serve to summon her presence into our imagination before we encounter the museum space. Yet what visitors encounter initially in the museum is the warehouse and the offices on the first two floors. The walls are decorated with photographs and biographies of the brave employees who hid the families. Video screens broadcast feature interviews with people who interacted with the families during the war. These mostly empty rooms are a fitting prelude

Figure 4.2 Crowds throng outside the Anne Frank House/Museum

to entering the Secret Annex space, for the stories recounted on the screens remind the visitor of the climate of arrests and deportations that prevailed in Holland and forced families to go into hiding (if indeed, that was an option open to them). In the rear of warehouse, we learn that pectin and ground spices were weighed and packaged for sale under the trademark Opekta (Metselaar et al. 2013). Objects associated with the warehouse such as bottles, labels and trademark rubber stamps are displayed to help the visitor imagine the busy commercial space that the warehouse once was. We are also alerted of the danger to the inhabitants of the Secret Annex. Apart from Johan Voskuijl, the warehouse workers do not know anything about the hiding place. Being discovered is a constant source of anxiety for those in hiding (Metselaar et al. 2013). As one contemplates this largely denuded space,[2] a large frieze of Anne's writing instructs us: 'We have to whisper and tread lightly during the day, otherwise the people in the warehouse might hear us [July 11 1942]' (museum display text, cited in Metselaar et al., p. 49).[3]

Throughout the house the authentic voice of Anne is often presented as a technique to constantly insert her presence into the space. This textual device, while by no means unique to this museum, is very powerful. The warehouse spaces create a sombre ambient for the visitor, helping them appreciate what was a stake for the families sequestered in the secreted part of the building where any movement or noise, like the flushing of the toilet cistern, might have betrayed their presence.

A small room that was once Victor Kugler's office is now also denuded of objects. A few everyday items are displayed that help the visitor understand the role he played in hiding the families. We learnt that to stave off boredom and isolation from the outside world, Kluger would bring the people in hiding different magazines and newspapers (Metselaar et al. 2013). As kind as these gestures were, they took a toll on him. Anne writes: 'Kluger, who at times finds the enormous responsibility for the eight of us overwhelming, can hardly talk from the pent-up tension and strain [May 26, 1944]' (museum display text, cited in Metselaar at al., p. 63).

These downstairs (non-hiding place) rooms are very powerful. They generate a great deal of anticipation and tension in the visitor's mind. So much was at stake for those hiding the families. As visitors reading the explanatory text, beholding the exhibits and listening to recorded testimony, we are primed for our eventual exposure to the hiding spaces.

Perhaps the most powerful part of the downstairs rooms is the storeroom, as it is referred to. Here the museum visitor can observe small scale models of the various Secret Annex rooms. These models were fabricated in 1961 with the guidance of Otto Frank and were reproduced to accurate scale with the express purpose of giving museum visitors an impression of the furnishings (Metselaar et al. 2013). Painstaking attention was paid to detail in constructing the models. The doors between rooms are architecturally realistic and the paint colours are true to their 1940s period tones. A miniature Persian carpet and wall frieze of pictures (which Anne cut out of magazines) demonstrate the degree of verisimilitude aimed for by the craftspeople who built the models. People cluster round the models, peering into the room through the glass enclosure. The dollhouse-like dioramas help animate our imagination for the real-life scale rooms we will encounter upstairs.

The models serve an important purpose. As Otto Frank observed, '[e]verything was hauled away during the war and I prefer it to stay that way' (cited in Metselaar et al. 2013, p. 90). Refurnishing the annex with period furniture and objects is entirely feasible. The museum catalogue, as previously noted, features two-page images of most of the rooms furnished circa 1940s. Notwithstanding the practical fact that navigating a refurnished house would render museum visits almost impossible due to the issue of clutter, refurnishing any of the house would be profoundly problematic. Museum visitors crave the aura of authenticity, and a period chair or table – however authentic in detail – would not satisfy the demand for authenticity. Writing in *Dark tourism and crime*, Dalton (2015) argues that emptiness weaves an affective spell on visitors to memorial spaces, provoking attentiveness in the visitor. Here, in the *Anne Frank House*, the *emptiness* of the rooms does not function as a conduit for imagination. The problem – if one is to frame it that way – is that the rooms are never empty. The steady streams of visitors literally fill the spaces to brimming. This is inevitable given the popularity of the museum, and yet it comes at a huge cost. One is so buffeted by other bodies in the space that any contemplative potential is somewhat thwarted. Trying to find an unguarded moment to linger and ruminate on an exhibit is challenging. The models thus offer visitors an opportunity to pause for a moment and stare downwards and ponder the lives of the family sheltering in these claustrophobic spaces.

The most palpably charged moment for most museum visitors comes as, having contemplated the models of the Secret Annex spaces, one finally gets the opportunity to enter the secreted spaces upstairs. In the storeroom, at last we come face-to-face with the hidden entrance to the families' hiding place. I overheard a young woman next to me utter one word to her friend: 'finally' as she smiled in anticipation. As each visitor steps over the threshold and enters the hidden part of the house, they no doubt reflect on the solemnity of this crossing, for we are entering a realm that hitherto was only captured by reading the diary. Again, the authentic voice of Anne adds gravitas to the experience: 'Now our Secret Annex has truly become secret. Mr Kluger thought it would be better to have a bookcase built in front of the entrance [August 21, 1942]' (museum display text, cited in Metselaar et al. 2013, p. 91).

The unassuming bookcase, laden with large-format cardboard ring binder folders to add to the charade, now stands ajar for museum visitors to enter. The effect appears to enthral visitors who silently contemplate the entrance and patiently wait their turn to enter. At the risk of sounding disingenuous, it is hard to convey to the uninitiated how transcendental stepping into the hidden entrance feels. Following in Anne's footsteps – entering the hidden spaces – feels like stepping into a sacred space like a church. People are hushed and very quiet as they step over the threshold and climb the stairs to experience the concealed spaces. Today 'the [original] stairwell is sealed off with a piece of glass' (Metselaar et al. 2013, p. 96). Nevertheless, the experience of entry is akin to the way the original inhabitants entered the space.

The sombre atmosphere in the secret room section of the museum is in part facilitated by the darkness that pervades the different spaces. We make our way from room to room, reflecting on memories of daily life as conveyed by the diary. The inhabitants slept here and bickered due the immense psychological torment of being unable to leave, and generally tried to remain quiet for the two years they sheltered here. At times, as Anne captures in her diary, the annex felt like a prison, and yet it was also a sanctuary from persecution before they were betrayed.

The only fixtures remaining are the toilet, the marble wash basin and stone counter, and the sink in the kitchen. There is precious little to see; nevertheless, the point is that this is not really a museum predicated on artefacts or exhibits. It is an *experiential* museum, and progressing from room to room, visitors are lost in private contemplation. Are they recalling their favourite passages from the diary? Did they even bother to read it at school? Or is the story of Anne Frank – one so entwined with the Holocaust that it will never be detached from the momentous event itself – so deeply engrained in the collective psyche that they have come to the house merely because they believe a visit to Amsterdam warrants such a pilgrimage? Whatever the lure that got them here, the elderly, the middle-aged and the very young are transfixed by the space. It is quite disarming to see the effect these largely vacant rooms have on visitors. People whisper in hushed tones; some look sad and reflective. A mood of quiet reverence permeates the spaces. The writer Paul Auster was so moved by his visit to the Anne Frank House in the 1980s that it – and Anne's life as a writer – became the inspiration for his novel

The invention of solitude. Auster's protagonist, 'A', recalls that in this house he was moved to tears (McLennan 2012). Tears seems appropriate in this museum. During my visit I saw some schoolgirls unashamedly wiping tears from their eyes. This is a very powerful space and people who grew to love and cherish Anne's story are deeply moved when they find themselves *in situ* – in the very rooms that provided her temporary sanctuary.

Finding Anne: traces among the teeming masses

> Our little room looked very bare at first with nothing on the walls; but thanks to Daddy who had brought my film-star collection on beforehand, and with the aid of a paste pot and brush, I have transformed the walls into one gigantic picture. This makes it look much more cheerful [July 11, 1942].
>
> (museum display text, cited in Metselaar et al. 2013, p. 118)

In the part of the museum that is designated as Anne Frank and Fritz Pfeffer's room, encased behind Perspex, one is able to view what the visitors' catalogue characterises as a 'room full of dreams' (Anne's World n.d., p. 4). We learn that, like many teenagers of her time, Anne would paste pictures and postcards on her bedroom walls:

> At first these images simply appear to depict random subjects: film stars, historical figures, records of childhood, works of art and royalty. But Anne's pictures tell a story: they give a clearly defined view of her world, her dreams and her development in the Secret Annex.
>
> (Anne's World n.d., p. 4)

The collage of images remains affixed to the wall, slightly faded by the passage of time but still the individual components are easily discernible. The Hollywood icon Greta Garbo is juxtaposed with a studio portrait of starlet Ginger Rogers. A photograph of the Dutch royal family in exile in Canada captures Anne's devotion to the House of Orange. More curiously, the English royal princess Elizabeth (later Queen Elizabeth II) is depicted in a portrait, as is her younger sister Margaret. Art and artists feature in the collage as well. The famous *Self Portrait of Leonardo da Vinci* sits alongside Rembrandt's sombre *Portrait of an Old Man*. Anne's interest in Greek and Roman mythology is captured by a photograph of an antique statue of the Greek God Hermes. Nature (so sorely missed by Anne in captivity) intrudes into the space with a Medici Society postcard, *The Lark's Song* by the English illustrator Margaret Tarrant, which depicts two girls picking primroses in spring. In another whimsical postcard toddlers who surely are too small to appreciate the rules, engage in a game of football.

Anne's collage literally stops people in their tracks. Perhaps because the rooms are denuded of objects, visitors crave some authentic trace of Anne in the space where she lived. The collage is profoundly moving. It captures Anne's aesthetic tastes and sensibilities; she loved cinema, royalty, art and artistic expression. Perhaps people imagine her cutting out the images and pasting them to the wall? Adding cheer to her hiding space, the act seems as defiant and as spirited as the diary itself. A woman near me wipes away a tear as she stares at the wall. Like the diary that affords us such an intimate glimpse into the psyche of this young woman in hiding, similarly the walls lay Anne's desires and aspirations bare. We recall that she once harboured a desire to act before formulating aspirations 'to become a famous writer and journalist after the war' (Anne's World n.d., p. 5).

In a sense, the closest we really get to Anne in the museum space is in being exposed to this 'room of dreams' as the museum guide call it. It is a slightly disarming exhibit where we behold something tangible. However, the spectre of Bergen-Belsen looms large in this room; we recall that Anne's dreams were extinguished in that infernal place and all that she might have been becomes apparent as we reflect on her collage. The diary brought her fame beyond measure, but her true destiny, had she not been murdered, is harder to fathom. The seriousness of her aspirations and interests aside, Anne *may* have created the collage in a frivolous and unplanned manner. Yet we, the spectators, stare at the collage with a type of forensic gaze as though it might reveal traces of the *real* Anne. To my mind, the images beguile and bewilder us in equal measure. How could Anne ever have predicted that millions of museum visitors would ponder this wall and try to invest it with meaning? It struck me that however unwittingly (on Anne's behalf), the presence of one image in the collage animates the way we behold the entire collage. A close-up photograph of Michelangelo's *Pietà* adorns the wall. The *Pietà* is a form of the Lamentation of Christ; we view it and ponder the suffering of Christ. In Anne's room, we look at this collage and it speaks to us like a lamentation for a young girl whose dreams were cut short by the homicidal intent of Nazism. In *Dark tourism and crime*, Dalton (2015) wrote about the power of synecdoche – the *part* that speaks to the *whole* – as deployed in museum spaces. Yet here (as will also be touched upon later), the collage is far too intimate and personal for us to think of other young women murdered during the Holocaust. The thoughts evoked by the collage cluster around Anne alone, which is perhaps fitting given it is *her* house, *her* hiding space, *her* former bedroom, *her* personal touch that created the visual medley. The Holocaust scholar Lawrence Langer argues 'those who canonize [Anne] as an archetypal victim of the Holocaust [are guilty] of a double injustice, to her and to the millions of other victims' (cited in Kirshenblatt-Gimblett & Shandler 2012, p. 6). The collage seems a powerful antidote to the canonisation of Anne. It is too unique an artefact from which to produce thoughts of archetypal victimhood.

The top-most rooms and attic: encountering the inner sanctum of the Secret Annex

For many of the museum visitors, the museum becomes more claustrophobic as one progresses through it. The final small rooms are strangely anti-climactic. That the attic – once accessed by a rudimentary wooden ladder in Peter van Pel's room – remains closed to visitors seems entirely appropriate. Notwithstanding its practical inaccessibility, it seems somewhat fitting that, despite the lure of the diary, we are not permitted to inhabit this attic space. The rest of the exhibits seem static and unengaging after encountering the collage. However, the bathroom, with one tiny sink and toilet that eight people had to share, provides a space upon which visitors can ruminate. Stencilled into a mirror is an extract from the diary which helps us understand that this tiny space was a type of sanctuary: 'Margot and Mother are nervous. "Shh . . . Father, be quiet, Otto, ssh . . . Comer here, you cannot run the water any more. Walk softly!" A sample of what's said to Father in the bathroom [August 23, 1943]' (museum display text, cited in Metselaar et al. 2013, p. 141). Still, the emotional dénouement of the *Anne Frank House* is yet to come. That experience – afforded by a massive extension that takes us into a new (adjacent) building – is the subject of the next section.

The museum portion of the house

> I see the world gradually being turned into a wasteland. I hear the ever-approaching thunder, which will destroy us too [July 11, 1944].
>
> (museum display text, cited in Metselaar et al. 2013, p. 175)

We make our way out of the annex and into the museum portion of the Anne Frank House by stepping through an elaborate glass cantilevered walkway. This architectural feature helps us perform a mental manoeuvre that orientates us in a distinctly different space. We leave Anne's world – a space of containment and shelter – to a space that places Anne, her family, and the others in hiding well outside the realm of their temporary shelter. Here the Shoah intrudes, as we all knew it would – an intrusion marked by an enormous pictorial frieze of the Auschwitz concentration camp. It is this section of the museum, to borrow Pollock's term, 'the political conditions of her [Anne's] *murder*' become evident (2007, p. 135, emphasis in original). As Pollock astutely reminds us '[w]e are not mourning merely a death, but a crime' (2007, p. 135), and the full magnitude of that crime becomes evident as we are confronted with what happened after the early morning arrests.

This part of the museum documents the fate of all the inhabitants of the Secret Annex. It tells the story of the raid on the house by the SD on 4 August 1944. Controversy about who betrayed the families remains to this day, with a police investigation after the war never providing definitive proof about the culprit's identity (Metselaar et al. 2013). The visitors learn of the fate of the people in hiding, their arrest and subsequent transportation to the Westerbork Transit camp from where they were dispatched to Auschwitz. The registration cards attest to individual fates. Hermann van Pels was murdered in Auschwitz sometime in 1944. Fritz Pfeffer died in Neuengamme concentration camp near Hamburg on 20 December 1944. Edith Frank was transported from Auschwitz to a labour camp in Liebau (Upper Silesia) where she died in a sick barrack on 6 January 1945 at the age of forty-four. Margot Frank was transported from Auschwitz with Anne to Bergen-Belsen in November 1944. In March 1945, Margot Frank dies of typhus and deprivation at the age of nineteen (Metselaar, et al. 2013). Anne, despite being fifteen, escaped the gas chamber at Auschwitz and ended up being afflicted by starvation, poor sanitisation and typhus. She died in March 1945, at the age of fifteen, just a few days after her sister and just a few weeks before liberation. Auguste van Pels spent time in Bergen-Belsen, Buchenwald and Theresienstadt. She was murdered by the Nazis in a gruesome manner: by being thrown under a train. She was forty-four years old (Metselaar et al. 2013). Peter van Pels spent considerable time in Auschwitz before being evacuated on one of the infamous death marches. He eventually arrived in Mauthausen where he died in April 1945 in a hospital barracks. Otto Frank (as if fated to bring Anne's diary to the attention of the world) managed to survive Auschwitz.

Filmic flights of fantasy: imagining the museum

Here it is fitting to refer to John Green's bestselling novel (later adapted into a commercially successful film) *The fault in our stars*, which stages part of its drama in the *Anne Frank House*. Green tells the story of two young teenagers, Hazel and Augustus, who are both battling aggressive cancer. While on a trip to Amsterdam they visit the Anne Frank Museum. A scene where the doomed lovers kiss in the museum to the applause of other tourists (recreated in the film on a set in Pittsburgh rather than being filmed in the actual museum) is central to the book and film's plot.

When the box-office hit film came out, debates erupted on social media and in popular culture discussion forums about the appropriateness of using the Anne Frank House as the location for such a fictive romantic scene. As terrible as two teens facing cancer is imagined to be, for many commentators introducing the Holocaust was a bridge too far. The logic at play was that it was egregious to juxtapose a young woman's fight to survive cancer with another woman's fight to survive the genocidal reach of the Nazis in occupied Amsterdam. Notwithstanding differing opinions about the quality of the acting or reducing the entire film to an exercise in teenage schmaltz, it strikes me as trite to construe the Anne Frank Museum as some sort of sacred space that cannot be depicted in literature or cinema. Ironically, Green's character Hazel is aware of the sensitivity of the museum space, as the film captures in a pivotal scene; Hazel ponders whether she should kiss her boyfriend Augustus in the Anne Frank House. She recalls that Anne kissed Peter and that she would probably approve of kissing in her former home; and so she succumbs to her feelings and kisses him.

All over the world, readers (of the book) and viewers (of the film) engaged in heated debates about the extent to which the plot may have exploited Anne Frank's life to invoke deep emotion and capitalise on Anne's tragic story. Such debates, to my mind, seems superficial and redundant. Anne may only function in Green's story as a cipher, but *her* story is not integral to *theirs*: teenagers fleeing death and looking for a fleeting reprieve from the disease that stalks them.

Museum spaces cannot be quarantined from the imagination of writers as though they are too sacred to meddle with. Anne, with her love of Hollywood cinema, would surely have approved of this scene in the film. In any event, critics of the scene are missing an obvious point. Featuring the Anne Frank House in the book (and subsequent film) piques curiosity about Anne's life and inspires even more teenagers to one day visit the museum to glean a more nuanced understanding of Anne Frank's life.

A profound observation in *The fault in our stars* enlightens us about the limitations of the Anne Frank House/Museum. Pondering a huge book on display in the museum featuring the names of the 103,000 dead from the Netherlands in the Holocaust, the reader is informed that beneath the name Anne Frank are four Aron Franks. It is then pointed out that these four Aron Franks are not memorialised or mourned with a museum bearing their name. This observation does not dilute the power or emotional impact of the museum, but it is a telling reminder that we cannot treat Anne Frank as a *synecdoche*, as one young victim who speaks for the *whole*: the countless other victims subsumed by the Shoah. Questioning the singular stature of Anne Frank as the representative victim of Nazism and of victimisation more generally, literary scholar Alvin Rosenfeld has cautioned 'there is a temptation to readily proclaim "We are all Anne Frank" but, in fact, we are nothing of the sort' (cited in Kirshenblatt-Gimblett & Shandler 2012, p. 6). Nonetheless, the unassailable fact is that we are all lured to the museum by Anne, no doubt because her diary is so powerful. Primo Levi's often cited aphorism – which appears enlarged on one of the walls of the museum – seems to sum the situation up well:

> One single Anne Frank moves us more than the countless others who suffered just as she did but whose faces have remained in the shadows. Perhaps it is better that way; if we were capable of taking in all the suffering of all those people, we would not be able to live.
>
> (cited in Metselaar et al. 2013, p. 239)

Encountering the diary

The final part of the museum leads into a small dark room where Anne's diary and other pages of writing are preserved behind glass. As Shandler notes, in the six decades after its publication, the diary has appeared in over sixty different languages and sold more than thirty-one million copies; 'making it the world's most read book' (2012, p. 26). Some versions are cheap paperbacks, while limited editions for collectors include a 1959 oversize edition with a frontispiece by Marc Chagall (Shandler, 2012). This exhibit brings the visitor face-to-face with the famous red plaid covered diary. Unexpectedly, few people seem to dwell on the diary or pay it much heed. Rather, in an adjacent space, visitors behold a wall filled with different publications of the diary from all over the world. I recognise the Penguin paperback edition with a smiling facsimile of Anne on the cover that I read in secondary school in 1984. It makes more sense that this exhibit attracts visitor attention in a way that the real (original) diary does not, for the published versions are the conduits through which we all know, admire and think fondly of Anne. It seems fitting that the item that lured us all here – the *published* diary – should be the last object we see before we are shepherded towards the exit.

Conclusion: Anne doesn't live here anymore

In our modern world, we often do profane things to the remnants of the real teenage girl, Anne Frank. In 2009, the Michigan-based firm Phojoe created the image of an eighty-year-old Anne with 'forensic compositing techniques that are usually employed to help solve crimes and find missing people' (Shandler 2012, p. 52). Shandler elaborates on the *effect* of such forensic imagining: 'Besides conjuring Anne Frank as living into old age, the composite photograph also implicitly imagines solving the crime of her murder by undoing it, thereby restoring the diary's "missing" author to her public' (2012, p. 52). The *effect* of beholding this image on the internet is monstrous. It performs, as Shandler identifies (2012), a slight-of-hand conjuring trick that mocks what we know. Anne died at the age of fifteen at Bergen-Belsen. The Holocaust subsumed her, and all the world is left with is her *authentic* remains – not a doctored photograph – but rather the diary of a vibrant young woman full of hope in a claustrophobic world of enforced concealment. It is this diary that summons visitors to the Anne Frank Museum in droves.

The Anne Frank House is something of a museological triumph; a space that transcends so many of the things that ought to completely spoil the experience of visiting this museum. As Reynolds (2018, p. 19) notes, 'the link between Anne Frank's story and Holocaust tourism is striking. Lines of tourists queue up to see the house in Amsterdam where the young girl hid with her family.' Most visitors queue patiently for as long as a few hours, only to find the museum space brimming over with bodies. Such is the lure of the name and image of this girl we know as Anne. The civility that seems to dominate the waiting visitors carries through to the museum space. People are largely quiet in the museum and seem to try and allow their fellow visitors an opportunity to commune with the exhibits and garner a deep appreciation for Anne's life; and yet the attendant noise that accompanies so many people is intrusive. Sanbonmatsu makes a very astute point:

> [O]nly museum employees, arriving in the quiet, early morning hours, one imagines, could have any feeling for the piercing solitude and vulnerability of that place, the heavy stillness that must have filled the air as the occupants calmed themselves as Otto Frank's employees arrived at work.
>
> (2009, pp. 118–119)

People stare earnestly at the remnants of the annex and patiently wait their time to get to the various stages (rooms) of the museum. One cannot really linger over most exhibits as one feels the momentum of the knowledge that others are waiting behind them. Sanbonmatsu captures the busy nature of the museum: 'During the day . . . it is difficult to linger over particular artefacts, let alone get any phenomenological sense of particular rooms, their aura and intimacy for those who once dwelled and worked inside them' (2009, p. 119). Moments to pause and take in the sights are compromised by the crowds; nevertheless, rumination and reflection are possible. During my two-hour visit, I beheld countless people lost in quiet reflection, whispering private comments to their companions as they pondered some aspect of life for Anne and her fellow captives. Framing the museum as offering a type of voyeurism where 'one gawks at the Frank's personal artefacts', Sanbonmatsu elaborates on his misgivings: 'What was once a private space has been brutally violated, turned into a public spectacle that feels strangely devoid of life' (2009, p. 118). This criticism seems simplistic. Voyeurism is a sexualised gaze; the gaze underpinned by the exhibits at the Anne Frank House is more akin to a reverential curiosity.

The memory of reading the diary is what attracts many visitors to the museum. The excerpts – scattered throughout the museum in enlarged captions as this chapter has documented – are a fitting fixture of the museum. They transport us back to the time we read it and suture Anne to the empty house. Author Cynthia Ozik provocatively wonders if 'a more salvational [sic] outcome' might have been, instead of the diary being rescued following her arrest, 'Anne Frank's diary burned, vanished, lost – saved from a world that made of it all things' (cited in Kirshenblatt-Gimblett & Shandler 2012, p. 6). Such speculation is somewhat redundant. The diary *did* endure and its siren song – a narrative that millions relate to – continues to draw visitors to the house to see, first hand, the space where Anne penned her anguished and heartfelt observations.

Anne Frank has become something akin to a brand (Kirshenblatt-Gimblett & Shandler 2012). The museum bookstore does a brisk trade, but thankfully books and postcards dominate the offerings. It is hardy the fault of the museum that people crave a souvenir of their visit. I purchased the book *Anne Frank House: a museum with a story* and a postcard that reproduces a sepia rear view of the street circa 1940 with the Secret Annex outlined in soft pastel blue. The aesthetic qualities of the image are slightly disarming. They render the hiding place an alluring visual appeal that perhaps belies the space as one of a failed sanctuary.

Ozick observes of Anne's plight:

> The atrocities she endured were ruthlessly and purposefully devised, from indexing by tattoo through systematic starvation to factory-efficient murder. She was designated to be erased from the living, to leave no grave, no sign, no physical trace of any kind.
>
> (cited in Hasian 2001, p. 369)

Despite this, her diary survived, and its popularity underpins the museum where 'Anne Frank's popularity offers proof that her "spirit" has not been snuffed out' (Hasian 2001, p. 370). This is indeed a museum with a *story*; one that is so familiar that everyone knows it. It is a story well told and the museum should be praised for managing to respect Anne with each curatorial gesture. However, the story does not end here, in the museum, with the arrest of Anne, her family and the four other inhabitants. We all know that the story of Anne Frank ends at the Bergen-Belsen concentration camp, and it is that geographical and memorial space that Chapter 5 of this book will subsequently explore.

Notes

1 Since this list was compiled in 2012 we might well add Anne Frank memes, an asteroid, a Facebook page, a graphic novel and a high-speed train to the ever-growing list.
2 The museum guidebook helps the visitor to the museum imagine the wartime 'look' of the different rooms. For example, a colour photograph depicts giant drums strewn around the room, baskets and giant wooden shelves are laden with tins and objects associated with the 1940s warehouse.
3 The use of the present tense in the museum textual displays (as extracted from the diary) is a powerful tool of engagement to help the visitor identify with Anne.

References

Anne's World (n.d.) *Pictorial publication of the Anne Frank House Museum*, Zwaan Printmedia, Netherlands.

Auster, P 2012, *Winter journal*, Faber & Faber, London.

Dalton, D 2015, *Dark tourism and crime*, Routledge, London.

Green, J 2012, *The fault in our stars*, Penguin, London.

Hasian, MA 2001, 'Anne Frank, Bergen-Belsen, and the polysemic nature of Holocaust memories', *Rhetoric & Public Affairs*, vol. 4, no. 3, pp. 349–374.

Kirshenblatt-Gimblett, B & Shandler J (eds) 2012, 'Introduction', in B Kirshenblatt-Gimblett & J Shandler (eds), *Anne Frank unbound: media, imagination, memory*, Indiana University Press, Bloomington, pp. 1–22.

Lee, CA 1999, *The biography of Anne Frank: roses from the Earth*, Penguin, London.

McLennan, R 2012, 'Anne Frank rescues the writer in Paul Auster's *The invention of solitude*', *Journal of American Studies*, vol. 46, no. 3, pp. 695–709.

Metselaar, M, van der Rol, R & Stam, D 2013, *Anne Frank House: a museum with a story*, 3rd edn, Zwaan Printmedia, Netherlands.

Pollock, G 2007, 'Stilled life: traumatic knowing, political violence, and the dying of Anna Frank', *Mortality*, vol. 12, no. 2, pp. 124–141.

Reynolds, D 2018, *Postcards from Auschwitz: Holocaust tourism and the meaning of remembrance*, New York University Press, New York.

Sanbonmatsu, J 2009, 'The Holocaust sublime: singularity, representation, and the violence of everyday life', *American Journal of Economics and Sociology*, vol. 68, no. 1, pp. 101–126.

Shandler, J 2012, 'From diary to book: text, object, structure', in B Kirshenblatt-Gimblett & J Shandler (eds), *Anne Frank unbound: media, imagination, memory*, Indiana University Press, Bloomington, pp. 25–58.

Williams, P 2007, *Memorial museums: the global rush to commemorate atrocities*, Berg Publishers, New York.

5   Concentration camp tourism in Germany

Two encounters

Introduction

While the concentration camp of Auschwitz-Birkenau has been subjected to sustained scrutiny as a site of tourism, a relative dearth of literature has been devoted to concentration camp tourism in Germany. Perhaps this is because the Auschwitz-Birkenau concentration/extermination camp complex is enormous, receives hundreds of thousands of visitors each year, and has come to symbolise the Holocaust by virtue of its iconic status in movies, documentaries and in wider culture.

This chapter will provide a brief overview of the current concentration camp tourism landscape that prevails in Germany. It will then seek to juxtapose two concentration camp tourist experiences that, for a variety of reasons, are quite distinct. These two camps are Dachau near Munich and Bergen-Belsen near Celle. In comparing both camps, it will become apparent that they offer the visitor markedly different tourism encounters.

Overview of concentration camp tourism possibilities in contemporary Germany

There are approximately twenty former concentration camps that can be identified in Germany. Many are referred to by the term KZ, the German abbreviation for *Konzentrationslager* (Lennon & Weber 2016, p. 26). Arguably the most infamous and notorious is Dachau, which was Germany's first 'model' concentration camp (Hodgkinson 2013, p. 26; Marcuse 2001, p. 6). Some of the most obscure camps in terms of public awareness include Hinzert, Osthofen, Flossenbürg, Landsberg, Kemna, Neuengamme, Malchow and Niederhagen (Hartmann 1989). Some camps were completely torn down after the war and offer no real point of focus for tourism. Other sites, despite signage that attests to their former use, offer no tangible traces of their earlier incarnation. Some obscure camps have been transformed into memorial spaces. A Gestapo 'educational work camp' near Kassel was turned into a memorial museum in 1982 (Macdonald 2009, p. 81), and the former concentration camps at Moringen, Drütte and Neckarelz were transformed into memorial museums in 1993, 1994 and 1998 respectively (Macdonald 2009).

Tourists crave authentic sites, but the paradox is that an authentic site – denuded of its former physical trappings as a concentration camp (e.g., barracks, guard houses and barbed wire) – offers little attraction as a location to visit. Many of the visitors who throng to Auschwitz each year are perhaps unaware that the majority of the sights they have come to see are a mixture of *preserved* (wooden block houses), *inauthentic* (e.g., the 'death wall'), and *replica* elements (e.g., the gas chamber at Auschwitz I) (see Dalton 2015). The ravages of time have led to many German concentration camp sites having so few original traces of their violent past that they offer no tangible opportunities for tourist scrutiny.

There is a handful of former concentration camps in Germany that offers tourism encounters that are aided by tour group opportunities, local tourism promotions and internet-based information-sharing facilitated by Facebook and other social media platforms. These camps are operated by local municipal authorities and are funded by the federal government. Buchenwald, Sachsenhausen and Ravensbrück are three camps that have a long history of tourism, largely attracting German tourists as veritable 'National Sites of Warning and Memory' (see Morsch 2001; Niven 2001; Hartmann 2018; Reynolds 2018).

Two concentration camps: two unique encounters

In the following section I wish to discuss two German concentration camps that attract considerable tourism from local and international tourists alike. I proffer the former concentration camps of Dachau and Bergen-Belsen as sites of discussion because they offer visitors profoundly different experiential encounters. Contrasted, they speak to the powerful ways that *extant* features (e.g., former block houses) and *absent* features (e.g., a site largely surrendered to nature) can both conjure a powerful aura of the suffering of former inmates. In both sections I will draw on my personal experiences of visiting these camps, augmented by other sources that will help elucidate precisely what these former camps offer visitors. My discussion of both camps will highlight the profundity of Niven's observation that 'the visitor must actively participate in generating his or her own impression' when visiting a concentration camp (2001, p. 39).

Dachau: remnants of brutality

Overview of the camp

In 1933, the Nazis opened a concentration camp on the grounds of a disused ammunition factory near Munich. It was the first state-run concentration camp established in the Reich. This prison became a place of brutality, torture and murder over its twelve years of existence. Historians estimate that 200,000 prisoners from over forty nations were imprisoned at Dachau and its sub-camps. Some 41,500 prisoners died here from starvation, disease, floggings or execution chiefly by shooting. Additionally, many prisoners perished due from succumbing to debilitating hard labour. After the US Army liberated the camp in April 1945, the

American military used the camp as an internment camp for suspected Nazi perpetrators (Hammermann & Pilzweger-Steiner 2017). The Dachau 'model', as it came to be termed, produced a school of violence that was subsequently adopted at other concentration camps (Dillon 2015). Moreover, the purpose of the model was to present the 'public image of the camp as a clean and efficient correctional camp' (Hodgkinson 2013, p. 24). Hodgkinson elaborates: 'This clean image created for propaganda purposes was, however, far removed from what the camp was actually like for those interred there' (2013, p. 26). The camp was no secret and soon word spread that this was a brutal place of correction. Citizens deemed 'regime opponents' (e.g., communists, social democrats, socialists, trade unionists, criminals and intellectuals) were imprisoned at Dachau. Later, Nazi racial and social ideology saw sexual and ethnic minorities including homosexuals, and Sinti and Roma, construed as aliens deserving imprisonment (Hammermann and Pilzweger-Steiner 2017).

After the camp was liberated in 1945, moving film images were taken of the mountains of corpses and emaciated survivors and were broadcast around the world as cinema news reels. As Lennon and Weber note: 'The distribution of these dreadfully iconic images meant that the name of Dachau became associated with some of the most extreme examples of Nazi persecution' (2016, p. 27). Dachau's notoriety, in part forged by its prominence in the public's imagination in the decades since its liberation, has seen the Dachau concentration camp memorial (hereafter the Dachau memorial for brevity) become 'the most visited camp site in Germany' (Hodgkinson 2013). The Dachau memorial opened in 1965 and to this day, the site's aim has been 'to remember the suffering and death of the prisoners, and to facilitate and foster analysis and discussion of Nazi crimes' (Hammermann & Pilzweger-Steiner 2017, p. 8).

Situating Dachau in the tourism landscape

As the most visited concentration camp memorial in Germany, Dachau attracts many day trippers who travel from Munich by coach. Hodgkinson (2013, p. 29) argues that most visit 'because of the proximity of the site and the ease of getting there'. Some arrive in guided tour groups and are cramming their visit into a busy schedule that includes beer halls and other Bavarian attractions. Long before the internet fuelled mass tourism with its travel blogs and TripAdvisor promotions, the phenomenon of the *Let's Go* travel bible (clutched by English-speaking young people all over the world) had identified Dachau as a 'must see' concentration camp destination. To that extent that many people garner a sense of what a concentration camp on Nazi soil was like, it is through exposure to this memorial site.

Many commentators have noted that visiting a concertation camp in the contemporary era is a strangely discordant sensory experience. I was struck at Dachau how suburbia now intrudes on the site, disrupting the individual's efforts to imagine the wartime essence of the camp. Tunbridge and Ashworth (1996) devised the phrase 'heritage dissonance' to describe how modern tourism amenities (car parks, toilets, cafés, restrooms) work to either interrupt or dilute the power of the imagination to conjure up an evocative sense of place. Perhaps the potential failure of a place like Dachau to animate the visitor's imagination is not merely linked to heritage dissonance but rather base ignorance. As Charles Hawley, a former tour guide at Dachau, framed it, Dachau is often perceived as another stop on the tourist's to-do list. Writing in *Spiegel Online*, Hawley (2005) remarked that to many of the tourists he encountered during his time as a tour guide: 'The Holocaust became something to sandwich in between a quick art museum visit in the morning and a session at the Hofbrauhaus in the evening. In short, they didn't know what they were getting into.' For the 'happy-go-lucky' party crowd, Hawley (2005) admitted that 'as petty as it sounded', his goal as a tour guide was to 'ruin their day' by compelling them to learn about the forced labour, medical experiments, brutal punishments and piles of bodies discovered by the American liberators. However, by way of balance, he pointed out that many visitors sat consumed in silent thought on the bus and train ride back to Munich or cornered him to ask questions prompted by their visit. This is not to assert that tour groups are the predominant form of tourism at Dachau; many visitors come alone or in intimate private groups.

The commodification of Dachau had its apotheosis in a recent event that demonstrates the ways that opportunistic commerce can rub up against concentration camp tourism in a manner that provokes outrage and distress. In 2017, the Dachau memorial took the local branch of fast food giant Burger King to court for distributing promotional brochures in its grounds. It claimed that uniformed staff were placing flyers under the windshield wipers of cars in an action that memorial site head, Dr Gabriele Hammermann, labelled 'disrespectful' (RT News 2017). The practice had allegedly been taking place for years despite the memorial officially requesting that it stop. Arch-rival burger franchise McDonald's faced a similar situation in 1996, but that company eventually complied with requests to stop distributing flyers in the car park adjacent to Dachau. McDonald's also issued an apology. The recent case is still being adjudicated by the courts. The burger franchise's defence asserts that it should have unhindered access to public places and that the car park is *just* a car park. The controversy reminds us that Dachau does not exist in social and commercial vacuum. It is a site that – for better or worse – attracts commercial interest from those who see profit as conjoined to Holocaust tourism (Cole 1999).

The permanent exhibition

As Lennon and Weber state, 'between 1968 and the late 1990s there were few fundamental changes to the site and exhibition content' (2016, p. 30). An advisory council comprised of historians, educators and Dachau survivors recommended that: 'A planned visitor tour should retrace the path that the entering inmates followed, starting at the entrance gate and continuing into the service building where the initial registration took place, then proceeding to the barracks area and crematorium' (Lennon & Weber 2016, p. 30). This trope of the 'prisoner journey' was much more pronounced when I first visited Dachau in 1992 than it was in 2016. That the guiding theme of the 'prisoner journey' has been toned down strikes me as apt. There was no *typical* prisoner journey at Dachau. Hundreds of thousands of individual prisoners journeyed through it; many perished, some survived and some were only incarcerated for a relatively short period. Apart from centralised registration, any tour that suggests a typical 'passage' through the camp is prone to distort a nuanced understanding. Indeed, the logic that such a tour 'ended' at the crematorium was problematic as it could underwrite a falsely dramatic message: that all inmates ultimately perished in Dachau.

The main exhibitions at Dachau are presented in the Shunt Room, where new arrivals were processed, and in the Prisoner Baths. I was pleased to note that since my previous visit, the exhibition space has been greatly simplified by curators. Discrete glass cabinets which one can peer into and vertical explanatory panels do not crowd the space.

Reconstructing horror: the problem of the simulacra

In his authoritative account of the post-war history of Dachau, Marcuse lamented changes to the memorial site that have occurred over the years and how it seems to have been 'repeatedly sanitized of authentic historical substance' (Marcuse 2005, p. 118). Indeed, the central problem relating to authenticity at Dachau is directly linked to the fact that many of its extant features are reconstructions. Vergo puts it more forcefully, noting 'a good deal of what we do see is in fact fake' (2008, p. 23). As architecturally faithful and as powerful these reconstructions are in instilling a sense of foreboding in visitors, the replica nature of some of these installations is problematic. Indeed, Hodgkinson places the problem of authenticity in the context of accommodating tourism: 'There is always a danger that by making a site more accessible to tourists the message of the history of the camp becomes diluted or simplified, or the authenticity is compromised by the need to reconstruct camp structures' (2013, p. 29).

Lennon and Weber note that 'by 1964 the old camp barracks had been demolished and two barracks had to be rebuilt to represent the original buildings' (2016, p. 29). During my visit, I overhead two English-speaking visitors make remarks to the effect that real people slept in this room. Seemingly oblivious to the signage, I did not have the heart to intrude and tell them that the bunkhouse is a simulacrum rebuilt precisely with the purpose of assisting visitors to imagine something about the tangible experience of being incarcerated here. Unlike the authentic (non-replica) bunks I observed at Birkenau during my 2007 visit (see Dalton 2015), these particular bunks seemed a discordant feature. Notwithstanding the good intentions at play, the replica barracks failed to capture my imagination. They struck me as an *empty* signifier; depleted of any authenticity they could not animate my imagination. I concur with Clark's observation:

> The bunkroom at Dachau in Germany, which was rebuilt for visitors to comprehend with ease the living conditions in the camps, is too clean to evoke

the horror of actual conditions and plays into the hands of Holocaust deniers through its artificiality.

(2014, p. 23)

Other tourists seemed enthralled by the bunks. Perhaps the artifice was not entirely misplaced? One must be cautious about denying the power of replica exhibits to animate empathy and sympathy in the minds of other visitors. Indeed, tapping into museological debates, Carden-Coyne has decreed 'a false dichotomy' exists 'between historical realism and authenticity versus abstraction and replication' (2011, p. 169).

Another problem of authenticity related to the notion of the simulacra is not just the reconstructed buildings, but some of the exhibits displayed at Dachau. An exhibit that receives a great deal of attention in tourist blogs is an implement of torture: a replica whipping block. This slightly concave wooden platform adorned with several whipping crop devices is exhibited in the former prisoner baths. Explanatory text outlines that prisoners would be laid across the block so that their back could receive up to twenty-five lashes. Nobody can dispute the historic reality that wooden devices like this were used to mete out horrific beatings at Dachau, but the need for artifice unnerved me. The whipping block exhibit, along with some other exhibits, was recently curated in what the memorial site termed a 'new presentation', which went to great lengths to contextualise the artefacts more carefully. The new presentation includes items of 'resistance and self-assertion' (e.g., illegal armbands and wall tiles that featured notes written upon them by prisoners). Such artefacts are welcome, for they challenge the notion that prisoners were wholly servile and too cowered to leave testimonials behind. A brave curatorial decision may have seen the whipping block retired from the exhibition space, much in the same way that *Wannsee House* in Berlin removed a large table from display because it was not authentic (see Chapter 1). Inauthentic items, however carefully made and historically faithful, do not belong in memorial spaces. Some would argue that they act as *props* to stimulate the imagination of the visitor. However, other less dramatic items can fulfil such an important role. For example, an original prisoner painting depicting sadistic SS officers whipping a prisoner on a whipping bench captures the barbarity of torture in a way that shows greater fidelity to the notion of authenticity.

Unused gas chamber

Many tourists are captivated by the gas chamber and morgue rooms that one can walk through. An unused gas chamber is something of a novelty in that one cannot contemplate the plight of the murdered in such a space, as sinister as such a space is. The corpse room – a former makeshift morgue – is arguably more disturbing because it was used to house bodies. These spaces are accompanied by clear signage. During my visit, I overhead visitors ruminating on the process of gassing. One man pondered to his companion, 'I wonder if they crammed as many people in here as they did in Auschwitz?' His question alarmed me although I was not game to respond (as he was not addressing me). I wondered how he could be oblivious to the fact that this gas chamber was never operational. In any event, he clearly had not seen the enormous dynamited gas chambers at Birkenau, or he would not have posed such a question out loud.

Overhearing the visitors' discussion felt like an intrusion on an unguarded moment. It suggests that however carefully and painstakingly memorials curate their spaces and exhibits, the tourist seems free to impose his/her flawed imagination on the exhibits and – in doing so – distorts their meaning. This, of course, is not the fault of the museum.

The open air remains of the camp

The vast proportion of what visitors encounter at Dachau is outside, away from the museum-like exhibition spaces. Whilst visitors can see the barbed wire and the reconstructed watch towers, the tranquillity of the space in the contemporary era is quite problematic as captured by Hodgkinson's observation:

> Many concentration camps are now in quite picturesque and pleasant surroundings, which conflicts with your knowledge of the terrible things that happened there, particularly if you visit in the height of summer and are surrounded by smiling family groups. This juxtaposition of the bleak history of the site, and the site today as a place of tourism, is disconcertingly incongruent.
>
> (2013, p. 30)

This sense of incongruity jarred my senses during my visit. The sunshine bathed the outside area in light and the lack of extant features did little to anchor one's thoughts back to the camp. Of course, such a feat is temporally impossible, but nevertheless, the vast swathes of emptiness at Dachau are hard for the visitor to imaginatively decipher. Giant concrete foundations cast in 1965 and strewn with gravel help the visitor imagine where thirty-two barracks once stood. Giant stone markers bear numbers that help the tourist envisage the magnitude of the camp. Fanning out in two neat rows, they attest also to the Nazi obsession with order. Many tourists walk swiftly past these foundations and many do not pay them much attention. Perhaps this is because their uniform sameness offers little novel value. Others stand transfixed, lost in contemplation and private thoughts.

Four memorial installations

In a space so denuded of objects, memorials at Dachau do much to harness interest from tourists. In this section, I wish to explore four memorial installations and comment on how they help animate what is essentially a largely barren space once one exits the museum at the front of the camp.

Skeletal bodies

Nandor Glid's bronze sculpture *Memorial of the Comité International de Dachau* was erected in 1968 (Niven 2001). It is located at the point where the prisoners first entered the camp in the middle of the former assembly square. Hoffmann-Curtius and Nurmi-Schomers elaborate on the sculpture's allegoric properties: 'The skeletal apparitions contorted until they are indistinguishable from the barbed wire are a reply to the straight lines of the decorative grating of the *jourhaus* entrance bearing the inscription "Work Liberates" [*Arbeit macht frei*]' (1998, p. 43). The sculpture features figures writhing in pain 'suspended in the barbed wire and indeed inseparable from it' and alludes to 'murder and suicide within the barbed wire of the concentration camp' (Hoffmann-Curtius & Nurmi-Schomers 1998, p. 43). To my mind, this sculpture is arguably the most powerful figurative element at Dachau. It conjures the *absent* prisoners in our mind's eye and, in doing so, reinstates them in their rightful place during our visit. It performs an invaluable commemorative task and one cannot imagine Dachau without this iconic sculpture instructing us about the suffering it attests to in such a sorrowful way.

Three links of chain bas-relief

At the front section of the camp, a simple but powerful memorial has stood since the 1960s. Offering a burst of colour, three stylised granite links of prison chain are adorned with approximately sixty KZ badges or 'chevrons' used to denote prisoner classifications (Hoffmann-Curtius & Nurmi-Schomers 1998, p. 42). Jews, asocials, homosexuals, political and religious prisoners (chiefly Jehovah's Witnesses) all had different symbols and colour combinations to enable the SS to readily identify their 'crimes'. The collage of overlapping symbols suggests a commonality of shared suffering despite individual difference. In a curious omission, green triangles denoting criminals, black triangles denoting 'asocials' and pink triangles denoting homosexuals are absent. These victim groups proved too controversial in the era that sculpture was erected (Hammermann & Pilzweger-Steiner 1998, 63). Nevertheless, it is a powerful memorial that cleverly evokes the masse of prisoners long banished from the memorial space.

The Jewish death ramp memorial

Marcuse documents that the next memorial under discussion arose out of the open and barely concealed contempt for Jewish victims that prevailed after the liberation of Dachau (Marcuse 2001). Zvi Guttmann's *Israelite Memorial at Dachau* was consecrated in 1967 (Kappel 2010). The architecture of the memorial, 'attempts to re-enact the extermination of the Jew symbolically' (Hoffmann-Curtius & Nurmi-Schomers 1998, p. 40). Located at the rear of the camp in an area that used to be the camp brothel, the imposing memorial to all Jews murdered during the Holocaust is 'made of black lava basalt rock with a parabolic plan that leads down into the depth, reminiscent of the "death ramp" that led to the underground rooms of the gas chambers of Birkenau' (Hoffmann-Curtius &

Nurmi-Schomers 1998, p. 40). The ramp downwards is 'fenced in by symbolic imitations of barbed wire that figuratively connects with Nandor Glid's bronze sculpture'. The building that appears to hover over the ramp is said to resemble the furnaces of the crematorium (Hoffmann-Curtius & Nurmi-Schomers 1998). The memorial has a distinctly experiential element as captured by Hoffmann-Curtius and Nurmi-Schomers' description:

> In the darkest, narrowest and deepest part of the sculpture the visitor's view is directed upwards . . . through an opening in the wall into the daylight, the strip of marble ending in a menorah as a sign of deliverance, the goal of eternal Jewish hope.
>
> (1998, p. 40)

It is hard to convey to the uninitiated the claustrophobic feeling of inhabiting the space at the bottom of the sculpture. Its profound power is that as a sculptural conduit, it transports the visitor to *other* camps, reminding us that Dachau existed as part of a constellation of concentration and extermination camps in the Nazi criminal universe.

The solitary prisoner

Fritz Koelle's bronze life-size sculpture of the *Unknown Concentration Camp Inmate* has stood as a silent sentinel in Dachau since 1949. Burnished a deep green verdigris, the solitary prisoner gazes out over the now empty camp, his hands secreted in his pockets.[1] Marcuse notes that the inscription on the pedestal – *To honour the dead, to admonish the living* – 'melds contemplation with accusation' (2010, p. 73). Apparently, former prisoners had a part in contributing ideas that Koelle used to ultimately conceive of his forlorn figure. Flowers often adorn the base of the sculpture; offering remembrance to all the nameless prisoners it represents. It is a very powerful memorial despite its formal memorial qualities harking back to 1940s realism. Its success, I suggest, relates to its properties as a memorial synecdoche (Dalton 2015). As a *part* – one unknown and unnamed prisoner – it speaks economically to the *whole* – the countless thousands of men who suffered or perished within the camp walls. Its gendered form may well obscure that women were imprisoned in Dachau, but that criticism must be tethered to the knowledge of its creation at a time when women were largely overlooked in memorial forms. The sculpture attracts much attention from visitors, partly because its position on a raised plinth invites veneration; but also because the *figure* of the prisoner *figures* so powerfully in our imagination. To the extent that visitors throng to Dachau, it is to vicariously experience something tangible about the plight of the prisoner. One can project all the sadness marshalled by the place onto this sculpture.

The crematorium

At the rear of the camp lies a giant carved granite block that mimics the crude shape of a tombstone. On it is carved the German text KREMATORIUM* DENKET

DARAN WIE HIER STARBEN, which translates in English as CREMATORIUM * REMEMBER HOW WE DIED HERE. This marking stone helps orientate the visitor to his/her location within the camp, but its simple text performs a much more important task as an individual's visit culminates. For it instructs us – German visitors and international tourists alike – to imagine death in this most terrible place. All the exhibits – memorials and extant camp features – coalesce in this moment. If one acquiesces to such a solemn plea, then one will recall the appalling facts gleaned in the museum space and *remember* that those who died here did so in a manner that few visitors can genuinely fathom. Loneliness, despair, starvation, anguish and torment attended every death in this place. Some deaths were also augmented by disease, medical experimentation and torture. The marking stone functions as a cognitive anchor that enables us to appreciate something of the sheer terror and fear that afflicted every prisoner incarcerated at Dachau.

Bergen-Belsen: savage beauty

Overview of the camp

Schulze notes that Bergen-Belsen was not the archetype of a Nazi concentration camp (2014). Established in 1943, it started out as a camp for Jews who were to be temporarily exempted from deportation to death camps in the east (Schulze 2014). Niven notes that the camp also housed Jews whom the Nazis planned to exchange for POWs (2001). In the final months of the war when Bergen-Belsen became a reception centre for the death marches from the east, the camp turned into 'the hell uncovered by the British troops, which is now associated with its name' (Schulze 2014, p. 122). Bergen-Belsen also functioned as a prisoner-of-war camp mainly for Soviet POWs. Some 50,000 people perished from starvation, disease and appalling camp conditions (Wiedemann 2008). All told, some 120,000 are estimated to have been interred at one of the camps on this site (Schulze 2006). Between 1945 and 1950, the liberated concentration camp was transformed into a displaced persons camp set up in former Wehrmacht barracks a mile from the Nazi camp (Schulze 2014). Like Dachau, Bergen-Belsen first entered the public's consciousness through the dissemination of atrocity pictures that were published by news agencies the world over. Images of emaciated corpses provoked public awareness of Nazi brutality.[2] The famous diarist Anne Frank and her sister Margot perished in Bergen-Belsen. While they were not archetypal Bergen-Belsen victims – the very concept gives rise to offence – it bears emphasising that many people visit the camp lured by *The diary of Anne Frank* or the experience of visiting *the Anne Frank House* in Amsterdam (see Chapter 4).

Situating Bergen-Belsen in the tourism landscape

In 1945, the British tore down or torched many of the wooden huts as soon as the liberated inmates had moved out, such was the fear of disease spreading. As Schulze notes: '[A]lthough done for good reasons' this eradication of the huts 'contributed to the process of getting rid of the evidence of what had happened at Bergen-Belsen' (2006, p. 218). Later, all remaining extant features were either removed or covered with a layer of topsoil. The German provisional government in Hanover was ordered by the British Military Government to set up an appropriate memorial to ensure that the memory of the infamy of the concentration camps does not fade (Schulze 2014). It was agreed by the authorities overseeing the project that the proposed memorial should not, by intention, invoke painful memories of the manner of the victims' deaths (Schulze 2014). Heeding this agreement, a memorial obelisk and a fifty-metre-long wall of remembrance was erected on the site (Marcuse 2010).[3] Schulze summarises the resulting situation:

> Bergen-Belsen had become a place of beauty, and of reverence, where those who had died could rest in peace, as the British had requested, but at the same time it was all but invisible to the uninformed visitor as the site of a prisoner-of-war and concentration camp.
>
> (2014, p. 123)

This problem of what might be termed an *invisible history* was gradually rectified. In 1966 some basic information about the camp was provided on the site and in 1990 – on the forty-fifth anniversary of the liberation of the camp – a small exhibition devoted to the history of Bergen-Belsen opened to the public (Schulze 2014).

Unlike Dachau – which is well promoted and serviced by a network of public transport and dedicated tour operators – Bergen-Belsen is comparatively remote, and is not well promoted or readily accessible by public transport. My journey on a Saturday necessitated a bus trip from the nearby town of Celle to the smaller town of Bergen and then a short taxi ride to the former camp. While waiting, I saved a young Japanese tourist from disappointment as she was on the wrong side of the road and would have missed the only bus running to Bergen that day. As the bus travelled to Bergen, she explained she had come on a pilgrimage to see Anne Frank's memorial.[4]

The new Documentation and Information Centre: a triumph of engagement

I arrived at the camp site and was immediately confronted by the dramatic, minimalist architecture of the new Documentation and Information Centre (hereafter Centre), which opened in October 2007.

To respect the fact that the site had been declared a Jewish cemetery and 'to avoid the creation of a "Bergen-Belsen-land" ', the new building to house the exhibition space was 'constructed just outside the historic site' (Schulze 2014, p. 124). A stony path leads to the entrance of a long and narrow building finished in raw concrete. The front exterior of the building is modern and unadorned, but it is the rear exterior space (that which is appreciated from *within* the camp grounds) that is a triumph of modern architecture. A seven-metre extension cantilevers over the

Figure 5.1 Entrance view of Bergen-Belsen Memorial Museum

camp's boundary. Its aesthetic properties will subsequently be explored. Schulze captures the importance of the exhibition space, observing:

> As the actual horror can never be recreated, and as it cannot be adequately described either, all the exhibition aims to do is to provide the visitors with the available evidence upon which they will then have to draw their own conclusions and form their own images as to what conditions at Bergen-Belsen were like.
>
> (2006, p. 226)

The plain concrete walls and prevailing colours of grey, white and black help lend the exhibition space an austere functionality that works well and 'is in line with a general effort against the Disneyfication of the Gedenkstätte'[5] (Schulze 2014, p. 132). In the large exhibition hall, which covers some 600 square metres, the floor slopes upwards. It contains an exhaustive exhibition of history of the concentration camp. Schulze summarises the intention of the exhibition: 'The exhibition aims to avoid trivialisation and simplification. It is a *tour de force*: rigorously designed to as a straightforward and sober documentation that sets out what occurred at Bergen-Belsen, but does not prescribe visitors how to feel' (2014, p. 127). Muted lights are used to delineate an uninterrupted view to the very end of the rear of the ground floor.

Figure 5.2 Interior view of Documentation Centre with mood lighting

The historical exhibition spaces sit off to the right in enormous banks that are equally distant and also subtly lit. A suite of light boxes that showcase archaeological findings are set into the floor. It is difficult to convey in writing how the space feels in its entirety. It is both sombre and calm, but also inviting and enticing. This is perhaps the most carefully thought-through and accomplished museum space I have ever encountered, and while the following sections will discuss some of the key attributes of the Centre, they are not strictly divisible. The emotional and cognitive effect imparted by a visit to the Centre is more than the sum of its parts.

It is a moving tribute to all those who suffered and perished here and sets a new benchmark for memorials to which museums and heritage sites the world over can aspire.

The new permanent exhibition is 'source driven' in the sense that its shows great fidelity to original texts, photographs, artefacts and testimony (Schulze 2014, p. 126). A broadly chronological approach documents three sections: the prisoner-of-war camp (1940–1945), the concentration camp (1943–1945) and the displaced persons camp (1945–1950), which is dealt with upstairs. The variety of exhibits is important because as Schulze observes, '[t]here is no single universal memory of Bergen-Belsen. Different groups have different memories' of the camp (2006, p. 222). In the following sections I will explore some of the particularly engaging attributes of the exhibition space, remarking on the ways the different exhibits captivate visitors.

It bears emphasising that the building is a museum and an archive at the same time (Wiedemann 2008, p. 45). To that end, the appearance of exhibition panels and display cases is 'deliberately reminiscent of archive shelves and thereby forms a mental link to the tens of thousands of documents and other items' that are stored here but not on display (Wiedemann 2008, p. 45). In conceiving the exhibition, the perspective of the prisoners was paramount in terms of curatorial decisions. The exhibition sought to give the former prisoners-of-war and concentration camp prisoners their voices back. This is both, as Wiedemann terms it, 'an act of justice' but also a process that 'enhances visitors' empathy with the victims of Nazi crimes and thereby forms an important basis for the educational approach' of the centre (2008, p. 45). Finally, it is worth emphasising that 'the artefacts, documents and photographs exhibited are testimony to violence in the civilised world' (Wiedemann 2008, p. 46). They are presented in a way that encourages visitors to ask questions but, as Wiedemann astutely reminds us, the exhibition also makes it clear that many 'questions cannot be answered at the moment and perhaps never will be' (2008, p. 46).

Whilst the exhibition space documents Nazi crimes using survivor testimony, photographs, film and artefacts, some heroic sentiment is suitably accommodated. For example, in contrast to the menacing and dread-inducing black SS officer uniforms displayed at Wewelsburg (see Chapter 3), a mannequin dressed in a regulation khaki British soldier's uniform, accompanied by a canvas kit bag, attests to the valiant work performed by the British army who liberated the camp and sought to save as many prisoners as possible from the clutches of starvation and imminent death.

Yet, as Reynolds notes, other exhibits counter any triumphant narrative: 'Photos of skeletal bodies, both living and dead, are reminders that liberation came too late for too many and testify to the failure to intervene sooner' (2016, p. 341).

The film tower (screening room)

Dalton (2015) emphasises the important preparatory work that film performs in concentration camp tourism contexts. According with this logic, in a small viewing

Figure 5.3 Mannequin dressed in regulation khaki British soldier's uniform accompanied
        by kit bag and cap

room separated by a heavy curtain, visitors can watch two short films recorded by
the British Army's Film and Photographic Unit for Movietone News. The films
are presented as 'authentic, singular historical records in their own right' (Gring &
Theilen 2009, p. 39). As an authentic mediated witness to the horror, film 'conveys
the historical events to the visitors very vividly and powerfully' (Wiedemann 2008,
p. 47). Gring and Theilen point out that 'the films do not just allegorically represent Nazi crimes, but also stand in for the loss of individuality on the part of the
victims and a more abstract view of suffering that does not take the individual into
account' (2009, p. 37). At the new Documentation Centre, the films are 'presented

as raw footage without any other editing as full reels of about one minute in length each' (Gring & Theilen 2009, p. 44). No commentary or voiceover is provided, but the original caption sheets prepared by the cameramen are projected in tandem onto a second screen. These captions sheets (or *dope sheets* as they were referred to as in the 1940s) capture information that eluded the technology of the camera: 'The dope sheets . . . supplemented the images on the films with descriptions of the heat, the deathly silences and, perhaps, most terrible of all, the smell' (Haggith, cited in Gring & Theilen 2009, p. 44). Condensed into one-minute viewing experiences, the films resist summary in terms of their brute power to shock and upset. Many people walked out on the day I visited: a visceral reaction to sights that are overpowering or feel like a voyeuristic intrusion to some.

Watching the films, the full catalogue of horrors unfolds: piles of emaciated bodies; bulldozers pushing bodies into mass graves; close-ups of the faces of survivors, many with inscrutable expressions; SS men and women reluctantly assisting with the burying of the dead. The 35mm footage is surprisingly sharp and vivid. Whilst these films are 'deeply engraved in our collective visual memory' (Gring & Theilen 2009, p. 37), it is very confronting to watch them *in situ*, so close to the site where they were filmed. The films 'serve to give an idea of the magnitude of the crimes committed by the Nazis' (Gring & Theilen 2009, 38). They are an important prelude to encountering the rest of the exhibition space and, subsequently, the outside of area of the camp.

Video testimonies

Throughout the exhibition space, a different type of film is encountered. Gring and Theilen (2009) document that some 365-odd biographical interviews (running to some 1,800 hours) with survivors of the concentration camp. They elaborate: 'These testimonies provide information on individual aspects, situations and events in the history of the camps' (2009, p. 45). We, as visitors, encounter these films as 'video points' that are integrated into the exhibition's spatial design 'to give the witness testimonies the same status as the other sources of material in the exhibition' (Gring & Theilen 2009, p. 47). Wiedemann elaborates on their intrinsic value: 'They convey an impression of the conditions under which these people lived and survived at Bergen-Belsen, a topic about which other sources tell us very little' (2008, p. 47).

The video testimonies provided helps us better grasp the black and white images of atrocity that we witness in the film tower. The historic footage was mute and the victims did not speak. Giving voice to the survivors' unique stories enables visitors to remember that the people who suffered at Belsen were unique individuals; a fact we are perhaps likely to overlook when contemplating the footage of amorphous piles of bodies being bulldozed into the soil. Still, we must also keep in mind in contemplating the testimonies that we, as outsiders, are never able to 'comprehend fully what it meant to be a prisoner at a concentration camp or to suffer the deadly conditions of a German camp for Soviet prisoners of war' (Wiedemann 2008, p. 47).

The lightboxes

As one moves through the exhibition space, one encounters approximately sixteen large light boxes set into the floor. Each box is laden with 'objects unearthed during archaeological excavations of the camp's structural remains' (Wiedemann 2008, p. 45). Their placement at the floor level forces visitors to look down and contemplate their contents, a gesture that reminds the spectator of the objects' archaeological provenance. One box contains pebbles, large rusted hinges (from a door?) and broken crockery brandished with an eagle carrying a swastika. Another light box features a naïve homemade necklace and cross juxtaposed with a crushed aluminium vessel and a rusted cup. Yet another box displays a brown felt purse, some tiny silver coins and several medallions including a yellow enamel one of splendour that appears to bear the number thirty-nine (perhaps alluding to the year 1939?). In another box, perhaps the most plaintive, twisted rusted barbed wire fragments are juxtaposed with a broken wooden fence paling conjuring up a reminder of the fence complex that imprisoned people at Belsen.

Some twenty-odd miniature glass or crystal bottles lay in an aesthetically interesting pattern in yet another box. Some have art deco shapes and appear to be luxury scent flacons. Another box contains rusted safety razors, broken spectacle frames, broken ceramic objects, a wooden handled spatula, expended aluminium tubes of ointment and other mysterious objects.

One box is devoted entirely to russet-brown rusted items: a rake, pitchfork, a green enamel watering can, a drill section and several keys.

Figure 5.4 Floor-set light box displaying rusted barbed wire fragments and broken wooden fence paling

Figure 5.5 Floor-set light box with safety razors, broken spectacle frames, ceramic objects, a wooden handled spatula, expended aluminium tubes of ointment and other mysterious objects

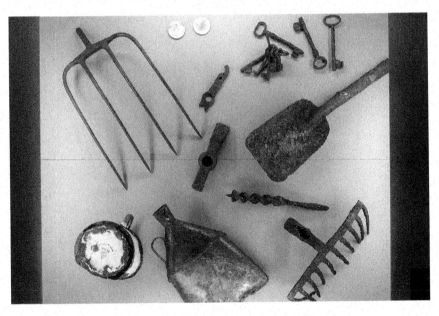

Figure 5.6 Floor-set light box with various russet-brown rusted gardening implements

In another light box, colourful Bakelite and pearl buttons sit alongside indeterminate rusted hinged items and numerous shoe, dress and belt clasps or buckles.

Vergo asserts that many concentration camp artefacts 'remain curiously mute and unrevealing' (2008, p. 23). He elaborates: 'Their simple juxtaposition may have the effect of coaxing the remains of the past into telling stories' (Vergo 2008, p. 24). Peering into the light boxes, we are encouraged to use our imagination to ruminate on the objects. Their enigmatic qualities make storytelling challenging, but they certainly exude a powerful testimonial authority. For they speak about the base experiences of the camp as a place inhabited by real people. The presence in the boxes of personal items attests to attempted survival. Cherished items, grooming items and items of utility tell us very simple, unadulterated stories; people lived and perished here. The artefacts linger in the mind. They accompany us metaphorically as we venture into the camp's space as powerful talismans of human occupation. They remind us of the humanity that resided here.

The rear of the exhibition hall: a glimpse into the camp

Wiedemann describes a feature at the rear of the exhibition hall where the building projects into the former camp itself: 'A large opening in the structure affords a view of the outside and thus includes the grounds in the exhibition' (2008, p. 44). Schulze captures the diorama one can appreciate from this perspective: 'By looking out this window, the visitors will be confronted by the duality of the historic

Figure 5.7 Interior view of camp revealing nature outside

site: concentration camp and cemetery' (2006, p. 225). He elaborates: 'The window almost draws the historic site into the building and makes it part of the exhibition' (Schulze 2006, p. 225). During my visit, many people stood transfixed in quiet contemplation, looking out at the beauty.

The window is a profound conduit of sorts. As we stare out at the scenic beauty, it is hard – some might say impossible – to stage any horrors in our mind's eye; yet, we are looking at the site where the horrors conveyed in the exhibition space took place in the past. Rather than disinhibiting solemn reflection, the quiet peaceful outside environs – so radically different to the outside sights of Dachau – seems a suitable blank canvas to just reflect. It is a powerful, emotionally charged zone within the exhibition hall where the outside beckons us to walk, reflect, and think after we have experienced the exhibition space.

Outside: beauty and reverence abound

Writing about a visit to Bergen-Belsen in the 1970s, the writer Paul Auster makes it clear he was visiting 'the site where Bergen-Belsen *once stood*' – firmly locating the camp's physical presence in the past (2012, p. 148, emphasis added). His reminder struck a chord with me as I walked the site. With the barracks and camp structures long gone, nature dominates the space.

Vergo points out that when we visit a former concentration camp, 'we are mistaken if by any stretch of the imagination we convince ourselves that by going to

Figure 5.8 Interior perspective of Documentation Centre as seen within camp grounds

the place itself, we are going to see it the way it really was' (2008, p. 21). While his observation is true of most former camps, it is most applicable here at Belsen when we exit the Documentation Centre:

> Walking through the grounds, parts of the original topography are still visible in places; some of the paths, the foundations of buildings and especially mass graves excavated and rapidly filled after the camp was liberated by British troops in spring of 1945.
>
> (Vergo 2008, p. 21)

He elaborates: 'It is thus immensely evocative: a place of memory, a memorial to the dead and a cemetery, all at the same time. But it does not claim to be a *museum*' (Vergo 2008, p. 24, emphasis in original). Rather, it is the new Documentation Centre that shoulders the 'crucial *responsibility* of a museum, that of mediating, explaining, and interpreting' (Vergo 2008, p. 24, emphasis in original).

So, when we venture outside, we are very mindful that the Documentation Centre has done most of the hard memorial work, an idea captured by Schulze:

> [A]fter walking through the exhibition it is hoped that the visitors will see the actual site with different eyes and realise that the peaceful and pleasant-looking landscape covered in heather and interspersed with birch trees and junipers is deceptive. Beneath the soil the dead lie in mass graves.
>
> (2006, p. 230)

Walking the central path, I was struck that Hübotter's original 1946 vision for the landscape design as 'a place of beauty and of reverence, where those who died here could rest in peace' had not really altered in all this time (cited in Schulze 2006, p. 219). The outside shows no traces of the crimes enacted here because it has been rendered, in the words of the writer Paul Auster, 'denuded and antiseptic' (2012, p. 148). However, this hardly matters. The Documentation Centre performs the role of revealing that criminality in an admirable way. The tranquillity of the space still carries echoes of the past; a past that poet Michaela Victoria Hoepffner captures in an extract from her poem, *Bergen-Belsen, April 1993*:

> only if you keep on: being there
> the bush might talk to you, perhaps
> a blade of grass, a leaf, a breeze
> voices of women behind you
> behind the next pine.
>
> (cited in Hoepffner 2013, p. 71)

Schulze (2006, p. 224) notes that no attempt has been made to reverse the radical intervention into the topography of the historic site which has taken place since the summer of 1945. Minimal markers document where particular buildings or roll call/assembly squares once stood. These signs bearing historic photographs and English and German text help the visitor better comprehend the level space and navigate it imaginatively. This relative lack of signage makes the space all the more evocative. A large but unobtrusive three-dimensional bronze map provides a scaled aerial view of the camp complex, replete with jutting pegs to indicate where watchtowers once stood. This also helps visitors better imagine the now-vanished camp structures. It bears emphasising that the outside space is constantly evolving. In time, 'a new *Place of Names* will be created in the new central corridor of the memorial' (Schulze 2006, p. 231). This will serve as a special place of remembrance for all the people who died here.

Anne and Margot Frank's memorial

Schulze notes 'Bergen-Belsen will be known to many visitors as the place where Anne Frank died shortly before the liberation of the camp' (2006, p. 228). The

Figure 5.9 Anne and Margot Frank memorial headstone adorned with gifts from visitors

exhibition space tells the story of Anne and her sister Margot, but does so carefully by tactfully showing that 'Anne Frank was one of many thousands of female concentration camp prisoners who were transported from Auschwitz-Birkenau to Bergen-Belsen in the autumn of 1944 in order to do slave labour and who perished in the final phase of the camp' (Schulze 2006, p. 228). Efforts to promote the plurality of female victims aside, the *singular* figure of Anne Frank acts as a lure and many thousands of visitors come to the memorial site to visit her symbolic grave, which is adorned by a headstone that bears her name and year of birth and death (and that of her sister).[6]

Lustiger-Thaler and Wiedemann (2012, p. 139) observe '[t]he contemporary commemorative practice by visitors, especially children, of leaving objects at the monument to Margot and Anne Frank that now stands on the grounds of the Bergen-Belsen Memorial'. On the day I visited, a sprig of mimosa, memorial candles, plastic flowers, ceramic books, a fabric doll and a famous photograph of Anne adorned the memorial. These offerings are not unique. Lustiger-Thaler and Wiedemann (2012, pp. 155–156) note that '[p]eople leave jewellery, notes, words etched on worn stones, stuffed animals, miniature flags and medals, among other things. They elaborate:

> These individualized responses arise from a mediated relationship to Anne of long standing, now taking place within the commemorative institution of Bergen-Belsen as a site of destruction, wedded to the memorial narrative of her brutal death, rather than to the diary and the palliative political and cultural uses made of it in the past.
>
> (Lustiger-Thaler & Wiedemann, 2012, p. 156)

Staring at the memorial, I reflected on my visit to the *Anne Frank House* with its maddening hordes of visitors (see Chapter 4). Here, in an almost empty memorial space very late in the afternoon, I reflected on the profundity of Lustiger-Thaler and Wiedemann's observation, which I had read in preparation to come here:

> Remembered from her unmarked grave, not from the Annex in Amsterdam, the transit camp at Westerbork, or even Auschwitz-Birkenau . . . Anne Frank demonstrates the potential of an appeal for justice as truth . . . thereby extending to Bergen-Belsen, as a site of mass murder, the ethical potential of memory.
>
> (2012, p. 157)

Anne's journey, like that of many others interred in this place, ended here. In this quiet, serene location – suffused with natural beauty – one is able to simply remember the precocious young woman whose diary can be credited as making the Holocaust familiar to millions the world over.

Darkness on the edge of town: accommodating atrocity

Wiedemann points out that no exhibition 'whether it is located on a historical site or not, could ever bridge the gap between the existential experience of the Holocaust and its representation' (2008, p. 49). This observation aside, my experiences at Dachau and Bergen-Belsen demonstrate that both former camps go to great lengths to engage visitors and educate them about the facts of the Holocaust as enacted on their soil. It is tempting to laud Bergen-Belsen's new approach over that of Dachau. In the former, great fidelity is shown to exhibits, survivor testimony and a largely unadorned natural camp space, whereas in the latter, reconstructions and faux elements strike a somewhat discordant note. Such a criticism must be tempered by the knowledge that Bergen-Belsen presented something of a blank slate for museum and memorial curators to work with, allowing them to heed the museological lessons learned from past concentration camp exhibitions. Perhaps we should elide these differences and focus on the fact that both Dachau and Celle do their very best to accommodate atrocity within their environs. Both places must coexist with these confronting reminders of Nazism on their doorsteps. In their unique ways, both camps work in concert to provoke visitors to confront evidence of Nazi atrocities.

However, if forced to recommend one site over the other to a potential visitor, I would reluctantly proclaim that Bergen-Belsen – in 'resisting the trend towards "Holocaust tourism"' (Schulze 2014, p. 121) – offers a more contemplative, moving experience than Dachau. While many tourists might crave the guard towers, fences, barbed wire and reconstructed trappings that help them 'imagine' being *inside* a concentration camp, the sparse nature filled grounds of Bergen-Belsen are arguably better animated by the exemplary exhibition space contained within the Documentation Centre. For at Bergen-Belsen, no external *props* are required to help the visitor imagine the horrors that unfolded in this most complex memorial space. This is not to denigrate the fine and fitting memorial work achieved at Dachau, but rather to laud the memorial work performed at Bergen-Belsen as more subtle and less dependent upon largely reconstructed, architectural drama.

Notes

1 The original design of Koelle's statue was entitled *Inferno* and featured a naked prisoner holding up an emaciated dead man and pointing at his listless body in an accusatory gesture. Marcuse (2010, p. 73) notes that this original design 'was withdrawn because it was too graphic'.
2 For an account of the central role atrocity film footage played in raising consciousness about Bergen-Belsen the world over, see Kushner (2006).
3 For a discussion of the way classical forms such as pyramids and obelisks have been 'typical of the earliest Holocaust memorials', see Marcuse (2010, p. 64).
4 For a discussion of the concept of pilgrimage in relation to concentration camps, see Cole (1999) and, in relation to Bergen-Belsen specifically, see Lustiger-Thaler and Wiedemann (2012).
5 The German term *Gedenkstätte* means memorial site.
6 The headstone is symbolic because it does not mark the precise place where Anne and Margot Frank are buried because that place is, of course, unknown.

References

Auster, P 2012, *Winter journal*, Faber & Faber, London.

Carden-Coyne, A 2011, 'The ethics of representation in Holocaust museums', in JM Dreyfus & D Langton (eds), *Writing the Holocaust*, Bloomsbury, London, pp. 167–256.

Clark, LB 2014, 'Ethical spaces: ethics and propriety', in B Sion (ed.), *Trauma tourism: death tourism: disaster sites as recreational landscape*, Seagull Books, London, pp. 9–35.

Cole, T 1999, *Selling the Holocaust: from Auschwitz to Schindler: how history is bought, packaged, and sold*, Routledge, New York.

Dalton, D 2015, *Dark tourism and crime*, Routledge, London.

Dillon, C 2015, *Dachau and the SS: a schooling in violence*, Oxford University Press, Oxford.

Gring, D & Theilen, K (2009, 'Fragments of memory: testimony in the new permanent exhibition at Bergen-Belsen', *The Holocaust in history and memory*, vol. 2, pp. 37–52.

Hammermann, G & Pilzweger-Steiner, S 2017, *Dachau concentration camp memorial site, a tour*, official memorial guide booklet, Stiftung Bayerische, Gedenkstätten.

Hartmann, R 1989, 'Dachau revisited: tourism to the memorial site and museum of the former concentration camp', *Tourism Recreation Research*, vol. 14, no. 1, pp. 41–47.

Hartmann, R 2018, 'Tourism to memorial sites of the Holocaust', in PR Stone, R Hartmann, AV Seaton, R Sharpley & L White (eds), *The Palgrave handbook of dark tourism studies*, Palgrave Macmillan, London, pp. 469–507.

Hawley, C 2005, 'A day in hell: touring a concentration camp', *Spiegel Online*, 27 January, www.spiegel.de/international/touring-a-concentration-camp-a-day-in-hell-a-338820. html, viewed 26 May 2018.

Hodgkinson, S 2013, 'The concentration camp as a site of "dark tourism"'. *Témoigner. Entre histoire et mémoire. Revue pluridisciplinaire de la Fondation Auschwitz*, vol. 116, pp. 22–32.

Hoepffner, MV 2013, 'Bergen Belsen, April 1993', *The Arts and the Holocaust*, vol. 6, University of Essex, Colchester.

Hoffmann-Curtius, K & Nurmi-Schomers, S 1998, 'Memorials for the Dachau concentration camp', *Oxford Art Journal*, vol. 21 no, 2, pp. 23–44.

Kappel, K. (2010) *Dachau Concentration Camp Memorial Site: religious memorials*, Deutscher Kunstverlag: Berlin.

Kushner, T 2006, 'From "This Belsen Business" to "Shoah Business": history, memory and heritage, 1945–2005', *Holocaust Studies*, vol. 12, no. 1–2, pp. 189–216.

Lennon, J & Weber, D 2016, 'The long shadow: marketing Dachau', in G Hooper & JJ Lennon (eds), *Dark tourism: practices and interpretation*, Routledge, London, pp. 26–39.

Lustiger-Thaler, H & Wiedemann, W 2012, 'Hauntings and sightings in Germany', in B Kirshenblatt-Gimblett & J Shandler (eds), *Anne Frank unbound: media, imagination, memory*, Indiana University Press, Bloomington, pp. 137–159

Macdonald, S 2009, *Difficult heritage: negotiating the Nazi past in Nuremberg and beyond*, Routledge, London.

Marcuse, H 2001, *Legacies of Dachau: the uses and abuses of a concentration camp, 1933–2001*, Cambridge University Press, New York.

Marcuse, H 2005, 'Reshaping Dachau for visitors: 1933–2000', in G Ashworth & R Hartmann (eds), *Horror and human tragedy revisited: the management of sites of atrocities for tourism*, Cognizant Communications, New York, pp. 118–148.

Marcuse, H 2010, 'Holocaust memorials: The emergence of a genre', *The American Historical Review*, vol. 115, no. 1, pp. 53–89.

Morsch, G 2001, 'Concentration camp memorials in Eastern Germany since 1989', in M Levy (ed.), *Remembering for the future: the Holocaust in the age of genocide*, Palgrave, New York, pp. 367–382.

Niven, B, 2001, *Facing the Nazi past: united Germany and the legacy of the Third Reich*, Routledge, London.

Reynolds, D 2016, 'Consumers or witnesses? Holocaust tourists and the problem of authenticity', *Journal of Consumer Culture*, vol. 16, no. 2, pp. 334–353

Reynolds, D 2018, *Postcards from Auschwitz: Holocaust tourism and the meaning of remembrance*, New York University Press, New York.

RT News 2017, 'Burger King in court amid outrage over flyers at Dachau concentration camp', 17 May, www.rt.com/news/388743-burger-king-flyers-dachau, viewed 29 May 2019.

Schulze, R 2006, 'Forgetting and remembering: memories and memorialisation of Bergen-Belsen', *Holocaust Studies*, vol. 12, no. 1–2, pp. 217–235.

Schulze, R 2014, 'Resisting Holocaust tourism: the new Gedenkstätte at Bergen-Belsen, Germany', in B Sion (ed.) *Death tourism: disaster sites as recreational landscape*, Seagull Books, London, pp. 121–137.

Tunbridge, JE & Ashworth, GJ 1996, *Dissonant heritage: the management of the past as a resource in conflict*, John Wiley & Sons, Chichester.

Vergo, P 2008, 'Museums and sites of memory: how best to memorialize the Holocaust', *The Holocaust in History and Memory*, vol. 1, pp. 21–25.

Wiedemann, W 2008, ' "Earth conceal not the blood shed on thee": the new documentation centre at Bergen-Belsen', *The Holocaust in History and Memory*, vol. 1, pp. 41–58.

6 The Jewish Museum Berlin
Encountering trauma

Introduction: experience

Writing about Daniel Libeskind's Jewish Museum Berlin, situated on Linden-straße in the Kreuzberg district, is a daunting task. It is a piece of architecture that 'eludes criticism and commands respect' (Mathes 2012, p. 175). A chief criticism is that 'the museum seems to be intentionally at cross-purposes with itself, both celebrating the past and mourning its irretrievability' (Reynolds 2018, p. 167). Since opening, the museum has attracted sustained academic scrutiny from a range of disciplines, much of which has marshalled praise for its groundbreaking architecture as providing a profoundly moving experience for tourists and visitors alike. Indeed, the museum unabashedly promotes itself on its official website and brochures as 'a museum you need to *experience*'. This emphasis on experience is deliberate, with Stead noting 'the Jewish museum . . . is engaged in establishing a new balance between history and experience' (2000, p. 13). She elaborates: 'Visitors . . . are not asked to experientially re-enact the Holocaust, but only to identify empathetically with aesthetic representations' (2000, p. 13).

The museum's form and function have been read through theoretical prisms as diverse as: Freud and the uncanny (Young 2000); Walter Benjamin's notion of aura (Pješivac 2014); W.G. Sebald's literary masterpiece *Austerlitz* described by Arnold-de Simine as an 'alternative Holocaust museum' (2012, p. 14); Paul Celan's poetry (Kligerman 2005); Michel Foucault's concept of heterotopia (Saindon 2012); the philosophy of Levinas (Ionescu 2017), Heidegger, Nietzsche and Adorno (Smith 2005); and the politics of regret and nostalgia (Sodaro 2013). Moreover, Alois Müller described the museum, in its entirety, as 'a metaphor for the perverted form of enlightenment that led to the perpetration of crime in broad daylight' (cited in Akcan 2010, p. 168). Spens summarises the museum as 'a container for sharing historical objects and memories, documented or attributed' (1999, p. 40). 'Resonant objects' as Chametzky terms them (2008, p. 233), are of particular importance in the museum. Branham argues that they are prized for their aura; exhibited as veritable 'relics of the Holocaust that are displayed as synecdochal devices' (1994/1995, p. 44), as this chapter will subsequently explore. Messham-Muir concurs with this view, noting: 'With artefacts, Holocaust museums attempt to recreate an element of the event experience of the victims and survivors for those who were not present at those events' (2004, p. 104).

This emphasis on artefacts is pertinent, considering most visitors to the Jewish Museum Berlin are young people who did not live through the era of the Holocaust and whose only experiences of the event have been mediated through film and the written text. For them, original artefacts are worthy of veneration for capturing an elusive aura of the past, even if such encounters with the objects 'can never equate with the lived experience of Holocaust survivors and victims' (Messham-Muir 2004, p. 106). Nevertheless, Hansen-Glucklich (2014, p. 125) stresses that for museum visitors 'Holocaust artefacts exhibit a power that exudes tragedy and fatefulness'.

Writing in the context of curatorial strategies employed by museums, Spencer Crew and James Sims assert that museum objects: 'are not eloquent as some thinkers in the art museums claim. They are dumb. And if by some ventriloquism they seem to speak, they lie' (cited in Branham 1994/1995, p. 35). Such a suspicious view that museum objects are mendacious fails to fully appreciate that, in the words of Holocaust survivor museum guide from the Sydney Jewish Museum, John Weiner, '[d]ocuments speak to the eyes, photographs speak to the imagination, but objects speak to the gut' (cited in Messham-Muir 2004, p. 106). They produce a visceral response in visitors, as is readily apparent when watching them transfixed in front of the exhibits in the Jewish Museum. To the extent that the objects are *speaking* to them, it strikes me that they are not telling lies. For Messham-Muir is right to proclaim that Holocaust artefacts 'are pivotal' in what she terms 'producing moving experiences for visitors' in Holocaust museums (2004, p. 98).

This chapter will draw upon the wealth of theoretical material generated in some of these musings to help us fathom this most complex and challenging museum space. My primary aim is to capture a sense of what it is like to *encounter* this awe-inspiring museum. To that end, I wish to invite the reader to share some impressions that I gleaned from my visit in September 2016. This is not to assert that a *vicarious* encounter (as mediated through written text accompanied by a few photographs) can in any way wholly capture the profoundly affective qualities of this museum. Rather, it is hoped that my individual impressions will resonate with those who have already experienced the museum themselves or inspire others to seek to encounter it in the future.

Genesis of the museum

The Jewish Museum in Berlin had a long and somewhat controversial gestation (Bishop-Kendzia (2018). In 1988, an open invitation was issued to architects in the Federal Republic of Germany to design a new extension to the existing Jewish Museum. In addition, another twelve architects from outside Germany were invited to compete. Some 165 designs were submitted before the competition closed in 1989. A Polish-Jewish architect, Daniel Libeskind, whose family were 'almost decimated by the Holocaust', grappled with the challenging brief to create 'a new Jewish extension of the Berlin museum' (Young 2000, p. 9). His audacious competition entry entitled *Between the Lines* (unconventionally written on sheet music paper) so impressed the judges that it was awarded first prize and the building was commissioned. Libeskind (1999) developed his project around three oft-cited concepts:

1   The impossibility of understanding the history of Berlin without comprehending the intellectual, cultural and economic contributions made by Berlin's Jewish citizens.
2   The necessity of integrating, both physically and spiritually, the meaning of the Holocaust into the consciousness and memory of the city of Berlin.
3   The need to thoroughly acknowledge and incorporate the 'erasure' of Berlin's past Jewish life into the fabric of the museum in the form of voids so that the city, and Europe, could have a 'human future'.

Hansen-Glucklich notes that 'the very title of Libeskind's design – *Between the Lines* – reinforces this notion by implying a mode of reading that transcends the literal' (2014, p. 49). She elaborates: 'The Jewish museum demands the active engagement of the reader-visitor who deciphers the text of the museum, which itself remains open to interpretation and analysis' (Hansen-Glucklich 2014, p. 49). Here again, the notion of experience is imperative to encountering and deciphering the museum.

Part of the controversy attached to the decision was the fact that Libeskind had never actually erected a building before (Ionescu 2017). Conceived of in 1989, the cornerstone was laid in 1992 and a decade passed before the museum finally opened. During that decade, the Berlin Wall came down, East and West Germany were unified, and building work was suspended for a time due to political uncertainty that threatened funding certainty.

In contemplating the role of memorial architecture in our contemporary world, James E. Young posed two powerful questions: 'How does a city "house" the memory of a people no longer at "home" there? How does a city like Berlin invite people like the Jews back into its official past having driven them so murderously from it?' (2000, p. 1) The answers to these questions are delivered by an austere museum that many architects and museological experts have declared a modern masterpiece that synthesises the trauma of the past and the hope for a compassionate future in a singularly unique and empathetic vision. Libeskind is referred to as a 'starchitect' (Reeh 2016, p. 3). His zig-zag shaped building, whose ground floor plan has been variously read as an: 'exploded' (Smith 2009, p. 146), 'unravelling' (Hansen-Glucklich 2014, p. 42), 'shattered' (Isenberg 2002, p. 160), 'fractured' (Kessler 2002, p. 226) or 'elongated' (James-Chakraborty 2018, p. 126) Star of David, defies conventions and visitor expectations. It is a 'highly symbolically charged' building that draws hundreds of thousands of tourists to visit it each year (Pieren 2004, p. 80).

Indeed, Reynolds notes that 'the building itself becomes a memorial, an architectural allegory that instantiates the loss of Berlin's Jewish past through the performance of tourism' (2018, p. 168).

Figure 6.1 Front perspective of Jewish Museum Berlin

Figure 6.2 Interior view of intersecting narrow windows

Figure 6.3 Exterior view of the different architectural styles that constitute the museum

When the museum first opened in January 1999, it was left empty for three years; attracting some 350,000 tourists drawn to see what was lauded as revolutionary architecture (Smith 2009). It is an enormous building yet deliberately offers visitors no formal or iconic entrance.[1] This, of course, runs counter to the logic of most museums. Zinc cladding envelopes the building in a grey skin from which angular, narrow windows intersect in discordant patterns.

Not merely aesthetic embellishments, the windows are topographical devices: an invisible matrix that points to the addresses of prominent Berlin Jewish citizens including Mies van der Rohe, Paul Celan, Heinrich Heine, Arnold Schoenberg and Walter Benjamin (Stephens 2010). Young observes that the museum's zinc-plated façade 'seems relatively self-effacing next to the ochre hues of its Baroque neighbour' (2000, p. 15). Here, Young is referring to the 1735 *Collegienhaus*, the former Prussian courthouse, which is now the conduit through which visitors enter the Jewish Museum. However, the 'practically untouched baroque building' and the 'avant-gardist extension' (Ionescu 2017, p. 1) exist in a kind of aesthetic harmony and are not jarring on the eye.

Despite its audacious form, the museum was built with conventional materials. Spens notes: 'relatively commonplace, ordinary materials and products' were used to construct the museum (1999, p. 46). This choice of everyday building materials seems fitting. Libeskind remarked in conceiving of the design: 'After all, the Holocaust was an everyday event. It was not special, even on the contrary, it was something that happened every day' (cited in Spens 1999, p. 46).

Overview of the museum: a voided labyrinth in which to get lost

Young remarks that Libeskind's original drawings of the museum: 'look more like the sketches of the museum's ruins, a house whose wings have been scrambled and reshaped by the jolt of genocide' (2000, p. 10). The shape of the zig zag or jagged bolt of lightning – whose symbolism is foregrounded in museum publicity as its signature logo (Smith 2009, p. 148) – is best appreciated from above as a drawn resemblance as 'it is not apparent in the building itself as a *gestalt*' (Stead 2000, p. 5, emphasis in original). The zig zag shape is not overtly discernible in terms of the grounded perspective of the tourist. Nevertheless, the museum's zig zagging internal layout is apparent in the axes that criss-cross the interior and resist easy directional choices as each visitor makes her/his way through the labyrinth-like corridors with their slanted floors,[2] dead-ends and stark surfaces. Young observes 'one never gains a sense of continuous passage' through the museum (2000, p. 16).

To enter the museum is to be enveloped in a space that defies convention. Smith captures the journey of discovery well:

> Visitors pass from the Collegienhaus into an abyssal entrance, down steep steps . . . You stand facing a choice between a set of three underground streets; none marked for preference, and no one insisting on you following an official itinerary. As you soon discover, each one has a single – indeed singular – destination.
>
> (2009, p. 148)

The three 'choices' are represented by a trio of axes, also known as streets, that beckon to the visitor. The first and longest, named the *Axis of Continuity*, leads to a main staircase that 'dramatically leads upwards – seemingly to nowhere' (Smith 2009) – but gives access to the permanent exhibition space *Two Millennia of German Jewish History*. This first axis intersects with two others that symbolise the emigration of the Jews – the *Axis of Exile* – and the extermination of the Jews – the *Axis of the Holocaust*. These two axes represent 'the two major, irreconcilable events that ruptured the continuous fabric of Jewish culture in Germany (Ionescu 2017, p. 153). Libeskind notes 'Physically, very little remains of the Jewish presence in Berlin – small things, documents, archive materials, evocative of an absence rather than a presence' (cited in Kligerman 2005, p. 42). We encounter some of these items in both of these axes.

Ionescu (2017, p. 155) points out: 'the Axes of Exile and the Holocaust trace an X of crossed destinies'. She elaborates:

> From the *Axis of Exile* the 'saved' continued their lives on the *Axis of Continuity*, yet those who managed to emigrate left relatives and loved ones behind on the *Axis of the Holocaust*; from the *Axis of the Holocaust* the few children sent on special transports to other countries and the camp survivors continued their lives on the *Axis of Continuity*.
>
> (2017, p. 155)

The architecture of the building powerfully insists on reminding us about these different destinies which Primo Levi framed as the 'drowned' and the 'saved' (1989) by supplementing the axes with two other unique architectural features in the museum. The first, the ETA Hoffmann *Garden of Exile*, is the culmination of the *Axis of Exile*. The second, the *Holocaust Tower*, is a dead-end edifice that one enters by following the *Axis of the Holocaust*, which gets narrower and darker as one approaches this foreboding space. A third reflective space, the *Memory Void*, is encountered on the ground level. It contains the interactive installation *Shalekhet* (*Fallen Leaves*) by Israeli artist Menashe Kadishman. The affective qualities of all three axes and the three distinct architectural spaces will subsequently be explored in detail in this chapter.

Encountering the voids: the paradox of *absence* made *present*

Perhaps the most celebrated feature of Libeskind's audacious museum is the voids that puncture the space and 'invite contemplation on the part of the viewer' (Isenberg 2002, p. 167). According to Libeskind, 'the voids echo the absence of Jewish culture, annihilated by the Shoah, in the midst of the museum dedicated to the history of Judaism' (cited in Reeh 2016, p. 9). A central void runs the entire length of building over 150 metres. Libeskind captures the omnipotent architectural quality of this straight void-line, which he says 'violates every space through which it passes, turning otherwise uniform rooms and halls into misshapen anomalies' (cited in Mathes 2012, p. 172).

Ionescu notes the void is divided into five separate parts and 'can be seen from small vertical windows in the bridges' that 'literally and architecturally connect the museum gallery spaces' (2017, p. 161). Kligerman stresses that 'the voids are blank spaces that cut vertically into the museum, interrupting both representational and temporal continuity along the museum's horizontal axis' (2005, p. 29). He elaborates on their architectural properties: 'the voids do not provide orientation and direction; instead they contribute to the estrangement that occurs along the labyrinthine halls of the museum' (2005, p. 29). The voids are completely impenetrable; described by Akcan (2010, p. 163) as 'unheated, unventilated, inaccessible spaces'. Additionally, nothing can be hung or exhibited in them. Young asserts: 'The voids make palpable a sense that much more is missing here than can ever be shown' (2000, p. 18). One encounters the voids sporadically and without warning in the space of the museum. They are inscrutable and offer no consolation. Resistant to any sort of revelation or catharsis, the voids are profoundly discomforting and disquieting. Stead claims that:

> The affective power of the museum's void spaces lies in their ability to provoke a crisis of subjectivity; the experience of each individual visitor, their sudden sharp awareness of presence, is juxtaposed chillingly with that which is missing, those others whose absence is also suddenly palpable.
>
> (2000, p. 14)

Like a mute witness to the crime of the Holocaust, the anguish of the silent still-ness of the enveloping, dank chiaroscuro blackness of the void instils a kind of dread in the spectator. This is not the dread of *anticipation* (for we know of the unquantifiable and unfathomable horror to which it gestures) but rather the dread of *regret* that the void has no recuperative or redemptive function. So many lives extinguished but no reverie of the past reverberates from the void. The void is a vacuum filled with *nothingness:* the paradox being that one suspects it contains an intangible, unseen pool of infinite sadness.

Sodaro affirms: 'the void is not just a symbolic rendering of absence, a com-mon trope in Holocaust architecture and memorialisation, but for Libeskind it also symbolizes Berlin's relationship to its history' (2013, p. 84). Libeskind captures this logic when he declares the void represents 'the space of Berlin, because it refers to that which can never be exhibited when it comes to Jewish Berlin history. It has been reduced to ashes' (1999, p. 30). Responding to the museum, Wiedmer concurs, noting: 'It is not then primarily the destroyed people who are referred to by the voids, but rather the loss their annihilation has left behind in the cultural and moral landscape of Germany' (1999, p. 129). The genius of the architectural voids embedded in the museum is that which speaks to the real voids outside the walls of the museum. This relationship is captured in what Kligerman terms 'one of the most stirring exhibits in the museum' (2005, p. 47). In part of the permanent exhibition, the visitor is confronted by a ten- by five-foot wall covered in hun-dreds of antique sepia postcards depicting synagogues throughout Germany and from as far afield as Köln (Cologne) and Dresden. Kligerman elaborates:

> Each picture functions as a metonym for the hundreds of Jewish communities that found themselves at home in Germany. But read next to the architectural void, these synagogues conjure up our mnemic reservoir the images of their destruction during *Kristallnacht* [the night of broken glass]. The wall is itself a map that puts on display the hundreds of voids spread across Germany.
> (2005, p. 47)

The postcard wall, displaying so many cardboard tourist souvenirs, is an arresting sight. Divested of their touristic veneer of happy visitations, these cards emerge as *leitmotifs* of genocide: synagogues reduced to ashes after *Kristallnacht*, and those who worshipped in them either exiled or themselves reduced to ashes in the exter-mination camps in the east. We do not know who sent these cards or who received them. As Kligerman profoundly asserts: 'In the space of the void . . . the viewer encounters the interpretive and perceptual limits of the Shoah' (2005, p. 47).

Axis of the Holocaust

Opotow notes that '[i]n addition to its dramatic spaces, the axes offer visitors their first exhibition experience in the museum' (2012, p. 61). The axes contain objects that belonged to deceased survivors. Such artefacts include letters, a blanket, jew-ellery, a handbag, a spoon, a brush, a typewriter and a Singer sewing machine.

Hansen-Glucklich added that these objects are framed to carefully 'highlight their special status as traces' (2014, p. 144). Young observes 'the great absence of life … now makes a presentation of these artefacts a necessity' (2000, p. 18). The visitor beholds these artefacts of genocide, or 'objects of memory' as the museum terms them (Opotow 2012, p. 62), in nineteen dimly lit vitrines set against the angled walls of the axes. Each object is accompanied by an explanation of its provenance; including where it came from, how it survived and how it found its way into the collection (Chametzky 2008). These objects, as Ionescu observes, 'silently testify to their owners' absence and aim to convey to the visitor a sense of irredeemable loss' (2017, p. 156). Reeh sums up the power of the exhibits when he writes: 'Standing in front of a dark display window of limited visibility, the individual visitor may silently experience how minuscule historical traces dialogue with Libeskind's architectural space' (2016, p. 13).

Ionescu notes: 'each object displayed in this section is a *memento mori* and represents a disappeared body, the frailty of humanity and civilisation as well as the need for recollection' (2017, pp. 157–158). As noted in other chapters, here the concept of the synecdoche – the *part* that speaks for the *whole* – is a trope that operates powerfully. Ionescu elaborates that the objects displayed are: 'representative as they stand synecdochically for the 6 million and as reminders in lieu of the presence of those unrelated people and families whose stories they encapsulate' (2017, p. 156).

A mood of quiet contemplation permeates this axis. Few people talk. People wait patiently for their turn to stand in front of the exhibits. Ellison notes, 'there is a lot to read and one must linger' (2011, p. 94). As Bendt has aptly remarked, 'it was the destruction itself that caused the collection to come into being. Otherwise, these objects would all be part of living, breathing homes – unavailable as museum objects' (cited in Young 2000, p. 18). Knowing that these objects are all that remains of murdered people changes how we perceive them. Drawing on the writings of Walter Benjamin, Pješivac stresses that 'the auratic object retains a "distance" no matter how close the object may be' (2014, p. 108). As I viewed the items in the showcases, the profundity of this observation resonated with me.

The right and left walls of the axis are emblazoned in bold letters with the Germanised names of Nazi ghettos, concentration camps and death camps. These names are intensely powerful. They remind the viewer that the little that is displayed can but gesture to the mind-boggling enormity of what is *not* on display: the objects looted and ultimately vanished during the Holocaust. The camps and ghettos could have produced some 200,000 items from all the Jews in Berlin.

One of the most powerful exhibits in the axis is a little five-inch stuffed-toy ape accompanied by a creased letter. The toy ape was owned by Gert Berliner, a fifteen-year-old boy who was sent to Sweden in 1939 on a children's transport. His parents, Paul and Sophie, remained in Berlin but were subsequently deported to Auschwitz in 1943 and murdered there. In 1941, his parents wrote to him. The heart-breaking letter (parts of it heavily censored) provides the title of the vitrine: '*My dear boy!*' where visitors read his family story. Gert became a painter, filmmaker and photographer, emigrating from Sweden to the USA in 1947. He donated his toy and precious letter to the museum to share his memories with the wider public (Opotow 2012). Opotow documents that part of the power of this particular exhibit is its universality and familiarity. Many people have beloved childhood toys and 'they therefore attract visitor attention' (Opotow 2012, p. 63). However, Opotow stresses that '[t]he museum values such objects in concert with the memories and stories connected with them rather than the object in isolation' (2012, p. 63).

The *Holocaust Tower*

The *Holocaust Tower* is arguably the most confronting space within the museum.

The tower's void is not a space for exhibition. Rather, as Kligerman frames it: 'in this crypt-like space, the walls are empty so that the visitor can contemplate a three-story chamber of stone and listen to the sounds emanating from outside' (2005, p. 45). Ionescu notes that the 'Holocaust tower, a 24 metre-tall empty concrete silo, was defined by Libeskind as a "voided void"' (2017, p. 166). According to the museum guide, the tower functions as a memorial within the museum. Visitors are instructed by a sign outside the tower to enter individually and allow the heavy steel door to shut behind them – a condition surely challenging or impossible given the sheer volume of visitors. Indeed, my time inside the tower was interrupted by the passage of other museum visitors which somewhat thwarted my ability to commune with the space in what Kessler (2002, p. 228) denotes as 'bleak and chilling solitude'.

Figure 6.4 Exterior view of *Holocaust Tower*

James-Chakraborty asserts that 'the experience of being in this space, which is illuminated dimly by a thin clerestory opening, is obviously intended to recall the gas chambers' (2018, p. 131). Much is made by theorists of the glimpse of light that one perceives standing within the enveloping blackness of the tower. Depending on the weather conditions, it appears as a thin streak or band of light that emanates from a slit. The light has an enigmatic quality. Sodaro notes:

> Libeskind's inspiration for the tower comes from the story of transport of a survivor, who was only able to survive the horrors of the train ride to camp by focusing on a sliver of light through the roof of the car.
>
> (2013, p. 85)

Ionescu describes the effect of being inside the tower: 'Once inside this symbolized antechamber of death, whose sense of helplessness is mitigated by the filtering light, the visitor comes face-to-face with him/herself in sheer emptiness' (2017, p. 167). I concur with Ionescu's impression. Being inside the tower is a profoundly personal experience that no doubt instils a myriad of responses. Ionescu captures the variety of these responses well, writing:

> Some visitors have feelings of claustrophobia (despite the vast emptiness inside) and despair or the sensation of suffocation, with chills sent down their spine by the oblique confrontation with the horrors of deportation and extermination; others just keep silent.
>
> (2017, p. 168)

During my time in the tower, my mind pondered how the door shutting behind me plunging the space into darkness captured something, however contrived and artificial, of the horror of having the gas chamber door sealed. This sensation immediately struck me as inappropriate, as a perverse feeling given that I was safe from harm. As my eyes adjusted to the light, I reflected in silence and *nothing* came to mind. My mind was empty of thoughts. I tried to solemnly reflect but the space did not summon any thoughts. It struck me after I departed the museum that this is the triumph of Libeskind's tower. Faced with the enormity of violence and loss occasioned by the Holocaust, the darkness cannot produce a condensed image to meet the totality of the horrific event. As Sodaro has astutely observed: 'Perhaps more than any other space in the building, the *Holocaust Tower* experientially produces the nothingness that Libeskind desired his building to represent' (2013, p. 85).

The *Axis of Exile*

As hitherto outlined the *Axis of the Holocaust* meets at the junction of the *Axis of Exile*. Effectively, this means that visitors can explore either section of the museum first. Indeed, when one is standing at the intersection, the museum does not delineate an obvious choice. The *Axis of Exile* is spatially almost identical to the *Axis of the Holocaust*. The walls are also emblazoned with text, but unlike the other axis, these words do not instil fear. For the cities all over the world in which Jews took refuge are named, including locations as far afield as Istanbul and Sydney. Ionescu notes how photographs are powerfully employed to help the visitor comprehend just how widespread exile was: 'different photographs of German Jews between 1934 and 1939 heading for Chile, the USA, Palestine, South Africa and Shanghai, travelling document's (*Ausweise*), suitcases filled with "objects of memory", sum up various family histories' (2017, p. 156). The mood of the *Axis of Exile* – while tempered with hope of survival linked to the knowledge of sanctuary abroad – is sharply tempered by its twin corridor, the *Axis of the Holocaust*. While they are distinct passageways in the museums, the visitor is constantly aware that the two spaces operate in symbiosis to afford each other meaning. For those who sought or were forced into exile, the shadow of the Holocaust haunted their banishment.

As is the case in the *Axis of the Holocaust*, in this second axis objects are displayed in dimly lit showcases that are recessed into the walls. These objects 'reflect the social conditions of Jews in Berlin during the Holocaust' (Opotow 2012, p. 62). Precious silverware, sets of dishes, paintings, a camera, gold wedding rings and other personal items testify to the scant possessions Jews who fled took with them. As Ionescu notes: 'The presentation on the *Axis of Exile* consists of snapshots of individual lives represented by artefacts, sometimes accompanied by commentaries about their respective donors or lenders' (2017, p. 155).

Ionescu elaborates on the power of the exhibits: 'Through these selective exhibits, the collective memory of a people is reduced to an aleatory assortment of heterogeneous, individual possessions' (2012, p. 155). Each object tells a tragic story, and while the objects are *personal* – named as belonging to particular individual or individuals who fled – they have a *universality* about them that adds poignancy to the entire suite of displays. For we, the visitor, are prompted to think of the countless *others* and wonder *what precious items did they manage to flee with?* Like the objects in the *Axis of the Holocaust*, the objects in this axis also stand synecdochically for other objects carried to the New World by those who fled. In doing so, they are powerful reminders that the *Axis of Exile* could theoretically house hundreds of thousands of artefacts and accompanying anecdotes. Perhaps that is why visitors seem to devote such careful attention to each vitrine. They seem to appreciate that *selectivity* – a necessity of the museum's spatial and temporal limitations – is a trope that paradoxically encapsulates the presence of a cache of other unseen objects that are conjured in the mind of the visitor. This is the power of encountering objects in Holocaust museums; they: 'individualize the Holocaust victim, and thus the encounter, by extricating each and every Jewish victim from the anonymous and alienating figure, "the six million"' (Branham 1994/1995, p. 43).

One of the most powerful exhibits in the *Axis of Exile* is an emigration pack containing works by Goethe and other great German writers that a German Jew took with him to Palestine. As Hansen-Glucklich notes: 'Even when driven from his homeland, this Jewish man included among his most treasured possessions volumes of German letters. This display thus testifies to the strength of the German-Jewish bond that survives even a cataclysm like the Holocaust' (2014, p. 144). Another object – a handkerchief from a 'German Jew preparing to go into exile' – is 'still folded today exactly as the mother folded it for her son before she placed it into his suitcase' (Hansen-Glucklich 2014, p. 144). This exudes an elegiac tone because it captures the poignant gesture of a loving mother.

The *ETA Hoffmann Garden of Exile*

The garden commemorates those victims of the Third Reich who either emigrated or were forced into exile by the Nazis. A heavy glass door must be pushed hard to enter the formally titled *ETA Hoffmann Garden of Exile.*

The garden was named after the author from whose writings Freud developed his theory of *Das Unheimliche,* or the uncanny (Kligerman 2005). Libeskind (cited in Young 2000) has stated that he dedicated the garden to Hoffmann because the writer was a lawyer working in a building adjacent to the site. While the fresh air is initially liberating, one soon realises that this is a space outside the museum and that it is nevertheless 'still fenced off within the perimeter of the museum' (Ionescu 2017, p. 163). Visitors encounter a disorientating floor that slants at twelve degrees. As Elton notes, '[t]he sloping ground is disorienting and makes you feel queasy' (2001, p. 45). The uneven ground is an appropriate metaphor for what Libeskind refers to as the 'shipwreck of history' (1999, p. 41).

Figure 6.5 ETA Hoffmann Garden of Exile

Ionescu notes the garden bears a striking resemblance to Peter Eisenman's *Memorial to the Murdered Jews of Europe* (see Chapter 7) and has been called its 'sublime cousin' (2017, p. 163). The space was 'designed to represent the experience of exiled Jews' (Akcan 2010, p. 176). It is an upside-down garden made up of forty-nine large concrete columns some seven metres high; spaced a metre apart. Forty-eight pillars are filled with the earth of Berlin, signifying the birth of Israel in 1948. One column is filled with the earth of Jerusalem to symbolise exodus (Akcan 2010). Willow oaks grow out of the tops of the pillars,[3] creating a surreal great, green canopy. Young writes: 'the columns stand at 90-degree angles to the ground plate, but the ground plate itself is tilted at two different angles, so that one stumbles about as if in the dark, at sea without sea legs' (2000, p. 18). This metaphor of being at sea and feeling off-kilter accords with Libeskind's notion of the shipwreck of history. Pješivac concurs with Young, writing that the garden: 'produces a feeling of strangeness, disorientation, weakness and confusion' that make 'moving uphill even more difficult' (2014, p. 105).

Kligerman describes the garden as a 'labyrinth of forty-nine tomblike pillars' designed to 'confuse the visitor's relation to space' (2005, p. 44). Elton (2001) points out that Libeskind's family arrived by boat in New York and the reference to the skyscrapers of the New World seems implicit in the design of the garden. The pillars tower over the visitors and add to the claustrophobic feel of the garden. As Kligerman informs, '[a]lthough the descriptive name may suggest a pleasurable space, the garden offers no consolation for the visitor. Lost amid the oblique cement blocks towering above our heads, we find neither comfort nor safety in this space' (2005, p. 45).

The garden is not a tranquil place and offers no respite or place to linger. Ionescu captures its uninviting qualities well: '[V]isitors are led to think they will feel some relief and finally reach hope after escaping from the labyrinth, but instead they still find themselves boxed in and forced to return inside the confined space of the museum' (2017, p. 164). While some theorists have noted that walking in the garden can produce a feeling of slight nausea – as Libeskind intended the space to produce – I found the space profoundly claustrophobic and only remained in the garden a few minutes to try and appreciate its properties.

The *Axis of Continuity*

The *Axis of Continuity* is encountered as soon as one enters the museum via a 'strangely off-centred and disorienting tunnel' (Kessler 2002, p. 226). The stairwell – like the labyrinthine corridors and crooked walls that dominate the rest of the museum – is a perplexing feature that diverges in strange ways as one descends it. As Kessler notes:

> Everything is askew: to suggest the permanently unbalanced, decentred and distorted nature of German society and culture following the eradication, or violent excision of the critical mass of Jewish creativity to which, until the Nazi onslaught, modern Germany had owed so much of its positive character.
> (2002, p. 226)

Figure 6.6 Interior view of *Axis of Continuity* staircase

Having explored the two axes (of the *Holocaust* and of *Exile*) and their affiliated inner sanctums (the *Holocaust Tower* and the *Garden of Exile*), visitors press on and at the end of the lower part of the *Axis of Continuity*, encounter a series of two further staircases that rise somewhat majestically upwards, luring each individual upwards towards the permanent exhibition.

Many commentators have invoked the mysticism of Jacob's ladder: of a steep and seemingly endless climb to describe the ascent. This is a fitting metaphor, for the stairs appear endless. As one slowly climbs them, one is encouraged to vicariously ponder the burden of continuity for all Jewish people who must live with the inherited memory of genocide. The climb feels both physically arduous and mentally taxing. All who ascend this axis do so under the weight of the symbolic burden of all that they have seen in the subterranean sections of the museum.

However, the ascent also has a positive symbolism as Mays captures: 'The ascent from the awkward, dark basement, up the building's grand staircase, to the lighter upper storeys symbolizes the passage of Germany's slowly growing Jewish community from a terrible, uneven history towards welcome participation in reborn, democratic Germany' (1999, p. 8).

The *Memory Void: Fallen Leaves*

Visitors approach the *Memory Void* – the only voided space that can be entered in the museum – by taking a short detour down a corridor halfway up the central

Figure 6.7 Interior view of installation *Shalechet (Fallen Leaves)*

staircase that forms part of the *Axis of Continuity*. As Hansen-Glucklich notes: 'Unlike the Holocaust Tower, this void is "filled" . . . with abstract forms that serve only to emphasize the depersonalization of the victims and the way that their humanity was stripped from them' (2014, p. 54). Upon approach, one hears 'admonitory clanging noises' echoing from the as-yet-unseen space (Ionescu 2017, p. 164). The dead-end space one discovers contains Menashe Kadishan's installation entitled *Shalechet (Fallen Leaves)*.

Of all the published descriptions of the art installation I have read, Ionescu's is the most evocative of its qualities:

> The permanent installation consists of over 10,000 open-mouthed faces coarsely cut from heavy, circular iron plates covering the floor, on which visitors have to walk gingerly in a receding, darkening dramatic space reverberating with the infernal rattle of these metal sheets against one another.
>
> (2017, p. 164)

The steel faces look 'frozen in horror' and are said to represent not only 'the suffering and memory of the Victims of the Holocaust' (Sodaro 2013, p. 85), but also 'all victims of violence and war more generally' (Saindon 2012, p. 28). The artist's intentions aside, I think the *specificity* of the space – a Jewish museum – works to dilute the *generality* of the work. The contorted faces of each steel plate are impersonal: 'frozen into horrifying expressions' (Ionescu 2017, p. 164). The

Figure 6.8 Close-up perspective of installation *Shalechet (Fallen Leaves)*

cut-out features of 'mouth, nose and eyes *in absentia*' (Ionescu 2017, p. 165) produce a trace of absent features that is industrial-looking. In fabricating the work, the faces were flame-cut out of sheet steel, a process that caused the molten metal to harden the outer surrounds and inner edges (Saindon 2012).

The faces are corroded, and their varying size signifies both child and adult victims. Indeed, the industrial aesthetic of the work gestures to the automated ways that people were murdered in the camps (so often referred to as *factories of death*).

Visitors are invited to walk upon the work. I reluctantly took up the offer, trepidation momentarily holding me back. It felt *wrong* to trample on the faces. Art critic Ulrich Schneider captures the incriminating lure of the installation: 'Of course, the way that *Shalechet* is installed involved the observer as an active culprit who is obliged to walk over the heads' (as translated and cited in Saindon 2012, p. 39). Saindon elaborates on the logic of complicity at play:

> The visitor is placed in a compromising position, stepping upon these anonymous faces seemingly in pain, as if actively participating in the perpetuation of violence. As one does, the faces shift beneath one's feet, producing a reverberating metal-on-metal sound reminiscent of forced labour camps.
>
> (2012, pp. 39–40)

I ventured about three steps but withdrew as the grating clanking sound and undulating feel of the faces under my feet was too awful a sensation to continue to endure. I watched three other visitors walk about five steps in before beating a hasty retreat. Saindon (2012) is right to claim that participating with the installation has a powerful impact on patrons of the museum. However, I do not agree with the somewhat grandiose claim that 'the act of walking on the "leaves" [faces] changes the temporal relationship the viewer has to violence' (Saindon 2012, p. 40). For me, encountering the work was more akin to the taboo we feel about walking over graves. I cannot say it felt like I inhabited the subject position of a perpetrator. My misgivings aside, it is clear that 'placing *Shalechet* in a special exhibition area immediately preceding the visitor's assent to the main exhibition functions is a preparatory statement for the museum's global audience' (Saindon 2012, p. 41). And it is to this permanent exhibition space that my attention now turns in the next section.

The upper floors: the permanent exhibition

Having left the axes, visitors ascend an expansive staircase and enter an exhibition area that recounts German-Jewish history and culture over two millennia. The uppermost two floors of the museum contain what is termed the *permanent exhibition*. Divided into fourteen distinct historical periods, visitors must navigate an extensive collection of art and objects that begins with the Middle Ages and culminates with contemporary Jewish life and culture in Germany. The exhibition – following modern museological trends – uses interactive elements to draw visitors in and make them part of the experience. Similarly, multimedia video displays are used to capture some of the drama of the Frankfurt-Auschwitz trials of 1965 with defendants exiting a police vehicle to enter the court (Sodaro 2013). Interactive kiosks raise visitors' awareness of the potential for anti-Semitism in the present by asking questions and displaying cumulative results (Chametzky 2008). Opotow notes that 'within the permanent exhibition is a thin narrow line of seemingly-endless wall text consisting of linked anti-Semitic statements' (2012, p. 65). The English and German text snakes around corners. These statements are a powerful reminder as we view the exhibits that anti-Semitism has endured for hundreds of years in Germany.

The space for the permanent exhibition is less dramatically askew than that one encounters in the axes (Opotow 2012). Nevertheless, the angled and irregular walls still gesture to the disorienting nature of the totality of the architecture. The ever-present voids, while feeling less menacing than those we encounter in the axes, intrude into the space: a constant insinuation to the devastation of the Holocaust. Sodaro notes that the Jewish Museum presents 'something of a paradox and a contradiction', elaborating:

> The building is considered by many to be a very powerful Holocaust memorial, yet the museum part of it – the exhibition – is explicitly not a memorial and strives to not be a Holocaust museum, but a very typical history or heritage museum.
>
> (2013, p. 87)

Two enormous floors are devoted to the exhibition: 'It uses everyday objects, ritual objects, art and documentation to narrate its story and emphasize not only the contributions of Jewish culture to German life but also the often-difficult relationship in Germany between Jews and non-Jews' (Sodaro 2013, p. 86). Thousands of exhibits are now presented, often via rotation, in the exhibition. When the museum was empty, Kessler lamented that: 'to fill this harrowing space now, after it has been experienced in this way [as empty] by so many dread-stricken visitors; with actual exhibits will only diminish its effect' (2002, p. 226). Reeh also lamented that filling the empty museum with objects would be problematic. Encountering the museum on a subsequent visit when it was replete with exhibits, he noted that '[t]heir sheer number seems to prevent the ever important reflection on the limits of historical representation' (Reeh 2016, p. 13). Mathes shares her concerns, writing 'the museum seems cluttered, stuffed with too many awkwardly placed items' (2012, p. 174). Ellison stressed that critics 'mourned the loss of Libeskind's stark and siring psycho-spatial drama, now cluttered with so much sentimental and commodified display' (2011, p. 92). Kessler notes, an empty upper two levels might have permitted an encounter with the 'moral emptiness and nullity of the Nazi regime and its purposes' (2002, p. 226). As fascinating as many of the exhibits are, I concur with the idea that the overwhelming array of things to look at diminishes the power of the museum in its entirety: transforming it into a more conventional museum that is strangely at odds with the bottom layers where less, paradoxically, is more. Of course, such a criticism is easily annulled. To the extent that the museum was intended to showcase two millennia of Jewish culture, it could hardly, as Spens notes, remain empty: 'history has been retrieved not simply in the form of objects of interest, but in the spirit and meaning of the *past*, the *present*, and above all the *future*' (1999, p. 46, emphasis added).

A lack of guards sees most exhibits encased in Plexiglass. For example, a Shabbat table in the section *Tradition and Chance* features bowls, plates, candelabra, cutlery and a wine bottle. This display of objects of 'everyday Jewish existence' unfortunately, to the initiated, evokes the Nazis' intended Central Jewish Museum in Prague – the so-called *Museum of Extinct Race*[4] – 'in which artefacts mundane and magnificent would provide anthological evidence of extinction' (Chametzky 2008, p. 235). Whilst the permanent exhibition celebrates Jewish culture, the spectre of this unrealised museum is invoked by the manner in which some of the displays present objects of ethnography. The terrible legacy of 'the Nazis' intention to house the material remains of an exterminated culture' (Chametzky 2008, p. 222) cannot be completely alleviated by this museum. However, the celebratory context of the entire collection does much, thankfully, to militate against this problem. For example, a pair of blue Levi Strauss jeans and a photograph of the KaDeWe department store founder Adolf Jandorf's birth house reminds us that 'historical German Jews still play a role in how Germans dress and where they shop' (Chametzky 2008, p. 235).

The Holocaust is explored in the permanent exhibition. Interactive displays capture many of the anti-Semitic decrees that one encounters in Renata Stih's and Frieder Schnock's 1992 street sign installation *Places of Remembrance* in the Bavarian Quarter (see Chapter 7). One particular exhibit in the Holocaust section really unnerved me. Chametzky captures it well writing: 'One can see how yellow stars were mass produced from bolts of fabric' (2008, p. 237). The roll of emblazoned yellow felt is grotesque and confronting in its industrialised design reminding anyone who beholds it that *mass* identification aided the process of *mass* murder.

Staring at modern paintings that are so self-evidently contemporary, the fact that the collection will continue to grow as time accrues stands as a powerful reminder that Nazi attempts to entirely eradicate Jewish life and culture failed. In that sense, the upper floors are a necessary counterpoint to the dark subterranean floors that narrate exile and the Holocaust.

Conclusion: experience

In relation to the Holocaust, Pješivac notes that the Jewish Museum Berlin is 'less interested in the *events* themselves . . . less interested in what actually *happened*' (2014, p. 106, emphasis added). The events and what transpired are comprehensively narrated at other memorial spaces in Berlin like the *Wannsee House* (see Chapter 1) and The *Topography of Terror* (see Chapter 2). Similarly, Kligerman notes of the museum that, 'Libeskind undermines any voyeuristic desire to see traces of extermination, displaying instead vast spaces of emptiness' (2005,

p. 42). Traces of genocide are best encountered *in situ* at places like Auschwitz-Birkenau (Dalton 2015). The real power of this museum is linked to its experiential properties rather than its instructive properties as this conclusion will explore.

Drawing on the theories of Mieke Bal, Opotow writes that 'traumatic events in the past have a persistent presence' (2012, p. 71). The audacious architecture of Libeskind's Jewish Museum in Berlin stages echoes of the past trauma of exile and the Holocaust, allowing us to experience something tangible of this *past* in the *present*. As Stead stresses, we engage with the museum 'in the *now* of lived experience' (2000, p. 12, emphasis in original). In the introduction to this chapter I noted that the trope of experience was the key to engaging with this museum. We are entreated by promotional material that this is a museum 'you need to experience'. Kligerman (2005, p. 41) takes up the fundamental theme of experience, writing: 'one does not "enter" the museum[5] to enjoy therapeutic experience with the Holocaust'; 'Instead, one experiences a series of perceptual wounds'. Kligerman's observation strikes me as profoundly apt. Whether walking along the various axes peering into the vitrines, reflecting in the *Holocaust Tower*, listening to the discordant grinding of steel-on-steel in the Memory Void or peering into the many voids that appear indiscriminately as one traverses the space of the museum, one's senses are assailed by the experience. The voids are particularly confronting; they function in Young's terms as 'reminders of the abyss into which this culture once sank and from which it never really emerges' (2000, p. 19). Kligerman is instructive in this regard: 'In the claustrophobic spaces of the void bridges, the viewer beholds the void through window slits and becomes not simply a witness of the shock, but its *recipient*' (2005, p. 41, emphasis added).

Stead emphasises: 'The Jewish Museum works by provoking an emotional and psychological disturbance in the visitor' (2000, p. 10). We visitors – Jews, non-Jews, Berliners and tourists alike – are vicariously drawn a little closer to the sorrow and horror of the Holocaust having experienced this museum. Pješivac argues that the Jewish Museum operates as 'a kind of permanent cut or open wound of Berlin' (2014, p. 108). It seems entirely fitting then that to encounter the space is not a therapeutic experience. Rather, as Pješivac (2014) and Stead (2000) assert, each visitor performs an act of commemoration as she/he passes through the space of the museum. Carol Duncan first proclaimed that 'museums do not simply resemble temples architecturally; they work like temples, shrines and other such monuments' (cited in Branham 1994/1995, p. 43). Her observation seems fitting in relation to the Jewish Museum Berlin. One part museum, with exhibits to behold, and one part shrine of remembrance, with enigmatic, mute voids, this particular museum transcends what we have come to expect from such spaces. Ionescu captures the allure of the museum well, remarking that it invokes in the visitor an 'irresistible need for historical recollection and an impossible communion' (2017, p. 1). Standing in the *Holocaust Tower* or staring into the void, one is struck by the profundity of Ionescu's observation. For while we can recollect the horror of the Shoah within the museum, a communion with the absent *others* is impossible. The voids constantly taunt us with the futility of seeking such a communion, and yet they also reward us for the effort of trying.

Notes

1 Young notes that the museum is indeed enormous: 'consisting of 30 connecting bridges, 7000 square meters of permanent exhibition space, 450 square meters of temporary exhibition space and 4000 meters of storage, office and auditorium space' (2000, p. 20).
2 Many of the slanted floors are illusory and not technically slanted or askew, but nevertheless, the effect of walking over these surfaces is to feel slightly disoriented.
3 Various articles attribute these trees as olive trees, but they are in fact oaks.
4 For a fascinating insight into this museum, see Bram Presser's multi-award winning *The book of dirt* (2017).
5 It should be stressed that Kligerman was not just reading the museum as an architectural space, but was also reading it through the lens of Paul Celan's poetry.

References

Akcan, E 2010, 'Apology and triumph: memory transference, erasure, and a rereading of the Berlin Jewish Museum', *New German Critique*, vol. 37, no. 2, pp. 153–179.

Arnold-de Simine, S 2012, 'Memory museum and museum text: intermediality in Daniel Libeskind's Jewish Museum and WG Sebald's *Austerlitz*', *Theory, Culture & Society*, vol. 29, no. 1, pp. 14–35.

Bishop-Kendzia, V 2018, *Visitors to the house of memory: identity and political education at the Jewish Museum Berlin*, Berghahn, New York.

Branham, JR 1994/1995, 'Sacrality and aura in the museum: mute objects and articulate space', *The Journal of the Walters Art Gallery*, vol. 52–53, pp. 33–47.

Chametzky, P 2008, 'Not what we expected: the Jewish Museum Berlin in practice', *Museum and Society*, vol. 6, no. 3, pp. 216–245.

Dalton, D 2015, *Dark tourism and crime*, Routledge, London.

Ellison, DA 2011, 'The spoiler's art: embarrassed space as memorialization', *South Atlantic Quarterly*, vol. 110, no. 1, pp. 89–100.

Elton, H 2001, 'Building on the shipwreck of history: the architecture of Daniel Libeskind', *Border Crossings*, vol. 20, no. 1, pp. 42–49.

Gross, AS 2006, 'Holocaust tourism in Berlin: global memory, trauma and the "negative sublime"', *Journeys*, vol. 7 no. 2, pp. 73–100.

Hansen-Glucklich, J 2014, *Holocaust memory reframed: museums and the challenges of representation*, Rutgers University Press, New Brunswick.

Ionescu, A 2017, *The memorial ethics of Libeskind's Berlin Jewish Museum*, Palgrave Macmillan, London.

Isenberg, N 2002, 'Reading "between the lines": Daniel Libeskind's Berlin Jewish Museum and the shattered symbiosis', in L Morris & J Zipes (eds), *Unlikely history: the changing German-Jewish symbiosis 1945–2000*, Palgrave, New York, pp. 155–179.

James-Chakraborty, K 2018, *Modernism as memory: building identity in the Federal Republic of Germany*, University of Minnesota Press, Minneapolis.

Kessler, CS 2002, 'A Berlin diptych', *Debate: Journal of Contemporary Central and Eastern Europe*, vol. 10, vol. 2, pp. 221–229.

Kligerman, E 2005, 'Ghostly demarcations: translating Paul Celan's poetics into Daniel Libeskind's Jewish Museum in Berlin', *The Germanic Review: Literature, Culture, Theory*, vol. 80, vol. 1, pp. 28–49.

Levi, P 1989, *The drowned and the saved*, Abacus, London.

Libeskind, D 1990, 'Between the lines: extension to the Berlin Museum, with the Jewish Museum', *Assemblage*, vol. 12, pp. 19–57

Libeskind, D 1999, *Jewish Museum Berlin*, G&B Arts International, Berlin.

Mathes, B 2012, 'Teutonic shifts, Jewish voids: Remembering the Holocaust in post-wall Germany', *Third Text*, vol. 26, p. 2, pp. 165–175.

Mays, JB 1999, 'Even empty, this building speaks: Daniel Libeskind's Jewish Museum embodies a rare thoughtfulness', *National Post* (Ontario), July 27, p. 8.

Messham-Muir, K 2004, 'Dark visitations: the possibilities and problems of experience and memory in Holocaust museums', *Australian and New Zealand Journal of Art*, vol. 5, no. 1, pp. 97–111.

Opotow, S 2012, 'Absence and presence: interpreting moral exclusion in the Jewish Museum Berlin', in E Kals & J Maes (eds), *Justice and conflicts*, Springer, Heidelberg, pp. 53–74.

Pieren, K 2004, 'Being Jewish is more than the Holocaust experience: what visitors see at the Jewish Museum Berlin', *Social History in Museums*, vol. 29, pp. 79–85.

Pješivac, Ž 2014, 'Between museum, monument and memorial: Daniel Libeskind's Jewish Museum in Berlin', *Култура/Culture*, vol. 8, pp. 101–109.

Presser, B 2017, *The book of dirt*, Text Publishing, Melbourne.

Reeh, H 2016, 'Encountering empty architecture: Libeskind's Jewish Museum Berlin', *Journal of Art Historiography*, vol. 15, pp. 1–14.

Reynolds, D 2018, *Postcards from Auschwitz: Holocaust tourism and the meaning of remembrance*, New York University Press, New York.

Saindon, BA 2012, 'A doubled heterotopia: Shifting spatial and visual symbolism in the Jewish Museum Berlin's development', *Quarterly Journal of Speech*, vol. 98, no. 1, pp. 24–48.

Smith, T 2005, 'Daniel among the philosophers: the Jewish Museum, Berlin, and architecture after Auschwitz', *Architectural Theory Review*, vol. 10, no. 1, pp. 105–124.

Smith, T 2009, 'Daniel among the philosophers: the Jewish Museum, Berlin, and architecture after Auschwitz', in G Hartoonian (ed.), *Walter Benjamin and Architecture*, Routledge, London, pp. 137–159.

Sodaro, A 2013, 'Memory, history, and nostalgia in Berlin's Jewish Museum', *International Journal of Politics, Culture, and Society*, vol. 26, no. 1, pp. 77–91.

Spens, M 1999, 'Berlin phoenix', *Architectural Review*, vol. 205, no. 1226, pp. 40–47.

Stead, N 2000, 'The ruins of history: allegories of destruction in Daniel Libeskind's Jewish Museum', *Open Museum Journal*, vol. 2, no. 8, pp. 1–17.

Stephens, AC 2010, 'Citizenship without community: time, design and the city', *Citizenship Studies*, vol. 14, no. 1, pp. 31–46.

Wiedmer, C 1999, *The claims of memory: representations of the Holocaust in contemporary Germany and France*, Cornell University Press, Ithaca.

Young, JE 2000, 'Daniel Libeskind's Jewish Museum in Berlin: the uncanny arts of memorial architecture', *Jewish Social Studies*, vol. 6, no. 2, pp. 1–23.

7 Berlin Holocaust memorials

Marking past atrocity in the space of the city

Introduction: encountering the memorials

Having situated the complex evolution of a Holocaust memorial culture in Germany over a fifty-year period in the Introduction of this book, this chapter draws on personal field experience to explore the variety of Holocaust memorials that tourists can encounter in the nation's capital, Berlin. These memorials differ vastly in form and scale and memorialise different classes of victim and aspects of the genocidal crimes of the Nazis. Some are (in)famous and well promoted, drawing throngs of tourists. Others are relatively obscure and are more likely to be stumbled upon by accident. Some are monumental in size; others are small and inconspicuous. One memorial is partially missing, and many tourists pass it by unless they know what to look for.

These memorial *sites* are also memorial *sights*, for they operate largely as visual spectacles which, in turn, provoke emotional responses. Usually there is explanatory text to read, but *looking* is always fundamental to engaging with these memorials. Whether *peering* between a gap between buildings, *looking up* at a street sign, *looking across* a field of stelae, *staring* into a screen (to watch a film), *glancing* downwards at the pavement, *scrutinising* a sculpture in a park or *observing* a soft blue hue in the afternoon light, all these encounters involve the sense of sight. Therefore, this chapter will vividly capture the experience of seeing these memorials *in situ* on the streets of Berlin.

Neumann observes: 'Every memorial has its own history. Some of these histories are complex and contradictory. They often stretch over many years, but rarely leave traces' (2000, p. 2). The chapter will not overly dwell on the genesis of the memorials discussed as these dramas have been rehearsed elsewhere.[1] Rather, in deference to the focus on tourism, I will capture the intrinsic qualities of the memorials and what sort of experience they offer tourists who encounter them.[2] Of course, this is not to say that an encounter is universal. For the memorials explored in this chapter provoke different responses in each individual visitor or tourist, depending on their personal background and knowledge of different aspects of the Holocaust.

Peter Eisenman's *Memorial to the Murdered Jews of Europe*

Peter Eisenman's *Memorial to the Murdered Jews of Europe* arose from a perceived need for a *lieu de mémoire* (Nora 1989), a permanent memorial, in the heart of Berlin. Despite concerns that the monument would end up as nothing more than a perfunctory stop on the Berlin tourist trail, the memorial opened in May 2005 'after 17 years of heated debates regarding its necessity, dedication and locale' (Dekel 2009, p. 72). Schlör captures the controversy of its form, writing: 'Too beautiful? Too perfect. Not torn enough, not ugly enough, not ambivalent enough even as far as it is supposed to somehow mirror Germany's relationship to its Nazi past' (2007, p. 429). Located in Mitte between the key tourist destinations of the Brandenburg Gate and Potsdamer Platz, the memorial soon became a veritable 'tourist magnet', attracting thousands of visitors a day (Quack 2015; Dekel 2013).

The memorial is spread over a strikingly vast site of some 19,000 square metres. Consisting of 2,711 grey concrete stelae, the memorial is a veritable field of pillars that one can enter and walk through. The stelae are of various heights, some so low as to be almost imperceptible, others some 4.7 metres in height.

They generally become taller towards the centre of the field. The ground surface undulates, creating a sense of unease, which is exacerbated the further into the memorial one ventures as the ground appears to sink. Aesthetically, the site looks like a giant graveyard, the stelae resembling square tombstones. Mathes goes so far as to suggest that the stelae exude a 'cool elegance' (2012, p. 170).

An Underground Documentation Centre framed as 'a complementary, instructive museum' (Åhr 2008) was added 'because of an insistence that the site be anchored pedagogically' (Harris 2010, p. 52). I concur with Sion's assertion that 'it is perhaps the part of the memorial in which the Holocaust is unequivocally

Figure 7.1 Peter Eisenman's *Memorial to the Murdered Jews of Europe*

Figure 7.2 Memorial to the Murdered Jews of Europe: view between stelae

present' (2010, p. 245), and Dekel's observation that 'victims are central to the memorial experience' (2014, p. 74). The centre,[3] which Eisenman was reluctant to incorporate into his vision for the memorial (Partridge 2010), details the fate of the victims and the authentic sites of destruction. The centre 'also provides information about those responsible for the crimes' (Quack 2015, p. 22). Ellison notes 'the Place of Information, while echoing the stelae above, serves as articulate memory. Names are recorded, processes are documented. The stellae may be mute, but the centre is prolix' (2011, p. 96).

Mügge describes the progression the visitor takes:

> [T]he visitor is confronted with a defined way through [the underground memorial] passing from the 'Room of Dimensions',[4] addressing the scope of the Holocaust (1), to the 'Room of Families'[5] (2), to the 'Room of Names (3), and finally to the Room of Sites.
>
> (2008, p. 714)

Mügge elaborates on the power of the subterranean information centre: 'The complex and open framework of the memorial with its semantic openness is transferred into an *allusion* to the above-ground memorial' (2008, p. 713, emphasis added). This is aided by 'various manifestations of stelae motif', which constantly remind visitors 'that they are beneath the memorial' (Quack & von Wilcken 2005, p. 44). The problem is that the allegorical power of the stelae to *allude* to murder is partly predicated on the tourist or visitor venturing underground. Many do not do so, thus their experience of the memorial is one based solely on an encounter where the *concrete* facts and faces of murder – as encountered underground – are not wholly conveyed by the *concrete* pillars above ground.

Gross notes that '[v]isitors come in masses, but the pillars function as sieves or filters separating them momentarily into discreet trajectories of experience' (2006, p. 89). Additionally, the memorial is imagined by Gross as producing '*individual* feelings of discomfort' (2006, p. 89, emphasis in original); however, on the day I visited, I beheld people experiencing the pleasure and joy of leisure. People sat chatting on smaller pillars conducive to seating. Some ate snacks or their lunch. Many took selfies, their exaggerated smiles capturing yet another 'I was here' moment. Other activities that researchers have noted regularly take place include kissing, sleeping on the stelae and sunbathing (Stevens 2012). Accordingly, Souto describes the memorial as a 'playful and vivid space' (2013, p. 89), and Quack observes: 'There is a surprising uninhibitedness even gaiety at this place dedicated to mourning and remembrance of victims of the Holocaust' (2015, p. 22).

Most of the rules prescribed at the memorial on plaques (e.g., no smoking, drinking alcohol or bringing dogs) appear to be obeyed with the exception of the 'no jumping between stelae' rule, which is flagrantly disobeyed. The most annoying activity I encountered was young children playing hide-and-seek, frolicking between the pillars. Some children collided with other bodies navigating the stelae, offering brusque apologies in German and English. Teenagers stood or sat nonchalantly chatting or gazing at their mobile phones. All these uses were intended, indeed encouraged, by Eisenman as he did not want the space to feel sacred. It does not feel remotely sacred; rather, it has the atmosphere of an outdoor shopping mall.

My attempts to commune with the memorial, to reflect on those who give the memorial its name – *the Murdered Jews of Europe* – were entirely thwarted by the hustle and bustle of the civic enterprise that envelops the space. I stood quietly trying to contemplate the suffering of the Jews, but two flirtatious teenagers ruined my efforts to concentrate. Despites its enormous size, the paradox is that there is little *space* to feel uncomfortable in this memorial. I ventured further into the memorial, in the hope that its promised feelings of unease and claustrophobia would emerge. Dozens of academic articles insist that walking through the field of stelae will induce a sensation of feeling of being lost, perplexed or trapped – a feeling analogous to the lives of those named by the memorial. For example, Harris writes: 'As one walks through the seemingly endless labyrinth of stones, feelings of inescapability and disorientation abound' (2010, p. 54). This was not my experience. To my dismay, I discovered that one never really *feels* vicariously trapped in this memorial. Even in its deepest recesses (where the stelae stand at their tallest), a line of sight always delineates a 'way out', so the metaphor of the labyrinth employed by so many academics to describe the memorial seems trite.

The chatter, frivolity and animation that characterise the space have been celebrated as the triumph of civic freedom in modern Berlin. That the memorial attracts such myriad uses is also characterised by the fact that it is not just a destination like a museum but a fluid space in the heart of the city that people, tourists and locals alike pass through. Yet the inability of the memorial space to harbour an unguarded moment to privately contemplate the murdered victims left me disturbed and convinced that it is something akin to a colossal failure. Stevens notes that Eisenman conceived of a space 'set aside from everyday life where all visitors could consciously focus their attention on the past and its meaning' (2012, p. 40). I found such a task impossible during my visit. Eisenman 'also envisaged the memorial as a space where visitors would experience the scope of contemporary German life and be reminded of its freedoms and faults' (Stevens 2012, p. 40). By that criterion, the memorial works if teams of happy, chatting visitors are evidence of freedom; nevertheless, none of them seem to suffer the burden to remember which Baptist argues 'is hoist upon each visitor' by the memorial (2012, p. 75).

The memorial's saving grace is the subterranean information centre, which must carry the solemn and necessary burden of testimony that the symbolic concrete stelae – despite their sheer number and bulk – cannot bear. As Dekel asserts 'Underground, there is knowledge: Jews were persecuted and murdered' (2013, p. 13). It is just a pity that many visitors to the site do not visit this centre. Countless tourists seem oblivious to its very existence. The shame of their missed opportunity is captured by Quack: 'When we leave the exhibition and go up to the memorial, we have more knowledge, and above all take the images and traces of the victims with us while we experience the memorial anew' (2015, p. 24).

While one must realistically expect that this large open-air memorial must accommodate laughter, cheerfulness, play, the vanity of selfie photography, and romance, it seems a shame that the *civic* and the *public* is privileged over the *individual* and the *private*. To the extent that the abstract field invokes thoughts of anything *but* the Holocaust (unless one visits the information centre or incessantly reflects on its name) the memorial strikes me as a failure. Despite being lauded by most academics, the memorial suffers from a sterility of form: an inability to conjure the suffering of the Jews, and an inability to memorialise despite its paradoxical monumentality. Perhaps this is entirely apt and forgivable given that

Gross, drawing on the writings of Shoshana Felman, insists that 'the Holocaust exceeds the tools we have to represent it' (2006, p. 91). In any case, I concur with Bettina Mathes when she writes 'I remain unconvinced by Eisenman's design and leave the site somewhat frustrated' (2012, p. 167).

Eisenman has famously insisted that the memorial is not necessarily 'anything to do with the Holocaust' but rather about 'being [and feeling] something different from everyday experience' (cited in Mathes 2012, p. 168). Such a view is somewhat disingenuous. As Reynolds notes: 'either it [the memorial] represents nothing in particular, or the movement through the center and out again symbolises something about the Holocaust' (2018, p. 170). I just wish that *my* experience of the memorial had been one where I could have done justice to the people who lend it their name. Like Sion, I think that the memorial succeeds as a public artwork and space of leisure, but 'fails to adequately perform remembrance' (Sion 2010, p. 243).

Karl Biedermann's *The Abandoned Room* (1988–1996)

Just off the well-trodden tourist paths in a small public park in Koppenplatz, north of Grosse Hamburger Strasse, I encountered Karl Biedermann and Eva Butzmann's sublime sculpture *The Abandoned Room* (*Der Verlassene Raum*), which is also referred to as *The Deserted Room*.

Di Bella eloquently describes the sculpture:

> This sculpture represents the sudden departure of Jewish citizens from their homes: on a rather large rectangle parquet floor is a rectangular bronze table surrounded by two brown bronze chairs, one of which is with its back on the floor, suggesting a violent confrontation or a swift departure.
>
> (2012, p. 62)

Senie concurs with Di Bella's reading of the sculpture, observing: 'Here the mundane, the unremarkable, become strange, even alarming, evoking a recent and sudden absence' (2016, p. 71). Jordan stresses 'no plaque announces the ensembles meaning or origin' (2006, p. 106). She elaborates: 'The only text accompanying the memorial is a poem by Nelly Sachs,[6] cast in the metal edges of the parquet floor, that begins "*Oh, the habitations of death*"' (2006, p. 106). *The Abandoned Room* is profoundly affective and 'hints at the Nazi rule of terror' (Davies 2007, p. 42). Jordan notes 'the aesthetics of the memorial are evocative and mournful, but not jarring' (2006, p. 110). The tableau it rehearses is reminiscent of the aesthetic of crime scene photography. One actively looks for *clues* as one tries to decipher what this oversized sculpture means.[7] The parquetry floor and ornamental style of the desk take us back to the early part of the twentieth century. Biedermann and Butzmann (cited in Neumann 2000, p. 3) elaborate: 'The pieces of old-fashioned furniture are to point to the irretrievable losses that occurred because a large group of people, their way of life and their culture, are missing.' But it is the *context* of the sculpture that ultimately helps us solve the puzzle, for

Figure 7.3 Karl Biedermann and Eva Butzmann's sculpture *The Abandoned Room*

we are in an affluent part of Berlin from which many Jews were deported, and only the ignorant would be oblivious to this fact of history. However, as Jordan notes: 'it would be possible to walk past this outdoor "room" without reading in it the message intended by the artist' (2006, p. 111).

Despite its ambiguity, few tourists would really be mystified by its meaning. As Bowring remarks of memorial aesthetics: 'Empty chairs embody a sense of departure, abandonment' (2017, p. 58). We have all seen films and read books that have rehearsed very specific versions of this bronze allegory in a public park. The specificity of the memorial does not dilute its power. Gazing at the sculpture, I imagined a couple sitting at this tiny table hearing the ominous sound of boots pounding up the stairs, subsequently summoned by a brutal hammering on their apartment door: their subsequent hauling away going curiously unnoticed by the neighbours. However, one thinks of so many *others*: sitting perhaps at larger tables with more chairs (perhaps art deco style) but facing the *same* fate. The creators might have called their sculpture *The Vanishing*. It is deeply moving and profoundly unsettling and it provokes attention and interrupts the civic pleasure of the park. I sat on a park bench, transfixed, staring at it for twenty-odd minutes as a few other tourists appeared in the park and encountered it. It gestures to the Holocaust in a way that is implicit and surreptitious, and it requires engagement and an inquiring mind. Its brilliance is that it transcends the temporal and the spatial in one deft gesture. For it locates us back in time – so that we can vicariously inhabit this room and imagine the terror and fear that *being there then* would have entailed. Also, it places a private, secluded zone – the *space* of the home – in the middle of a public park.

Biedermann described his co-conceived work in the following terms: 'The bronze sculpture is an appreciation of all Jewish citizens who lived and worked in Berlin over seven centuries. The sculpture should warn against the disregard of life and remind us of our humanistic heritage' (cited in Jordan 2006, p. 111). To the extent that '[t]he Koppenplatz monument attempts to insert a reminder of the Nazi past – and here specifically the treatment of the Jews – into an ordinary city-scape, recalling the lives lost in the neighbourhood' (Jordan 2006, p. 110), it does so very successfully. By insinuating itself into the landscape of the park – a place of peace and tranquillity – *The Abandoned Room* powerfully summons memories of past trauma and reminds us with its scene of domesticity torn asunder that the catastrophe, as Levi ruminates, can happen again:

> We are too dazzled by power and money to forget our essential fragility, for-
> get that all of us are in the ghetto, that the ghetto is fenced in, that beyond the
> fence stand the lords of death, and not far away the train is waiting.
>
> (1985, p. 172)

Senie, in her reading of the sculpture, also sees latent menace in its form: '*The Abandoned Room* signals that all may not be as it appears in the newly comfort-able present, may not be taken for granted, and may not hold' (2016, p. 71).

Christian Boltanski's *The Missing House* (1990)

Despite knowing the precise address and setting out to locate it, I walk past French artist Christian Boltanski's *The Missing House* memorial twice before I realise I missed noticing it.[8]

This is perhaps not surprising given Czaplicka (1995, p. 157) observes that the artwork 'employs a visual rhetoric of absence'. Solomon-Godeau (1988, p. 3) notes that the history of the house partly explains why it is relatively difficult to discover: 'The building at 15/16 Grosse Hamburger Strasse, in the former East Berlin, had its central part blasted away in the allied bombings of 3 Febru-ary 1945'. Eventually, the remaining parts of the building were reconstructed, and 'their standing walls braced and reinforced, leaving a vacant space, and a vacant lot, between two supporting walls' (Solomon-Godeau 1988, p. 3). By the time I visited, the vacant lot described by Solomon-Godeau was occupied by a low building, but the walls of the two buildings still bear Boltanski's brilliant 1990 installation. It consists of twelve black and white plaques which are '[m]ounted on the facing walls, storey by storey, indicating the family name, profession and period of residency of each tenant who had lived in the bombed-out building' (Solomon-Godeau 1988, p. 3).

Di Bella (2012, p. 62) stresses that the plaques 'indicate the approximate space occupied by former Jewish and non-Jewish residents, testifying to a diversity that was lost' once Nazi decrees forced the removal of the Jewish population from

Figure 7.4 Christian Boltanski's *The Missing House*

Berlin. The plaques allow us to reconstruct fictive biographies of the people who lived there, thereby allowing us to try and imagine something about their lives (Arandelovic 2018). In a clever aesthetic manoeuvre, 'Boltanski presents this personal data in bold black letters against a white field of large name plates in black frames that imitate the death notices [*Todesanzeigen*] of German newspapers' (Czaplicka 1995, p. 167). Solomon-Godeau emphasises that by the time the building had been bombed, many of the building's former Jewish tenants had already been 'evicted, displaced, deported and presumably liquidated' (1988, p. 3).

So many tourists in this busy part of Mitte pass by this enigmatic memorial completely oblivious to its presence. Czaplicka (1995, p. 161) remarks that 'the ability of the *Missing House* to inspire thought and reflection depends on the receptivity of the beholder'. We tourists must look up and actively engage with it to decipher what it might mean. It is hard to read some of the details on the plaques affixed to the off-white painted stucco walls that testify to the former residents, and so the specific personal details of the past occupants can still be elusive despite discovering the memorial. Solomon-Godeau states that *The Missing House* is a memorial to loss and absence describing the memorial: 'as a commemorative space in which a nothingness has been inscribed with a historical reference, but a reference whose significance remains troublingly enigmatic' (1988, p. 7).

Solomon-Godeau argues that although the passer-by 'can readily infer that the plaques denote the dead or dispersed former residents, there is no way to reconstruct the existence of the immediately *previous* residents, the Jews evicted from the building and deported before 1942' (1988, p. 7, emphasis in original). Nevertheless, the installation is interpreted through the prism of what Solomon-Godeau terms 'Holocaust Consciousness' (1988, p. 7). How is one to read this most challenging memorial? Solomon-Godeau stresses that it was conceived as 'a meditation on the ruins of the past, the past tense of the war, the past tense of the obliterated part of 15/16 Grosse Hamburger Strasse and its former residents' (1988, p. 7). Who do we remember when we stare up at the plaques? The brilliance of the memorial is that it testifies both to the wartime death of the building's German Aryan inhabitants at the time of the bombardment, but also to the death of the now vanished Jewish residents. Haladyn argues that: 'Similar to the *Anne Frank House* [see Chapter 4], Boltanski's *The Missing House* addresses the architecture that remains after the violence of war is over' (2009, p. 59).

However, whereas the former stands as a monument to loss – 'one that serves in a sense as a site of comfort and remembering' – the latter 'highlights the impossibility of situating this memorialisation of the missing victims of war, both Jewish and German alike' (Haladyn 2009, p. 59). I realise this profound truth as I stare up at the scarcely legible plaques. All we are left with is a gap, a void with sunshine streaming between the buildings: a lacuna that can never be filled despite our contemplation. Haladyn captures the dual power of the memorial well, writing: 'Architecture designates and substantiates wartime encounters, whether it be the dislocation and likely extermination of the original Jewish tenants or the death of the German occupants: both histories overlap in and through the walls of this now *Missing House*' (2009, p. 59). Solomon-Godeau argues *The Missing House* 'leaves unexamined the whys and wherefores of its own mute testimonial' (1988, p. 19); it is nevertheless a profoundly affecting memorial that invites tourists and passers-by alike to look up and contemplate its significance as a powerful testimony to absence. Czaplicka also sums up the power of this memorial well, writing: '*The Missing House* effectively engages it beholders in the retrieval of a complex past by combining the allusive aesthetic of the ruin, historical facts, and the powerful symbolism of a destroyed house' (1995, p. 168). Furthermore, Czaplicka asserts *The Missing House* 'teeters always on the edge of oblivion; it does not *stand out*' (1995, p. 187, emphasis added). It is a hidden, somewhat secret memorial, and yet if discovered, it is a profoundly 'elegiac work' (Bergman-Carton 2001, p. 3) that rewards close scrutiny.

Memorial to the Homosexuals Persecuted under the National Socialist Regime

Dedicated in 2008, Michael Elmgreen and Ingar Dragset's *Memorial to the Homosexuals Persecuted under the National Socialist Regime* sits in a corner of a park in Berlin's Tiergarten, where tourists might easily remain oblivious to its existence (Haakenson 2010).

The memorial engenders historical recognition for one of Nazism's most-forgotten group of victims, gays and lesbians. Some 54,000 homosexuals were arrested by the Nazis and some 7,000–15,000 have been estimated as murdered (Jensen 2002). Sometimes referred to as the '*HomoMonument*', it 'memorializes all those who were persecuted as homosexuals and invites questions about what it *meant* and *means* to be gay, to be lesbian or queer' (Wilke 2013, p. 156, emphasis added).

Sharing 'an obvious architectural similarity with . . . the nearby *Memorial to the Murdered Jew of Europe*' (Haakenson 2010, p. 150), the memorial consists of a large concrete grey block that is twelve feet tall and six feet wide. It has a some-what brutalist aesthetic, strangely reminiscent of a bunker or World War II battle-ment from which a cannon's barrel might protrude. An impenetrable structure, a

Figure 7.5 Memorial to the Homosexuals Persecuted under the National Socialist Regime

small window allows the visitors to peer inside. As Haakenson notes, what visitors see may surprise them: 'a 90-second film, in black and white, showing two men walking toward each other, kissing, and sharing a whispered, intimate secret. The film is looped, repeatedly playing out the encounter' (2010, p. 146). The film's subjects – whose clothes and hairstyles are contemporary – jarred with my expectations of seeing something tangible in the opening that might evoke the infamous victims of paragraph 175 of the penal code (which criminalised homosexuality). The suffering of these victims has been likened to a 'Hidden Holocaust' (Grau & Shoppmann 1995).[9] Souto concurs, describing the film as 'an overly simplistic treatment of the subject' (2013, p. 85). A friend who visited this memorial a few years later noted that the film had been replaced with a new one that featured various vignettes of lesbian, gay and heterosexual couples kissing. The inclusion of pearls, a nose ring, black nail polish and modern clothes also place this film in the modern era. In a moment of whimsicality, a little boy witnessing two women kissing smiles before he is led away by a woman. This substitution is in keeping with the logic that every second year, for a ten-year period, the current film will be substituted with 'other artists' filmic interpretation of an intimate homosexual encounter (Haakenson 2010, p. 151).

Haakenson describes how the pavilion-like opening compels visitors

> to peer inside the structure allowing . . . [the] monument to address a dual purpose: the need to render visible a forgotten and ignored historical fact and to draw provocative parallels with the apparently less visible marginalization of homosexuals in the present.
>
> (2010, p. 151)

The problem with this memorial is that it privileges the *contemporary* at the cost of the *past*. I yearned for some footage or images that might better represent the suffering of gays and lesbians during the Nazi era. It also struck me as trite that, in a society that celebrates sexual difference, the memorial would dare invoke the idea of contemporary queer marginalisation and inequality as though it were on some sort of continuum with the incarceration of gay men in places like Dachau. While the 2001 Life Partnership Law did 'not fully equalise homosexual and heterosexual relationships', the notion that two men kissing could be genuinely 'risky' in contemporary Berlin struck a false note with me. Haakenson celebrates how the monument encourages visitors to recognise 'how simultaneously invisible yet omnipresent homosexuality can be' (2010, p. 151). However, the static flat text that recounts the basic history of Nazi persecution renders *that* past obscure. That text – while informative – cannot compete with the filmic text that anchors us firmly in the present. Haakenson argues that the memorial is deployed in the service of educating us about the Nazi past, but to my mind it fails because its filmic texts do not adequately capture the so-called 'ominous warning' (2010, p. 152) written on a plaque near the monument that instructs the visitor that 'a simple kiss could land you in trouble'. A kiss could certainly land you in trouble in the 1930s – it could land you in a concentration camp. However, that same logic – deployed in the *present* – seems empty and robbed of its menace. In that sense, as Haakenson notes, the 'inscription appears to trivialise the horrors that the monument is seeking to represent' (2010, p. 152).

The Memorial and Information Point for Victims of National Socialist 'Euthanasia' Killings

A lesser-known aspect of the memory of Nazi atrocities that 'still occupies a marginal place' (Knittel 2010, p. 127) was the murder of tens of thousands of patients with mental or physical disabilities.[10] Classed as socially undesirable under a eugenic logic, and an economic burden on the Reich, the murder of these people was the first systematic mass crime carried out by the National Socialist regime.

The 'euthanasia'[11] programme was codenamed Aktion T4[12] and was planned and coordinated by sixty employees in a villa to the south of Berlin's Tiergarten Park. Doctors and administrators gathered information on patients from psychiatric clinics and care facilities. They selected those who would be killed and organised their transportation to six purpose-built gassing centres on German soil, including Grafeneck Castle (Knittel 2012). Some 70,000 people were gassed in disguised shower rooms. An additional 90,000 people died from starvation, medical experiments, electrical shocks (Klee 2012), deliberate neglect or an overdose of medication as part of the same wider programme to eradicate people perceived

Figure 7.6 The Memorial and Information Point for Victims of National Socialist 'Euthanasia' Killings

to be a burden to German society. As Klee notes: 'The crime was unprecedented in world history: psychiatrists exterminating their patients' (2012, p. 76).

In 2011, a competition was launched to design a memorial to those murdered under the T4 programme. The winning entry – by architect Ursula Wilms and the landscape architects Nikolaus Koliusis and Heinz Hallmann – was built outside the Berlin Philharmonic concert hall.

This was an appropriate site since it formerly housed the T4 administrative headquarters villa. The memorial is twenty-eight metres long and consists of two concourses of grey granite. Adjacent to the higher of the two concourses is a tall section of suspended blue glass, which aesthetically dominates the space. One of the granite slabs is angled at 35 degrees to afford visitors an opportunity to walk alongside the memorial and view video exhibits, texts and photographs. This long concourse provides the history of the T4 programme and its legacy in present times, while touching upon quests to bring the perpetrators to justice. The exhibition includes a very powerful work of art by Wilhelm Werner: a man diagnosed with idiocy and subsequently asphyxiated by carbon monoxide at the Pirna-Son-nenstein killing centre in 1940. In the drawing 'Triumph of Sterelation' [sic], a swastika arm-banded woman is depicted sterilising Werner. In an interview with one of the creators of the memorial, Koliusis revealed that that his team conceived the memorial as both an installation and a sculpture, and that the blue coloured glass was chosen because the dimensions of the tragedy that planned at this place 'cannot be described in words and images' (cited in Arandelovic 2018, p. 357).

Whether by day or night (when it is illuminated by lights), this beautiful swathe of blue glass lures tourists and locals alike from Potsdamer Platz to discover this memorial and learn about the T4 murders. Reynolds argues 'there is a dimension of kitsch to this blue wall that seems out of place with the heartless murders conveyed through image and text in the nearby granite' (2018, p. 164). I do not concur with his view. It is hard to evoke the exquisite beauty of the blue glass wall in words alone. Koliusis (cited in Arandelovic 2018, p. 359) notes that he continues to receive feedback that: 'whether sunshine, rain or dusk, in summer or winter . . . people visit this place around the clock'. This observation accords with the two visits I made to the memorial during the day and the evening. By 'creating a poetic moment to give the individual the chance to encounter art in everyday life' (Koliusis, cited in Arandelovic 2018, p. 359), this memorial is profoundly satisfying. The same, alas, cannot be said for Richard Serra's controversial sculpture *Berlin Junction*, which was not originally created as a memorial, yet was installed outside the Philharmonic Hall and dedicated to 'euthanasia' victims in 1987. People responded to it 'as just another abstract sculpture by a famous artist' and in response a bronze plaque was installed in 1989 detailing historical information regarding the tragic events (Arandelovic 2018, p. 353). The rusted curved sculpture left me unmoved and uninspired; the controversy over its inadequacy to evoke anything tangible about T4 seems justified.

At the T4 memorial site, I had anticipated encountering a life-size replica concrete Mercedes-Benz bus with sleek 1930s proportions. I had seen photographs of this bus parked outside the Berlin Philharmonic and erroneously presumed that it was permanently placed there. Designed in 2005 by the artist Horst Hoheisel and the architect Andreas Knitz, the memorial came to be known as the *Monument of the Grey Buses* or *Grey Bus Memorials* (Niven 2013). Two buses exist. As Herzog notes 'they are cast in the exact size and shape of those originally used for transporting the disabled to the killing facilities' (2011, p. 308). One stands permanently at the Centre for Psychiatry Weißenau near Ravensburg to commemorate the deportation of more than 550 patients to Grafeneck in 1940. In an audacious move, it blocks the gate and compels visitors to encounter it (Herzog 2011). The second bus was conceived as a 'moving memorial that travels from place to place' (Knittel 2012, p. 91).[13] Knittel describes how the buses are split down the middle: 'Visitors can walk through the narrow space and read the inscription *Wohin bringt ihr uns?* [Where are you taking us?] echoing the words reportedly spoken by a patient about to be transported to the euthanasia killing centre at Grafeneck' (2012, p. 91). The memorial bus proved so popular that the creators were 'inundated with requests to bring it to towns, museums and other sites connected to the memory of euthanasia all over Germany' (Knittel 2012, p. 91). I lamented the absence of the concrete bus when I visited the site. The sublime beauty of the blue glass that now dominates the space shies away from the brutality of the murders. In contrast, the menacing grey buses immediately locate us back to the 1940s, affording us an opportunity to *board* the bus (as it were) and encounter the haunting inscription *Wohin bringt ihr uns?* which works as a powerful empathetic tool to imagine the plight of those who boarded the real buses so long ago. I concur with Knittel (2010, p. 130) when she writes: 'The memorial not only transforms the perpetrators' means of deportation into a vehicle that transports the memory of their victims but it also an uncanny manifestation of a repressed memory'. Here she is referring to the fact that the buses were a frequent sight on the roads and people knew that they signified transportation. As with the departure of the Jews, people choose to avert their gaze and remain ignorant.

Memorial to the Sinti and Roma Victims of National Socialism

Located in Simsonweg in Tiergarten close to other Holocaust memorials, the *Memorial to the Sinti and Roma Victims of National Socialism* is dedicated to 'the 220,000 to 500,000 people murdered during *O baro Porrajmos*, or The Great Devouring[14]' (Kapralski 2013, p. 235). Given that 'scant attention was paid to Nazi crimes against those they labelled Gypsies [*Zigeuner*] for a long time' (Zimmermann 2007, p. 22), this 2012 memorial is a welcome addition to Berlin's Holocaust memorial landscape and its existence sutures 'a gap of remembrance in the national historical narrative of persecution' (Blumer 2013, p. 205). Designed by the Israeli artist Dani Karavan and dedicated in 2012, the memorial is effectively a large circular memorial pool. One enters the memorial space through a rusted red steel entrance flanked by information boards that provide a chronological account of the genocide of the so-called 'gypsies' by the Nazis. The text is legible and provides enough detail to adequately familiarise the visitor before s/he crosses the threshold of the entrance. Once inside the memorial, one encounters the large circular reflecting pool ringed by a black border. Dozens of irregular shaped pavers surround the pool. Some bear engraved inscriptions of the names of concentration camps and places of annihilation in which the persecuted gypsies were tormented and murdered (Zimmermann 2007). At the centre of the pool sits a slightly raised triangular stela invoking the symbol that many concentration camp inmates wore on their clothing. A fresh field or wild flower is placed on this retractable plinth each day (Arandelovic 2018). The words of the poem *Auschwitz* by Italian Roma Santino Spinelli are written in bronze letters around the edge of the pool in English, German and Romany. The elegiac poem alludes to the indescribable horror of genocide. The Reichstag looms over the park but a canopy of trees and shrubs help afford the space a solemn atmosphere. On the sunny day that I visited the memorial, I lingered for half an hour and during that time no other tourist or visitor stopped there. Perhaps the much larger field of stelae devoted to the *Murdered Jews of Europe* with its drama and worldwide exposure allows tourists to symbolically tick a box and move on to other locales, thereby depriving *other* memorials of prospective visitors.

I could not help but wonder if the form of the *Memorial to the Sinti and Roma Victims of National Socialism* works against it. While the scale is adequate, the nature of the pool is problematic. Unlike the imposing reflecting pools at the *World Trade Center Memorial* in New York (Dalton 2015), this pool is flat and distinctly unremarkable. The central triangular plinth seems disproportionally small to attract the kind of focus intended. I stood trying to conjure something tangible about the Roma and Sinti genocide, but the memorial seemed to obscure any relationship with the victims. Despite the art of memorials in the twentieth century employing 'pictorial motifs that are generally readily understandable' (Zimmermann 2007, p. 4), I wondered whether the triangle-shaped plinth was well-intentioned by misguided strategy. Some eight different classes of prisoners wore triangular badges as an aid to identification in the concentration camps (Neumann 2000); thus, here the *specificity* of the triangular symbol works to erode the memorial work performed. In any event, the memorial struck me as far too timid to really evoke the suffering of the Roma and Sinti people. Before this memorial was erected, Zimmermann (2007, p. 5) worried that the 'mode of remembrance' would be 'less extensive' than that possible at the *Memorial to the Murdered Jews of Europe*. I left this space with a sense that my visit had done little to enhance my appreciation or understanding of the Romani Holocaust and that Zimmermann's concerns had proven well-founded.

Places of Remembrance

Renata Stih and Frieder Schnock's *Places of Remembrance* memorial sits in the former Jewish district of West Berlin known as the Bavarian Quarter (the *Bayerisches Viertel*). The locale of Schöneberg is off the tourist trail but is arguably the most powerful Holocaust memorial in the city of Berlin. Knight (2005, n.p.) describes it as a 'genuinely moving and unsentimental Holocaust memorial'.

Clark characterises this memorial work as an 'intervention in the urban land-scape' because it draws attention to the fact that 'many traumas are not localized at memorial sites' but rather are dispersed throughout the city (2014, p. 29). Inaugurated to some controversy in 1993, the memorial consists of eighty double-sided signs hung on lamp posts so that one must look up to see them clearly. Each sign alludes to one of the hundreds of Nazi laws passed from the 1930s onwards that gradually dehumanised the Jews and paved the way for their eventual deportation and murder. The memorial 'recreates on linguistic and pictorial levels the political violence that went on in everyday life' (Wiedmer 1999, p. 107). One of the artists, Stih, captures the intention of the work: 'The overall idea was to show this crime with double-sided signs. We didn't want to show it from the point of view of the victims but from perpetrators' (cited in Johnson 2013, n. p.).

Reynolds notes that employing 'a strategy of camouflage, the memorial catches the viewer by surprise' (2018, pp. 160–161). The genius of the signs is that one side depicts the text that summaries the anti-Jewish decrees and other side depicts a colourful stylised picture. So, depending on the direction one walks, one either encounters *the picture* or *the script (law)* first. This prompts the individual to want to see the reverse side, to satisfy their curiosity and decipher the meaning of the sign. By doing so, one gleans 'the full picture' as Wiedmer (1999, p. 112) puts it. The signs are scattered all over Schöneberg. Three large tourist information boards in the area and, more recently, the use of a mobile phone application, help visitors learn the location of each of the signs by small green dots assigned on the map. The sign text is German but English translations are provided on the boards. Additionally, each of the billboards 'show pre- and post-war maps of the area, one from 1933 and the other from 1993, superimposed upon one another' (Wiedmer 1999, p. 111).

In a deliberate strategy employed to engage the reader in the *here and now* of daily life, the anti-Jewish Nazi rules and regulations are often condensed and written in the *present* tense (however, the precise year of the relevant decree is provided at the end of the text). So, as we encounter the signs, we are prompted to reflect on what it must have been like for a Jewish person to encounter such a law in their daily life. Indeed, the governing principle of the memorial is, in Stih's words 'to make visible the conditions which led in an insidiously logical way the destructions of the Jewish inhabitants' (cited in Wiedmer 1995, p. 2).

Wiedmer astutely notes that 'there's an instructive difference between reading the poster and actively seeking out the signs amid the quotidian sights and sounds of the neighbourhood' (1999, p. 111), and in deference to this observation I wish to ruminate on several of the signs I encountered as I wandered around Schöneberg.[15] One sign depicts a large sourdough loaf of bread with the text: 'Jews in Berlin are only allowed to buy food between four and five o'clock in the afternoon – July 4, 1940' (most people might note the irony that during wartime by that time of day, many shops would be sold out of food).

An orange sign with musical notes proclaims 'Jews are expelled from all choral groups – August 16, 1933'. Another sign depicts a mottled cat accompanying the decree 'Jews are no longer allowed to have household pets – February 15,

Figure 7.7 Sign: Renata Stih and Frieder Schnock *Places of Remembrance* (Bread)

1942'. A sign bearing an electrical plug on a blue background bears the law that 'Jews must hand over all electrical and optical appliances, bicycles, typewriters and records – June 12, 1942'. The spectator is reminded of the profound isolation and deprivation of pleasure engendered by such a law. Another sign bears a pearl necklace on a regal blue background with the decree (again – as always – on the reverse side), 'Jewellery. Items made of gold, silver, or platinum, and pearls belonging to Jews are to be turned to the State – February 21, 1939'.

The state sanctioned theft as a prelude to genocide. A German shepherd dog on a green background instructs us: 'Jewish Veterinarians may not open practices – April 3, 1936'. A thermometer against a red background bears the law 'Jewish doctors may no longer practice – July 25, 1938'. A sign bearing a clock face with the hands struck at seven o'clock against a yellow background instructs the tourist or local visitor: 'Jews are not permitted to leave their apartments after 8pm (9pm during the summer) – September 1, 1939'. Another sign, located in front of a children's playground, depicts a hopscotch game outline with a decree that attests that: 'Aryan and non-Aryan children are not allowed to play together – 1938'. As Wiedmer notes:

> In this direct association of anti-Semitic rules with today's world, the conditions of fifty years ago are re-staged, and the beholder is forced to come to terms with her or his own reaction to violence presented in such a matter-of-fact way.

> (1999, p. 111)

Figure 7.8 Sign: Renata Stih and Frieder Schnock *Places of Remembrance* (Pearl necklace)

The most powerful sign in my eyes is one that depicts a close-up of a dramatic red theatre curtain, its draped contours lost in shadow. The accompanying decree reads: 'Employment ban for Jewish actors and actresses – March 5, 1934'.

To my mind, the sign's specificity is misleading, for we know that the term 'curtains' is a short-hand metaphor for death: and death was the intended fate for all Jews living in Berlin – not just actors. Indeed, another sign bearing a golden Christian goblet warns: 'Baptism and conversion of Jews to Christianity have no bearing on the issue of race – October 4, 1936'. A colourful red cut-throat razor bears the decree: 'Jews may no longer purchase soap and shaving cream – June 26, 1941'. A sign portraying a black milk churn is accompanied by the decree: 'No fresh milk for Jews – July 10, 1942'. On another sign, red and yellow striped swimming trunks bear the law: 'Baths and swimming pools in Berlin are closed to Jews – December 3, 1938'. A stylised empty art deco ashtray bears the decree: 'Cigarettes and cigars are no longer sold to Jews – June 11, 1942'. A sign next to the Post Office depicts a telephone handset and proclaims: 'Telephone lines to Jewish households will be cut off – July 29, 1940' and 'Use of public telephones is forbidden – December 21, 1941'. As Stih observes, 'everything was meant to exclude Jews from daily life, from social structures, and to threaten them' (cited in Johnson 2013, n.p.). Another sign does not refer to a specific law, but we can guess that it invokes deportation. A picture of a white envelope on a yellow background bears mournful sentiment: 'The time has come. Tomorrow I must leave, and naturally, it is a heavy burden . . . I will write to you . . . – Before being deported

Figure 7.9 Sign: Renata Stih and Frieder Schnock *Places of Remembrance* (Theatre curtain)

January 16, 1942'. One sign features a solid black rectangle. No image is affixed. The other side decrees: 'The emigration of Jews is forbidden – October 23, 1941'.

The sign powerfully alludes to death enshrined in this decree, with so many Jews trapped and awaiting deportation to the extermination camps.

Wiedmer sums up the power of these memorial signs when she writes:

> Experienced together, the three aspects of image, writing, and location powerfully re-stage the persecution of a people within the space of the neighbourhood, and conversely, any of the three maps on the large billboards turn the neighbourhood into a peerless mnemonic landscape.
>
> (1999, pp. 112–113)

The suite of signs one encounters in Schöneberg is profoundly moving. Despite having lectured on Nazi anti-Jewish decrees for more than ten years at a university, encountering these laws on the streets – so beguilingly framed in the *present tense* and accompanied by 'pictograms that mimic the informational aesthetics of today's advertisements' (Wiedmer 1999, p. 110) – (re)invested them with a palpable menace that had been eroded by merely reading about them in history books. Watching some tourists contemplating one of the information boards in Bayerischer Platz, I hope this decentralised memorial might lure more tourists

Figure 7.10 Sign: Renata Stih and Frieder Schnock *Places of Remembrance* (Black)

off the beaten track to encounter these signs that signify the magnitude of social exclusion that preceded genocide.

Stumbling Stones

Gunter Demnig's *Stumbling Stones* (*Stolpersteine*) first appeared in 1995.[16] Individuals or groups commission these brass-covered cobblestones engraved with the names of Holocaust victims and their fate at an approximate cost of €120 each (Knittel 2012; Apel 2014). The project was designed to bring the names of Holocaust victims to the places where they previously lived (Gould & Silverman 2013). Demnig (cited in Cook & van Riemsdijk 2014, p. 145), framed the impetus for the project as the 'idea that we have to restore their names', noting 'in the concentration camps they were just numbers'. Accompanied by an assistant, Demnig personally embeds each stone into the pavement 'directly in front of the house where the person lived' (Knittel 2012, p. 91). When individuals and groups commission the installation of *Stolpersteine* they are 'intentionally re-placing a victim in the physical space from which they were removed' (Cook & van Riemsdijk 2014, p. 146). The profundity here is that: 'Demnig's stones commemorate a real person, who actually lived at the address – not just an anonymous victim of history' (Cook & van Riemsdijk 2014, p. 146).

Originally conceived as an art project for Cologne and Berlin, some 56,000 *Stolpersteine* have been laid in more than 750 towns in Germany and in twelve other countries occupied by the Nazis (Cook & van Riemsdijk 2014). The term 'stumbling stone' is a biblical metaphor implying both a potential 'tripping' or 'stumbling' (Harjes 2005). The term for the memorial is beautifully apt, as Harjes notes: 'Rather than being located in a meditative, isolated place one has to seek out like a museum or a park, *Stolpersteine* memorials are placed in unexpected locations'(2005, p. 144).

The plenitude of *Stumbling Stones* means that tourists and locals who bother to look down, can *stumble* over them unexpectedly. The stones are set flush with the street surface, often between cobble stones, and are sometimes lovingly polished (by locals) to gleam brightly in the sunshine and attract attention. No explanations at all accompany the memorials, rather their meaning 'relies entirely on already existing sources of Holocaust memory' (Harjes 2005, p. 147). As Knittel asserts 'the stumbling stones are indeed compelling: they make people aware of the forgotten or repressed history of their immediate surroundings' (2012, p. 92). The *repressed* history is captured by the specificity of each stone. An individual's name, year of birth and year of death (if known), along with their fate (deported, killed in concentration camp, suicide, etc.) are engraved on each ten by ten centimetre cube (Cook & van Riemsdijk 2014, p. 140). Most poignantly, the phrase 'HIER WOHNTE' (Here lived) provokes the person encountering the stone to pause and reflect, however momentarily, that one of the countless many lived adjacent to the stone. Many of the stones culminate in the German phrase 'ERMORDET' (murdered). To those who encounter them, they are most affecting 'because they connect a name with a nameless crime' (Cohen 2008, p. 549).

As Gould and Silverman (2013, p. 793) contend: 'the Stumbling Stones subtly illustrate how the vernacular urban landscape exists as repository for multiple voices, memories and histories'. My first encounter with a cluster of five stumbling stones (an entire family) is bidden by a group of Japanese tourists who stand solemnly staring downwards deciphering the inscriptions of *Stolpersteine* on a street in Mitte. The German language does not appear to confuse them. The last word on each of the five stones AUSCHWITZ helps dissolve any inherent ambiguity about what they might mean. Apel (2014, p. 185) perceptively asserts: '*Stolpersteine* offer relief because they make it possible to confront emotionally burdensome and barely comprehensible crimes by reducing the complex instances of persecution to simple relationships by expressing empathy with individual innocent victims.'

On the numerous occasions that I stumbled upon individual or family *Stolpersteine* while walking the streets, I was taken with the simplicity of Demnig's vision. For these modest memorials are so inconspicuous that they almost blend into their surroundings, and yet, once discovered, they compel tourists to stop, look down, read and solemnly reflect. Apel proclaims that *Stolpersteine* 'provide knowledge in fragments'. Those who encounter *Stolpersteine*:

> acquire a connection to the living environment of the victim: where she grew up, went to school, raised a family or established a business, and was

ostracised by her neighbours, which made it possible to deport her to be murdered out of sight.

(Apel 2014, p. 192)

As testimonials to murder, we should applaud that '[i]n a city that at times has
tried to hide, destroy, and move on from the past, Demnig's *Stolpersteine* rein-
scribe the past in Berlin's sidewalks for all to encounter' (Cook & van Riemsdijk
2014, p. 147).

Grunewald Station Track 17 memorials

Writing in the article 'Ghosts on display', Ladd asserts that 'smaller memorials
throughout the city call attention to sites associated with persecution and deportation' (2004, p. 32). The Grunewald rail freight ramp is one such 'authentic site of
Third Reich crimes' (Ladd 2004, p. 32). Situated in an exclusive suburb of Berlin,
it is documented that the Nazis feared protests if a more central station was chosen
to transport Jews to the east, and so Grunewald freight yard was chosen as a less
conspicuous alternative (Waters 2010). Davies (2007) notes that the high-ranking
Nazis who occupied the local villas adjacent to the station were not expected to
object.

There are, in fact, two memorials that one encounters. The first, erected in
1991, is entitled *Grunewald Deportations Memorial* by artist Karol Broniatowski.
Schlant evokes this sculpture well, writing: 'Cut into the wall are the outline of
human figures moving in the direction of the station. The figures themselves are
non-existent; it is the surrounding cement that makes their absence visible' (2004,
p. 1). This is thus 'a monument in which presence is stated as absence, and in
which the solidity of the wall serves to make this absence visible' (Schlant 2004,
p. 1). The sculpture is profoundly affecting. The figures are *absent*; long since
harried to their deaths. It works as an evocative prelude for the second memorial
that one encounters on the tracks. Writing about her encounter with the sculpture,
Gigliotti (2009, p. 217) observes: 'I went to leave, and the hollow people, in the
concrete walls, seemed to disappear.' The genius of the sculpture is that, should
one glance back, the figures are not discernible to the eye. This is, of course, a
fitting artistic conjuring trick. Already *gone* – deported on so many trains so long
ago – we approach Track17 already mindful of the absence of some 50,000 Berlin
Jews having followed 'the path of deportees who have been etched as silhouettes
into concrete walls' (Gigliotti 2009, p. 204).[17] Waters (2010, p. 10) notes that the
Grunewald memorial cleverly plays on the sense of place of this location. He
laments 'why did it take the German railways so long to construct a memorial
to the Holocaust, considering their involvement, to some extent, in it?' (2010,
p. 10). Gigliotti acknowledges that the memorial, which was inaugurated in 1998,
nevertheless 'acknowledges the complicity of the DRB in deportations' (2009,
p. 204).[18]

Alexander notes that: 'Gleis [track] 17 is a well-preserved platform and section
of railway track bordering a large and pretty woods' (2018, p. 12). On the day

I visited, I was struck by the simplicity of the memorial as captured by the description of Dwork and van Pelt (2015, p. 20): 'The Grunewald railway siding . . . is paved with metal plates. An inscription on the edge of each plate records a date, a number of Jews and a destination – mostly Auschwitz'. They elaborate: 'The relentless succession of dates, numbers and the name Auschwitz presses the point' (2015, p. 20). The rusted metal appearance of the plates helps locate us in the past. I strolled up and down the platform taking in the details and realised that a plate exists for each recorded transportation, totalling some 186 in total. Blank plates leave room for additional commemorations if new deportation dates are discovered. Di Bella (2012, p. 61) observes that each grate representing a transportation is 'assembled in chronological order and set in the ballast next to the platform edge'. Writing about his exposure to the memorial, Cox (2016, p. 7) asserts, '[a] person walking alongside the train tracks could very easily imagine people standing in the exact same place, waiting to be shipped off to the ghettos . . . or to a concentration camp such as Auschwitz or Theresienstadt'. The mood of the platform is desolate. On the morning I visited, no other tourists arrived to intrude on my refection for the half-hour duration of my time there. Perhaps the Eisenman memorial with its saturation exposure robs this smaller, less dramatic memorial of visitors.

Alexander evocatively captures the mood of the memorial: 'Birch trees – some taken from Auschwitz – grow up amongst the track's far end, and weeds sprout between the sleepers next to a disused brick hut, indicating a railway that has long ceased to know the sound of trains and passengers' (2018, p. 12). This is, as Alexander observes, a place of reflection and silence (2018). He elaborates: 'Walking slowly along the silent platform, the clearest sound is of one's own footsteps, overlapping freely with associations of solitude, lonely railway stations and fear' (2018, pp. 12–13). What else can we, the tourist, *hear* here among the solitude? Alexander is instructive of the imaginative potential at play here: 'A silenced platform . . . resonates loudly . . . the mute tracks, dramatically stilled, stand in material and aesthetic opposition to the sounds of terror that they represent, and of which they were a part' (2018, p. 13). We need to carefully imagine the sounds that accompanied deportation: screaming, yelling and crying accompanied by the shrill whistle and cacophony of the idling steam engine. Perhaps even the sound of gunfire that accompanied the shooting of reluctant Jews who refused to cooperate. Alexander notes the paradox at play: 'silence becomes a way of *hearing* the past' (2018, p. 14, emphasis added).

As poignant as the Track 17 memorial is, it offers little instruction about the process of transportation. In her masterly exploration of transportation to the ghettos and concentration camps in freight cars, Gigliotti (2009, p. 222) cautions us not to deceive ourselves that we can imagine the horror this entailed. Gigliotti asserts: 'Deportees journeyed with the living and the dead, were witnesses to and victims of suicide, became violated and violators in cramped conditions, and were bathed in the sensory reminder of their pestilential degradation and deprivations' (2009, p. 214). Treated and forced to behave 'like animals' (the term many survivors used to describe their experience as documented by Gigliotti 2009, p. 210), deportees suffered the additional olfactory shame of the stench of death, urine and excrement. Gigliotti reminds us that '[m]ore than trains *to* death, they were trains *of* death' (2009, p. 214, emphasis added). And so the Grunewald memorial cannot adequately capture the pandemonium of waiting to board such a freight car, let alone traveling in one for several days. Alexander notes: 'The unremarkableness of the track itself jars bitingly with the places of death wrought in iron along its side' (2018, p. 13). It is these names, wrought in capitals – THERESIENSTADT, AUSCHWITZ, LODZ, LUBLIN, RIGA and UNBEKKANT – that transport us to known and unknown places of terror and extermination; and help us fully grasp the meaning of this most elegiac memorial.[19]

Conclusion: *assembling* the memorial pieces

Berlin offers an abundant memorial landscape in which tourists can reflect on the diversity of Nazi crimes. Some memorials, like the centralised *Memorial to the Murdered Jew of Europe*, have become essential tourist destinations, drawing thousands of people every day to wander in the field of stelae. Other memorials are not nearly as well promoted and require a more intrepid type of tourist to seek them out. These more intimate memorials lack the monumental scale of the field of stelae, but arguably offer a more contemplative experience. Karl Biedermann's *The Abandoned Room* struck this tourist as a sublime memorial that captured the sense of chaos and terror of arrest and deportation. Similarly, Renata Stih and Frieder Schnock's *Places of Remembrance* offers the tourist a powerful lesson in the legal deprivations that paved the way for the dehumanisation of Jewish people, culminating in genocide. While the *Memorial to the Homosexuals* and the *Memorial to the Roma and Sinti* are not completely successful, one must laud the city of Berlin for including them in the wider Holocaust memorial landscape. The blue glass of *The Memorial and Information Point for Victims of National Socialist 'Euthanasia' Killings* audaciously beckons tourists to come learn about a largely neglected category of Nazi victims. Arguably the most poignant memorials in the cityscape are the *Stumbling Stones*. Discovered by chance as one walks the city streets, these decentralised memorials are profoundly touching. For they name past citizens who also once walked these streets and gesture to their fate. The *Stumbling Stones* offers a key to deciphering many of the other *abstract*, *metaphoric* and *allegorical* memorials in the city of Berlin. To the extent that the pillars rise out of the ground in the centralised field of stelae in the *Memorial to the Murdered Jews of Europe*, these flat stones – embedded all over the city – are the foundations upon which so much memorial meaning is carried. Each victim left behind an actual deserted room to which they never returned, a poignant reality we recall when contemplating Biedermann's *The Abandoned Room* sculpture.

Notes

1 For example, for a discussion of the controversy surrounding the use of the anti-graffiti protection for the concrete stelae being provided by the company Degussa, whose

sister firm produced Zyklon B for the gas chambers, see Knischewski and Spittler (2005) and Quack (2015).

2 Some obvious caveats apply to my exploration of the memorials. Evidently, my impressions are based on the 'here and now' of my visitation. I visited these memorials on days bathed in autumn sunshine. Visiting the memorials in the middle of winter with dreary grey skies, snow and/or rain invariably adds a more sombre mood to any encounter.

3 The centre is sometimes referred to as a Place of Information.

4 The Room of Dimensions is also known as the Room of Silence.

5 The Room of Families is often referred to as the Room of Fates.

6 Sachs' poem was published in 1947. She was a German-Jewish writer who fled to Sweden in 1940 (see Arandelovic 2018, p. 7).

7 By oversized, I mean that the sculpture is not life-sized. The chairs and table are roughly 20 per cent larger than those one would encounter in ordinary life. No doubt this technique was a deliberate tactic to engage attention by rendering the sculpture slightly absurdist in its proportions.

8 Czaplicka (1995) notes that *The Missing House* was, at the time of its installation, paired with a second piece entitled *The Museum*. This second work consisted of ten vitrines exhibited near the Lehrter train station. Boltanski filled the vitrines with copies of documents, photographs and postcards 'concerning the former residents of the missing house, many of whom had been deported to the death camps' (1995, p. 161). These materials had been discovered as a result of the historical research conducted by Boltanski's assistants. The vitrines were removed at the close of the exhibition after they had been vandalized (Czaplicka 1995).

9 The Nazi persecution of homosexuality was based on the logic that homosexuality was a disease that could infect other men, eroding the power of the nation-state. As such, the Nazis sought out and eliminated individuals who committed homosexual acts. Branded with the pink triangle in the concentration camps, gay men suffered the stigma of being unmanly subjects and were often treated as the lowest of the low. However, in line with the perverse logic of Nazism, some men who were deemed rehabilitated and fit to help procreate the nation were occasionally released from concentration camps.

10 Recently, a big-budget film has helped bring this obscure crime to the attention of the world. Florian Henckel von Donnersmarck's Oscar-nominated film, *Never look away*, explores – as part of its plot – the crimes undertaken by the Nazis as part of their murderous eugenics programme. The film's main protagonist, Kurt, had a beloved and talented aunt who was murdered by the Nazis because of her mental illness. The film graphically depicts her sterilisation and subsequent murder by gassing.

11 Inverted commas are always applied to the term *euthanasia* when discussing this memorial as a strategy to draw attention to the fact that these acts were not mercy killings but calculated acts of murder.

12 The codename derived from the address of the villa, 4 Tiergartenstraße, where the murders were planned.

13 The second bus was 'parked' in front of the Berlin Philharmonic for a year, between January 2008 and January 2009.

14 This is the term used to describe the Romani Holocaust.

15 All English translations of the German sign text are supplied by the artists as the official memorial instructive text which is available on apps and posters in the nearby park.

16 Apel (2014, p. 187) notes that the starting point for the *Stolpersteine* project was the commemoration of the Sinti and Roma, since for a long time the focus was almost exclusively Jewish victims.

17 Fastidious Nazi records inform us that some 50,000 Jews were deported from Grunewald between October 1941 and February 1945.

18 DRB was the German rail company that was replaced by the company name, Deutsche Bahn DB after the war.
19 UNBEKKANT is German for unknown. It serves as a powerful reminder that for many victims, where they were ultimately sent and where they perished continue to remain largely unknown.

References

Åhr, J 2008, 'Memory and mourning in Berlin: on Peter Eisenman's Holocaust-Mahnmal', *Modern Judaism: A Journal of Jewish Ideas and Experience*, vol. 28, no. 3, pp. 283–305.

Alexander, P 2018, 'Sounding the Holocaust, silencing the city: memorial soundscapes in today's Berlin', *Cultural Studies*, pp. 1–24.

Apel, L 2014, 'Stumbling blocks in Germany', *Rethinking History*, vol. 18, no. 2, pp. 181–194.

Arandelovic, B 2018, *Public art and urban memorials in Berlin*, Springer International Publishing, New York.

Baptist, KW 2012, 'Shades of grey: the role of the sublime in the Memorial to the Murdered Jews of Europe', *Landscape Review*, vol. 14, no. 2, pp. 75–85.

Bergman-Carton, J 2001, 'Christian Boltanski's *Dernières années*: the history of violence and the violence of history', *History & Memory*, vol. 13, no. 1, pp. 3–18.

Blumer, N 2013, 'Disentangling the hierarchy of victimhood: commemorating Sinti and Roma and Jews in Germany's national narrative' in A Weiss-Wendt (ed.), *The Nazi genocide of the Roma: reassessment and commemoration*, Berghahn, New York, pp. 205–228.

Bowring, J 2017, *Melancholy and the landscape: locating sadness, memory and refection in the landscape*, Routledge, New York.

Chametzky, P 2008, 'Not what we expected: the Jewish Museum Berlin in practice', *Museum and Society*, vol. 6, no. 3, pp. 216–245.

Clark, LB 2014, 'Ethical spaces: ethics and propriety', in B Sion (ed.), *Trauma tourism: death tourism: disaster sites as recreational landscape*, Seagull Books, London, pp. 9–35.

Cohen, A 2008, 'Memory and history in Germany', *International Journal*, vol. 63, no. 3, pp. 547–552.

Cook, M & van Riemsdijk, M 2014, 'Agents of memorialization: Gunter Demnig's Stolpersteine and the individual (re-) creation of a Holocaust landscape in Berlin', *Journal of Historical Geography*, vol. 43, pp. 138–147.

Cox, BK 2016, 'A personal reflection on the nature and value of public memory in Holocaust memorials', *Conversations: A Graduate Student Journal of the Humanities, Social Sciences, and Theology*, vol. 3, no. 1, pp. 1–12.

Czaplicka, J 1995, 'History, aesthetics, and contemporary commemorative practice in Berlin', *New German Critique*, no. 65, pp. 155–187.

Dalton, D 2015, *Dark tourism and crime*, Routledge, London.

Davies, M 2007, *Absence and loss: Holocaust memorials in Berlin*, David Paul, London.

Dekel, I 2009, 'Ways of looking: observation and transformation at the Holocaust Memorial, Berlin', *Memory Studies*, vol. 2, no. 1, pp. 71–86.

Dekel, I 2013, *Mediation at the Holocaust memorial in Berlin*, Palgrave Macmillan, London.

Dekel, I 2014, 'Jews and other others at the Holocaust Memorial in Berlin', *Anthropological Journal of European Cultures*, vol. 23, no. 2, pp. 71–84.

Di Bella, MP 2012, 'Walking memory', *Journeys*, vol. 13, no. 2, pp. 55–70.

Dwork, D & van Pelt, RJ 2015, 'A distant shore: the Holocaust and us', *Holocaust Studies*, vol. 11, no. 1, pp. 5–26.

Ellison, DA 2011, 'The spoiler's art: embarrassed space as memorialization', *South Atlantic Quarterly*, vol. 110, no. 1, pp. 89–100.

Gigliotti, S 2009, *The train journey: transit, captivity, and witnessing in the Holocaust*, Berghahn Books, New York.

Gould, MR & Silverman, RE 2013, 'Stumbling upon history: collective memory and the urban landscape', *GeoJournal*, vol. 78, no. 5, pp. 791–801.

Grau, G & Shoppmann, C 1995, *The hidden Holocaust? Gay and lesbian persecution in Germany 1933–45*, Routledge, New York.

Gross, AS 2006, 'Holocaust tourism in Berlin: global memory, trauma and the "negative sublime"', *Journeys*, vol. 7 no. 2, pp. 73–100.

Haakenson, TO 2010, '(In) visible trauma: Michael Elmgreen and Ingar Dragset's Memorial to the Homosexuals Persecuted under the National Socialist Regime', in B Niven & C Paver (eds), *Memorialization in Germany since 1945*, Palgrave Macmillan, London, pp. 146–155.

Haladyn, J 2009, 'The missing house', *On Site Review*, vol. 22, pp. 59–60.

Harjes, K 2005, 'Stumbling stones: Holocaust memorials, national identity, and democratic inclusion in Berlin', *German Politics and Society*, vol. 23, no. 1, pp. 138–151.

Harris, C 2010, 'German memory of the Holocaust: the emergence of counter-memorials', *Penn History Review*, vol. 17, no, 2, pp. 34–59.

Herzog, D 2011, 'Gray bus', *Women's Studies Quarterly*, vol. 39, no. 1–2, pp. 300–314.

Jensen, EN 2002, 'The pink triangle and political consciousness: gays, lesbians, and the memory of Nazi persecution', *Journal of the History of Sexuality*, vol. 11, no. 1–2, pp. 319–349.

Johnson, I 2013, '"Jews aren't allowed to use phones": Berlin's most unsettling memorial', *The New York Review of Books*, 15 June, www.nybooks.com/daily/2013/06/15/jews-arent-allowed-use-telephones-berlin-memorial, viewed 29 May 2019.

Jordan, JA 2006, *Structures of memory: understanding urban change in Berlin and beyond*, Stanford University Press, Stanford.

Kapralski, S 2013, 'The aftermath of the Roma genocide: from implicit memories to commemoration', in A Weiss-Wendt (ed.), *The Nazi genocide of the Roma: reassessment and commemoration*, Berghahn, New York.

Klee, E 2012, 'Those who honour the perpetrators murder their victims a second time: some thoughts on psychiatry in Nazi Germany', *The Holocaust in History and Memory*, vol. 5, pp. 74–83.

Knight, C 2005, 'Concrete, yet not', *Los Angeles Times*, 25 June, www.latimes.com/archives/la-xpm-2005-jun-25-et-berlin25-story.html, viewed 29 May 2019.

Knischewski, G & Spittler, U 2005, 'Remembering in the Berlin Republic: the debate about the central Holocaust memorial in Berlin', *Debatte: Journal of Contemporary Central and Eastern Europe*, vol. 13, no. 1, pp. 25–42.

Knittel, SC 2010, 'Remembering euthanasia: Grafeneck in the past, present, and future', in B Niven & C Paver (eds), *Memorialization in Germany since 1945*, Palgrave Macmillan, London, pp. 124–133.

Knittel, SC 2012, 'Beyond testimony: Nazi-euthanasia and the field of memory studies', *The Holocaust in History and Memory*, vol. 5, pp. 85–101.

Koonz, C 1994, 'Between memory and oblivion: concentration camps in German memory', in A Bakshi (ed.), *Topographies of memories: a new poetics of commemoration*, Palgrave, Cham, Switzerland, pp. 259–280.

Ladd, B 2004, 'Ghosts on display: reconstruction and the meanings of history in Berlin since 1989', *The Planning Review*, vol. 40, no. 156, pp. 30–34.

Levi, P 1985, *The drowned and the saved*, Abicus, London.

Mathes, B 2012, Teutonic shifts, Jewish voids: remembering the Holocaust in post-wall Germany, *Third Text*, vol. 26, no. 2, pp. 165–175.

Mügge, M 2008, 'Politics, space and material: the "Memorial to the Murdered Jews of Europe" in Berlin as a sign of symbolic representation', *European Review of History – Revue européenne d'histoire*, vol. 15, no. 6, pp. 707–725.

Neumann, K 2000, *Shifting memories: the Nazi past in the new Germany*, University of Michigan Press, Ann Arbor.

Niven, B 2013, 'From countermonument to combimemorial: developments in German memorialization', *Journal of War & Culture Studies*, vol. 6, no. 1, pp. 75–91.

Niven, B & Paver, C (eds) 2010, *Memorialization in Germany since 1945*, Palgrave Macmillan, London.

Nora, P 1989, 'Between memory and history: les lieux de mémoire', *Representations*, vol. 26, pp. 7–24.

Partridge, DJ 2010, 'Holocaust *Mahnmal* (memorial): monumental memory amidst contemporary race', *Comparative Studies in Society and History*, vol. 52, no. 4, pp. 820–850.

Quack, S, 2015 'The Holocaust Memorial in Berlin and its information center: concepts, controversies, reactions', in *The International Handbooks of Museum Studies*, Wiley-Blackwell, Hoboken, NJ, pp. 3–28.

Quack, S & von Wilcken, D 2005, 'Creating an exhibition about the murder of European Jewry: conflicts of subject, concept and design in the "Information Centre"', in Foundation Memorial to the Murdered Jews of Europe (ed.), *Materials on the Memorial to the Murdered Jews of Europe*, Nicolaische, Berlin, pp. 40–49.

Reynolds, D 2018, *Postcards from Auschwitz: Holocaust tourism and the meaning of remembrance*, New York University Press, New York.

Schlant, E 2004, *The language of silence: West German literature and the Holocaust*, Routledge, New York.

Schlör, J 2007, 'Memory in Berlin: a short walk', *Urban History*, vol. 34, no. 3, pp. 427–430.

Senie, H 2016, Memorials to shattered myths: Vietnam to 9/11, Oxford University Press, New York.

Sion, B 2010, 'Affective memory, ineffective functionality: experiencing Berlin's Memorial to the Murdered Jews of Europe', in B Niven & C Paver (eds), *Memorialization in Germany since 1945*, Palgrave Macmillan, London, pp. 243–252.

Solomon-Godeau, A 1998, 'Mourning or melancholia: Christian Boltanski's "Missing House"', *Oxford Art Journal*, vol. 21, no. 2, pp. 3–20.

Souto, A 2013, 'Architecture and memory: Berlin, a phenomenological approach', in S Bandyopadhyay & G Garma Montiel (eds), *The territories of identity: architecture in the age of evolving globalization*, Routledge, London, pp. 77–90.

Stevens, Q 2012, 'Visitor responses at Berlin's holocaust memorial: contrary to conventions, expectations and rules', *Public Art Dialogue*, vol. 2, no. 1, pp. 34–59.

Waters, D 2010, 'Berlin and the Holocaust: a sense of place?', *Teaching History*, vol. 141, pp. 5–10.

Wiedmer, C 1995, 'Remembrance in Schöneberg', *Alphabet City*, no. 4–5, pp. 1–4.

Wiedmer, C 1999, *The claims of memory: representations of the Holocaust in contemporary Germany and France*, Cornell University Press, Ithaca.

Wilke, C 2013, 'Remembering complexity? Memorials for Nazi victims in Berlin', *International Journal of Transitional Justice*, vol. 7, no. 1, pp. 136–156.

Zimmermann, M 2007, 'The Berlin Memorial for the murdered Sinti and Roma: problems and points for discussion, *Romani Studies*, vol. 17, no. 1, pp. 1–30.

Conclusion

Nazi crime-related tourism in contemporary Germany

The Holocaust perpetrator sites, memorials and museums explored in this book are so eclectic in form that they defy neat categorisation in terms of their power to educate and dismay tourists about the crimes of the Nazi regime. This is in keeping with Reynolds' astute observation: 'Tourism, as an engagement with space, confronts the Holocaust's physical immensity and its many variations of scale, location, and execution, as well as the differences in how its traces and artifacts are preserved from one place to another' (2018, p. 14).

From the colossal – a former villa in Wannsee where genocide was planned – to the allegorical – a sculpture of an abandoned room in a park in Mitte – traces and reminders of Nazi criminality abound in Berlin and all over Germany for tourists to encounter. Nazism is often invested with a mystique: an allure that is the unfortunate consequence of popular culture's treatment of the icons and iconography (swastikas and SS runes) of the Third Reich (Rohr 2010). There can be no doubt that a prurient motive lures some tourists to sites associated with the Nazi rule. However, many 'memory tourists', to adopt Dekel's term, possess more wholesome motivations – a desire to pay homage to the victims of Nazi terror and perform 'public acts of performed sorrow' (2013, pp. 25, 174). Here, tourists perform a kind of duty to vicariously witness the remnants, traces and reverberations of the Holocaust and its legacy of absence that underpins every tourist encounter. Reynolds concurs, asserting that 'tourists play an undeniable even indispensable role in Holocaust memorialisation' (2016, p. 349). In addition, Dekel (2013, p. 2) notes that the experience of visiting a memorial 'always exceeds their physical boundaries and the temporal confines of the visit'. Indeed, tourists make links with *other* sites and *other* memorials; contemplating the past and piecing together the true horror of Nazism with each distinct site, museum or memorial they encounter. The effect is cumulative; the enormity of Nazi persecution and criminality is honed with each distinct encounter. Moreover, as Reynolds notes, 'tourists encounter not only direct evidence of the *past* but also its preservation and presentation in the *present*' (2018, p. 70, emphasis added). In doing so, they 'bear witness in a general sense to the memory of the Holocaust' becoming 'stewards of that memory'. Czaplicka (1995, p. 156) observed:

> [M]ere historical conventions, the assembled material facts, statistics, and documents in archives and museums . . . sometimes seem only to mimic

the cool factual calculations of a criminally efficient regime: they leave one without much empathy for the victims whose suffering and demise deserve a human response.

It is precisely such a 'human response' that the tourist sites explored in this book elicit from visitors who come primed to respond to the memorials in an empathetic manner.

The chapters in this book have explicated that the various sites and memorials do much to divest Nazism of any vestige of allure. Taken in their totality, the sites, museums and memorials explored herein offer profoundly confronting encounters where tourists come face-to-face with the unassailable reality of terror, suffering and death inextricably linked to Nazi criminality. Even the SS castle of Wewelsburg – a museum that walks a fine line between explication and glorification – goes to great pains to demystify the SS and instil in the visitor a strong impression of the organisation's blatant criminality.

Niven writes: 'There is now a broader awareness of the true extent of National Socialist Criminality and of the range of victims' (2001, p. 5). The tourist sites explored in this book have done much to promote this awareness. He elaborates: 'by remembering National Socialist crimes and the victims of these crimes, Germans will maintain a sense of the need to uphold and defend democracy' (Niven 2001, p. 7).

Indeed, the need to uphold and defend democracy is seen as a lesson that tourists can take away having been exposed to sites that reveal the genocidal logic of the National Socialist government. Gross (2006, p. 95) asserts that '[t]he mediating link between tourism and commemoration is the ritual practice of memory'. Throughout this book, the transmission of memory – of suffering borne by others – was shown as being instrumental in engendering tourist empathy for the victims of Nazi terror. We should not imagine that this process does not come without an emotional cost for tourists. Liyanage, Coca-Stefaniak and Powell (2015, p. 282) conducted a study that found that:

> Emotions that surface during a tourist's visit to a concentration camp destination can linger after they have left the site. In fact, feelings of sadness, depression, anger and existential questions can haunt visitors for a considerable amount of time after their visit.

Similarly, Brown found that tourists are often overwhelmed by their exposure to memorials in Berlin and attest 'to feelings of sadness, shock, anger, despair and incomprehension' (2015, p. 244).

Lehrer and Milton observe that 'museums, monuments, and heritage sites not only exist as texts that visitors read, but also as sites of practice that are social, embodied and generative' (2011, p. 3). These chapters have demonstrated the truth of this profound observation in relation to tourism. Tourists do not just passively read texts, rather they actively engage with the museum exhibits and seek embodied encounters that might challenge what they think they know about the Holocaust. Whether staring into the voids at the Jewish Museum Berlin, walking in the field of stelae at the *Memorial to the Murdered Jews of Europe*, listening to concentration camp survivor testimony at Bergen-Belsen, trying to decipher one of the colourful *Places of Remembrance* memorial signs, contemplating the enigmatic sculpture *The Abandoned Room*, sitting in silent contemplation in the garden of the Wannsee House, pondering the faux medieval architecture at Wewelsburg, or walking the trench ruins at the *Topography of Terror*, tourists genuinely engage with traces of Nazi criminality. They generate photographs, Facebook and Instagram posts, tweets and emails to friends and family back home, and other personal commemorative gestures that attest to being profoundly moved by their encounters. In turn, these other texts work in tandem with the museums, monuments and memorial sites to inspire others to follow in their footsteps.

I wish to conclude this book by exploring five concise case studies that probe the experiential limits of Nazi-themed tourism in Germany. These case studies explore:

- whether 'tainted' architecture can be wholly divested of its trace of Nazi history when converted into a modern tourist facility;
- how voyeurism underpins undesirable tourism in relation to the Führerbunker in Berlin;
- how the Documentation Centre at Obersalzberg works to thwart undesirable nostalgia for Hitler;
- how the power of an audacious artwork conjures memories of Nazi criminality; and
- whether 3D technology can genuinely augment memorial sites that are empty and thereby enhance a tourist encounter.

Prora: divesting a monumental structure of its Nazi trace

Prora was the name assigned to a vast vacation complex designed in 1936 and built by the Nazis on the island of Rügen along the Baltic coast. Every one of the 10,000 rooms in the slated building complex had a view of the white sandy beach. A veritable Nazi 'megastructure' (Hagen & Ostergren 2006), Prora is – after Albert Speer's rally grounds – the second largest architectural remnant of the Third Reich (Curry 2017). Curry notes: 'the vast beachfront complex, only partially completed before the start of World War II . . . became a mainstay of Third Reich propaganda, which promised affordable seaside vacations of loyal German workers' (2017, n.p.).

The complex never operated as a dedicated holiday complex but was promoted so heavily in propaganda that Nazi workers believed it existed as a holiday destination funded by and affiliated with the Nazi *Kraft durch Freude* (KdF or 'Strength through Joy') programme. One cannot claim that the buildings characterise classic Nazi architecture. Rather, many architects point out that its architectural style is sympathetic to the Bauhaus and Le Corbusier. An architect named

Jürgen Rostock asserts: 'Still, the scale of the project unmistakably bears the ideological imprint of the Nazi regime . . . the way it was built, the way it was planned, the way it looks is all because of Nazi ideology' (cited in Curry 2017, n.p.).

During the war, military battalions trained at Prora. They later participated in the murder and deportation of hundreds of thousands of Jews (Curry 2017). After the war, the buildings – which span as far as the eye can see when contemplating them from the beachfront – fell into disrepair and became something a decrepit ruin. For twenty years the concrete shell decayed until, after reunification, the government converted a part of Prora into a massive barracks and training centre (Curry 2017). Activists founded the Prora Documentation Centre which presented a very basic history of the site to tourists. Jürgen Rostock (cited in Flanagan 2015) notes that the centre emphasises that 'these are not harmless buildings . . . the original purpose for Hitler was the construction of a resort in preparation for the war to come'.

Recently, several portions of the massive building complex have been sold off and redeveloped for middle- to upper-class Germans looking for investment opportunities or a holiday apartment. As Curry (2017, n.p.) indicates in his exploration of the redevelopment, brochures, radio and print advertising emphasise the 'timeless modernist lines of the building' while neglecting any mention of the Nazis. In 2017, the success of the redevelopment meant the last available Prora building – which contains the Prora Documentation Centre – was earmarked for conversion to holiday apartments. As part of the approval process, politician and developers were lobbied to ensure that the development plans might allow for funding for a modest museum, along the lines of the one that already existed. Lucke stated: 'we are not saying that Prora can't be used. It wasn't a concentration camp, or a Gestapo prison . . . but its past needs to be talked about honestly' (cited in Curry 2017, n.p.).

In assessing the redevelopment of this 'onetime Nazi resort', Curry posed the thorny question 'Will the complex's redevelopment whitewash its dark origins?' (2017, n.p.). Nobody is suggesting that this beautiful beachside resort should not be reclaimed and enjoyed as a tourist attraction for those able to holiday here. I would venture to answer Curry's question with an observation. Standing on the beach, the sheer monumentality of the structure cannot be obscured by the developer's fresh paint and floating glass balconies. From the shorefront, the meandering silhouette of the buildings stretch with the horizon, conjuring in the mind's eye the monumentality envisaged by the Nazis. Seen from afar, the buildings' visage will always bear the imprimatur of its Nazi heritage. We can only hope that the Prora Documentation Centre – a mere few rooms in this expansive complex of thousands of rooms – is permitted to remain *in situ* to help an inquisitive tourist better imagine just how such a monumental building came to completely dominate this beautiful beach landscape. While a tourist might only dwell on this history for a moment given the mood of relaxation and tranquillity that envelops the landscape here, such an interlude would be deferential to the complex history of this beguiling place.

The Führerbunker: a voyeuristic tourism simulacra encounter

Jordan notes that 'the centers of Nazi power' have the 'ability to capture the public's fascination evident in television documentaries, films, walking tours and years of newspaper coverage' (2006, p. 184). The Führerbunker is such a site. Celebrated as Hitler's subterranean lair in television documentaries and, more recently, the award-winning feature film *Downfall*, tourists are aware that Adolf Hitler and his mistress Eva Braun spent the last months of their lives sheltering in an underground concrete bunker complex before deciding on a suicide pact in the face of imminent defeat.

In a recent *Irish Times* news article, Scally (2015) pondered why the site of Hitler's death is still a tourist attraction seventy years after the end of the war: 'Groups of tourists arrive and depart at this very site every few minutes and stare in quiet fascination at what little there is to see.' The site, partially destroyed by the Soviets and later obliterated by the East Germans in a joint effort to wipe out landmarks from the Third Reich, now contains no physical trace of its former use. The central irony here is that tourism – a practice long predicated on visitors taking in sights – is reduced to the antithesis of a tourist site, for there is literally nothing to *see*. Indeed, if it were not for a simple square board added in 2006, tourists would be oblivious to the presence of the bunker. Also Ladd observes, even if one could peer underground, there would still be little to *see*: 'Apparently little more than its floor still remains, forty feet below an expanse of playground, parking lot, and lawn adjoining a new apartment building' (1997, pp. 133–134). And yet – in keeping with Scally's observation – on the day that I visited the former bunker location, tourists approached the site, staring at this non-descript domestic space as though it might reveal something worth *seeing*. The head of the municipal archaeology office, Alfred Kernd'l, noted some twenty years ago that 'the thorough removal of the above-ground traces of Hitler has made the search for the Third Reich a largely archaeological one' (cited in Ladd 1997, p. 133). Here tourists must excavate their own memories of television and film documentaries if they are to imagine the bunker at this site which offers so little imaginative stimuli.

Tourists crave sights and experiences and recently a company has sought to capitalise on curiosity about the Führerbunker. Kirschbaum (2016, n.p.) noted 'it was only a matter of time before something about the bunker was added to the city's list of tourist attractions'. In what might be construed as commercial opportunism, in 2016, a German company erected a privately funded exhibit entitled *Berlin Story Bunker* in a former air-raid shelter a short walk from Potsdamer Platz on the tourist trail of central Berlin. Tourists pay €12 to experience the exhibit, which requires them to take a ninety-minute guided tour of the dingy premises. Any extremists are denied entry and if any neo-Nazi sentiment is expressed during the tour, the offender is summarily removed (Kirschbaum 2016, n.p.).

In this building located some two kilometres from the site where the Nazi leader's actual bunker once existed, a replica of Hitler's office has been recreated. The exhibit also contains a cut-away model reconstruction of the entire Führerbunker complex, replete with scarred trees, fortified silos and ventilation shafts. The model's dollhouse-like simulation of the original thirteen-feet-thick concrete roof is missing. One can peer inside this miniature simulacrum and stage the dramas one might have witnessed in the film *Downfall* in the seventeen rooms that are visible. Nevertheless, this scale model is something of a consolation prize, for the main attraction is the recreated office lair of Hitler that one reaches at the culmination of the tour.

In homage to the original room which is supposedly modelled on period photographs and historic records, the verisimilitude extends to carefully curated period furniture and accoutrements: 'The exhibits first visitors were greeted by copies of Hitler's desk, couch, grandfather clock, a portrait of King Frederick II on the wall and an oxygen cylinder in the corner' (Deutsche Welle 2016). Books, an art deco desk clock, magnifying glass, inkwell, Bakelite telephone, ink blotter, a brass miniature statue of Hitler's dog Blondi, table lamp and newspapers adorn the oak desk. Heavy concrete walls help strengthen the impression that one is peering at an underground room. The exhibit has been described as a reconstruction of the space, a tiny room, where Hitler took his own life on 30 April 1945.

What do tourists think as they ponder this strange tableau of the death chamber behind a glass barrier? For some, it may fuel fantasies about Hitler and offer a furtive voyeuristic pleasure. Perhaps others see this replica space as a pathetic prison-like room in which the deranged, dictator cowered from the air raids that were signalling the downfall of his supposed Thousand-Year Reich. The installation has proven controversial. Despite its creators insisting the replica bunker was designed to be educational, officials from state-backed exhibits such as the nearby *Topography of Terror* (as explored in Chapter 2) have dismissed the Führerbunker exhibit as sensationalism (Kirschbaum 2016). Arnd Bauerkaempfer from Berlin's Free University was not convinced about the exhibit's merits. He mused that the replica's 'fake authenticity' carried with it a 'danger that it personalizes the history of Hitler in his bunker' (cited in Kirschbaum 2016, n.p.). Furthermore, to extend his argument, this personalisation could aid in humanising Hitler and his suffering in the bunker. The *Topography of Terror* spokesperson, Kay-Uwe von Damaros, was more strident in her criticism of the showmanship performed by the replica bunker: 'We explain history, document it, and stick to the facts. That is why we cannot support such productions . . . Sensationalism isn't our thing' (Deutsche Welle 2016). The curator of the exhibition, Wieland Giebel, proclaimed that the aim was not to 'create a Hitler show' (Deutsche Welle 2016). And yet the inauthenticity of this exhibit, despite its alluring veneer of realism, has the imprimatur of the worst form of Nazi tourism that carries with it a risk of veneration of a space perhaps best quarantined from sight. Resembling a rudimentary Disney-esque Hitler phantasia, *Berlin Story Bunker* may well provide tourists an experience of what we might crudely term Hitler-land that they desire, but some desires are best left unfulfilled.

Obersalzberg: documenting criminality and combatting nostalgia for Hitler

Aschauer et al. (2017) argue that Obersalzberg is considered a major historical site in the history of National Socialism. Indeed, the Obersalzberg is considered a 'site of perpetrators because here war crimes were planned on a major scale and carried out elsewhere' (Aschauer et al. 2017, p. 159). Hitler is reputed to have proclaimed of the Berghof:[1] 'all of my great plans were developed there' (cited in Neumann 2010, n.p.). Historic photographs from the time show Hitler walking deep in conversation with Heinrich Himmler. It seems plausible to speculate that some aspects of the Holocaust were discussed in this Alpine retreat on the many private walks Hitler took with his SS leader.

Located just above the Bavarian town of Berchtesgaden, Hitler's holiday chalet became a popular pilgrimage spot of avid Nazi supporters who flocked there in the late 1930s hoping to catch a glimpse of their beloved Führer (Kaplan 2007; Landsman 2004; Walden 2014). The area was secured by security fences, adding to the mystique that this was Hitler's private mountain idyll and the spiritual home of Nazism. Kaplan notes that in propaganda films taken at the Obersalzberg: 'Hitler poses with animals or children, conveying a relaxed alpine man-of-the-people image' (2007, p. 246). Accordingly, the Obersalzberg functioned in the Nazi imaginary as 'the beautiful, secretive, mysterious place in which the Führer became himself' (Kaplan 2007, p. 262).

Knauss captures the importance of Obersalzberg, writing: 'It was the innermost citadel, the real fortress for which the Second World war was fought, the "Alpine Fortress", the most profound and precious heart of Hitler's Reich' (cited in Kaplan 2007, p. 262). A seemingly never-ending supply of vivid-coloured documentary footage of Hitler on the terrace of the Berghof and dramatisations like *Band of Brothers* have done much to keep Obersalzberg and in the imagination of tourists. However, two factors thankfully work to delimit Hitler-themed tourism in the area. First, after the bombed ruins were set on fire by the SS, looters took away or destroyed any relics associated with the site. American soldiers also took any small objects they could salvage – such as swastika-emblazoned porcelain plates and silver cutlery with eagle motifs – as war souvenirs. A visiting war photographer, Lee Miller, noted at the time: 'There isn't even a piece left for a museum on the great war criminal' (cited in Kaplan 2007, p. 265). Second, no physical traces of the Berghof remain to sustain any Nazi-themed tourism. In 1996, Bavaria's state government took over control of what Neumann termed 'a historically charged compound' (2010, n.p.). She elaborates:

> To keep away those who might harbour nostalgia for the Nazi past, officials drew up plans to build a luxury hotel and a documentation center on the site, and the government began demolishing the Berghof's remaining walls and digging out their foundations below ground.
>
> (2010, n.p.)

In the face of a landscape divested of any trace of Hitler's Berghof, the Documentation Centre, which opened in 1999, must now bear the weight of tourism scrutiny in Obersalzberg.

Aschauer et al. note that: 'Virtually nothing remains of Hitler's Berghof as a key site where decisions relating to National Socialist crimes took place and the bunker lies hidden beneath the idyllic scenery'(2017, p. 164). Housed in the renovated ruins of Hitler's former guest house, the building was renovated at a cost of 4.7 million Deutschmarks and consists of some 900 text documents, images and historical items (Landsman 2004). Some have criticised the centre's architecture as being timid and 'indistinguishable from other villas in Berchtesgaden' (Landsman 2004, p. 64). The logic is that its presence is deliberately camouflaged. However, an architecturally audacious design may have looked very unsympathetic in the landscape. In any event, the centre is well-promoted and, while not a tourist magnet like the museums and memorial in Berlin, attracts respectable tourist numbers for its modest size.

When the Documentation Centre opened, a journalist remarked that it would function as 'an alibi, providing a green light to "build over the old shame"' (cited in Landsman 2004, p. 65). The journalist was alluding to plans to build a new Inter-Continental resort hotel in the area. Such a criticism seems ill-conceived, for the notion of building over shame is a flawed analogy. The ruins of the former Nazi buildings in Obersalzberg have already been long hidden from view. The power of the Documentation Centre is that it pays homage to the former existence of these Nazi dwellings in a manner that is not sensationalistic. To that end, an interactive display case in the centre contains a scale model of the Obersalzberg. Push buttons highlight infamous sites such as the so-called 'Eagles' Nest' (*Kehlsteinhaus*), Hermann Göring's Alpine lodge, and other long since vanished buildings from the National Socialist period. The model helps visitors imagine the vast extent of the Führer's off-limits area, without venerating it with enlarged period photographs.

Landsman describes the experience of encountering the exhibition well, employing an evocative altitudinal metaphor: 'As if tracing a precipitous descent from the breathtaking heights of the mountaintop to the lowest depths of Nazi terror, the exhibition leads one further and further downwards into a set of bunkers' (2004, p. 61). Fittingly, in the bunker one is confronted with the horrors of the Holocaust. One can listen to recorded audio testimony of two Jewish women describing their experiences in Auschwitz and Bergen-Belsen. The Holocaust has also been situated at the Documentation Centre in the realm of the visual. As Aschauer et al. (2017, p. 169) note, a 'confronting photograph of four female victims [from Latvia] stands for an individual fate in a period of mass murder: the horror of the Holocaust is given a face'. Indeed, Aschauer et al. laud the power of the Documentation Centre to facilitate arresting tourist encounters: 'a visit to the Obersalzberg is an emotional experience that for many people that "gets under the skin" and can possibly never be forgotten' (2017, p. 169).

In documenting the Holocaust – a Nazi crime so geographically removed from our communal images of the Obersalzberg – the Documentation Centre demystifies this space as a mountain idyll, reminding us that crime was implicated in this alternative seat of Nazi government. Any vestige of nostalgia for Hitler, underwritten by filmic images of him relaxing with Eva Braun on the terrace of the Berghof, dissipates when one ventures into the bunker and encounters photographs precipitating murder of Jewish women in the depths of the Documentation Centre.

Gottfried Helnwein's *Selektion*: exhortation and lamentation

Huyssen (2003) has argued that the memory of historical trauma has a unique power to generate works of art. This fourth case study explores the art of Gottfried Helnwein, 'an artist who has committed himself to reminding the world of the Holocaust' (O'Donoghue 2008, n.p.). O'Donoghue argues that by placing his work in the public realm 'he attempts to keep Holocaust memory alive by instigating a dialogue' (2008, n.p.). Helnwein's enormous paintings often conflate Nazi and religious imagery – as typified by *Epiphany I (Adoration of the Magi)* – in which a beautiful Aryan woman holds a baby whose face resembles that of an infant Hitler while five SS officers look on admiringly. However, it is artwork entitled *Selektion (Ninth November Night)* that I wish to discuss here as I think it illustrates how a spontaneous pubic encounter can rupture the present and provoke passers-by, locals and tourists alike, to think about the Holocaust in a radically new way.

Selektion was first exhibited in 1988, the fifty-year anniversary of *Kristallnacht* (the night of broken glass)[2] in which an unprecedented wave of violence was unleashed on synagogues, Jewish-owned businesses and Jewish citizens on the evening of 9 November 1938 (Jacobs 2008). In an interview, Helnwein explains why *Kristallnacht* so captured his attention and inspired the creation of *Selektion* and his adoption of the phrase 'Ninth November Night' as part of the title of the work:

> *Kristallnacht* was really a crucial point in time because it was the moment when suddenly the Germans openly went against the Jews. Thousands of synagogues burnt down in one night, all the businesses and stores were destroyed, they were chased in the streets, the people were dead and that was open killing.

> (as cited in O'Donoghue 2008, n.p.)

While there are some fifty fixed *Kristallnacht* memorials all over Germany, most are conventional sculptures of torn and charred Torah scrolls (Jacobs 2008), whereas Helnwein's artwork is impermanent. For *Selektion*, Helnwein photographed children in muted pastel colours with sepia tonal properties. Some children look directly at the viewer, other look downwards and avert our gaze. Affixed to ropes and strung using tension on giant steel awnings, individual spotlights afforded each individual portrait an eerie spectral presence when illuminated at night.

O'Donoghue (2008, n.p.) notes that Helnwein had difficulty finding a sponsor, as 'his planned installation of haunted children's faces was unlike the muted, conceptualist holocaust memorials usually commissioned by City Councils in Germany'. The City of Cologne was worried about controversy and refused permission to exhibit the work, but eventually Helnwein was able to organise the first public exhibition of *Selektion* on a private site sanctioned by Deutsche Bahn AG railway in Cologne. Having secured this location, the resonance of the work became even more marked as Helnwein noted 'it was the railways that deported them to the concentration camps' (cited in O'Donoghue 2008, n.p.).

The first exhibition of *Selektion* stretched from the Ludwig museum in Cologne to the main train station, a spectacle encountered by thousands of people a day commuting to other cities (O'Donoghue 2008, n.p.). O'Donoghue captures the provocative nature of the work well, writing: 'Each passer-by was confronted with larger-than-life children's faces; painted white, they appear almost death like, lined up in a seemingly endless row as if for concentration camp selection' (2008, n.p.). Controversial artworks, particularly those that evoke memories of crime, are often attacked and vandalised (Young 2005). After hanging for two days, the mural was vandalized and someone 'slashed' the throats of some of children in the panels. Helnwein patched the damage up crudely with black masking tape, but left evidence of the attack evident for others to see when they encountered the work (O'Donoghue 2018, n.p.). *Selektion (Ninth November Night)* has since garnered support from municipal authorities all over Germany and has been exhibited in Heilbronn (1990), Saarbrucken (1993), Oberhausen (1995) and Berlin (1996). It has also been exhibited internationally in Japan, Austria, Russia, Switzerland and Ireland.

An audacious artwork, *Selektion (Ninth November Night)* offers no consolation to any tourist who might have stumbled across it in the streets of the cities in which it was exhibited. For it insinuates the Holocaust into the present. As we contemplate the pallid deathly faces of the children, their T-shirts, and contemporary hairstyles place us firmly in the *here and now*. Divested of any trace of nostalgia, the beseeching and forlorn expressions in the portraits remind us of children we know and love. While we do not think of them as imperilled – we know the spectre of Nazism is long gone – we nevertheless recall they are photographic proxies. For they stand in for murdered children whose faces we cannot see. We pause to think 'imagine a child I love selected for death', and the horror of the Holocaust assails us. Gazing at this artwork, we are exhorted to imagine a suffering that is almost unimaginable: the industrialised murder of children. To my mind, the artwork's power is that it also works as a powerful lamentation for the countless children who are not depicted in the work; the ones whom we know were shipped like cattle to the extermination centres in the east. In collapsing the *past* and the *present* – the *seen* and the *unseen* – Helnwein provides us with a work that tests the limits of memorial culture by daring to conjure the spectral presence of dead children in an artwork that borrows living children to evoke the fate of their former *doppelgängers*. It is a sublime ephemeral artwork; one that deserves to be rehearsed in other German cities for visitors and locals alike to encounter.

Memoryscapes: virtual tourism versus 'being there'

Recent developments in digital technology are creating novel ways through which people can connect with Holocaust memories and testimony. A concept called *Virtual Holocaust Memoryscapes* is being devolved at by Leeds University to create an immersive experience that uses virtual reality technology – as employed in 3D gaming – to facilitate a connection with Holocaust memories. The logic underpinning *Virtual Holocaust Memoryscapes* is that a 360-degree map of a site can be populated with relevant archive material such as films, photographs, diary extracts, news footage and oral testimonies to 'create an interactive and immersive virtual environment' (Worldwide Universities Network 2018). In an interview, Dr Matt Boswell stated: 'We want to see how it changes our understanding of the past and history and the way we engage with places like Bergen-Belsen, where so little remains on the ground' (Worldwide Universities Network 2018). While one cannot dispute that digitisation of Holocaust memories and images is a profoundly important pursuit, particularly with fewer survivors left with each passing year, I have reservations about the core logic underpinning this project as it relates to tourism. The *Virtual Holocaust Memoryscapes* research makes two key claims: 'The virtual memoryscape could be accessed via an app or website – allowing people anywhere in the world to visit a Holocaust memorial site – or be used on the ground, making a visit to the sites a more powerful experience' (Worldwide Universities Network 2018). Visiting a site from anywhere in the world may well have educational benefits, particularly for those who are curious but have limited time or financial resources to travel. In the context of the Holocaust, Pollock has cautioned against 'vicarious tourism by film' (2003, p. 186) and I wonder if we might extend her concerns to include vicarious tourism aided by 3D technology. Having visited Bergen-Belsen recently (see Chapter 5), I am not convinced that a so-called immersive experience would make for a 'more powerful' experience. The recently completed Documentation and Information Centre already offers a profoundly moving experience where tourists can encounter original camp artefacts, survivor testimony, photographic and moving images that capture the essence of suffering and death that prevailed during the camp's history. Does this wealth of extant resources and archive material really need to be augmented with 3D technology that reconstructs the long since demolished buildings and barrack structures?

The trope of *absence* has informed my discussion of many Holocaust and memorial sites discussed in this book. Sometimes absence works to remind us of what has been lost and forces us to employ our imagination. The need to fill a void with meaning is understandable, but I wonder if resurrecting a demolished structure to create a virtual landscape is a flawed pursuit, despite its digital allure. Would peering through a 3D headset and seeing a barrack photograph (or simulated likeness) *really* make an encounter at Belsen more powerful that the vast sway of nature that now envelopes the space? In terms of memorialisation, I think we sometimes need to resist the urge, however well intentioned, to fill absent spaces with things to look at. The Documentation Centre provides so much to *see* and *hear* to fill this largely empty landscape with meaning. Sometimes, as many tourists well know, there is no substitute for 'being there' – even if that 'there' is a vast empty space where nature now intrudes.

An explanatory document that promotes the memoryscape technology asserts: 'And – for sites like Bergen-Belsen – how different will it feel to connect those now open spaces to archive material showing what happened there over seventy years ago?' (Worldwide Universities Network 2018). Such a claim seems misguided. For one can already immerse oneself in the Documentation Centre and use its emotionally charged content to assemble a powerful sense of what this vanished camp looked like and comprehend what happened here. Tourists crave so-called 'immersion experiences' (Dalton 2015; Knudsen 2011) whereby role playing, and other techniques can supposedly supplement a site's ability to engender empathy for the plight of former prisoners. The irony here is that Bergen-Belsen already offers an immersive experience. Anyone who has recently taken in the harrowing exhibits and then ventured outside – into the vast emptiness – already knows that this is the case. To my mind, offering a set of 3D glasses to tourists would, paradoxically, occlude their imagination of this extremely solemn site.

Coda: the tourist encounter as commemorative act

Reynolds wisely reminds us: 'The fact that tourists can never inhabit the Holocaust itself, only its traces and its representations, opens the door to questions about absence and presence, about the past and the present' (2018, p. 23). The chapters in this book have explored how tourists readily seek out imaginative encounters with memorials, museum artefacts and other conduits in the space of the city that enable them to fathom the paradoxical absence/presence of victims of Nazi violence and crime in contemporary Germany. Some traces are *authentic* (e.g., Wannsee House or *Topography of Terror*), others are contrived, designed to disrupt the ordinariness of the space of the city and insinuate Nazi crime into the *here and now* of the moment. Tourists encounter these traces by conscious choice (e.g., visiting the Jewish Museum or Holocaust Memorial) or happenstance (e.g., walking over *Stolpersteine*, glancing up a street sign adorned with a colourful picture). The manner of the encounter is not important, but rather what happens when that encounter occurs.

Ruminating on what she terms 'imaginative encounters' at sites of mass murder, Popescu insists that:

> Simply accepting the ruin and the loss, and acknowledging that the sites do not speak, is not easy to come to terms with. One is compelled to draw on imagination to animate the artefacts and geography of the place and invest them with meaning. Searching for meaning means creating a meaningful experience.

> (2016, p. 285)

Her comments strike me as applicable to tourists who crave a similar commemorative experience in a public space devoted to some aspect of Nazi criminality in Germany. Face-to-face with a murder site, a museum that gestures to the crimes or a memorial that testifies to the victims, this book has explored the vital role that imagination – borne out of an experiential memorial encounter – plays in helping the tourist bridge the cognitive dissonance of being here *now* and trying to imagine the *then* of the past. Each encounter that a tourist has at a Holocaust site or memorial, planned or unplanned, has the potential to become a commemorative act; so long as that individual tourist is prepared to harness their empathy and linger in the space long enough to hear the faint – almost imperceptible – whispers of the departed.[3]

Notes

1 The Berghof was Adolf Hitler's home in the Obersalzberg of the Bavarian Alps near Berchtesgaden in Bavaria.
2 *Kristallnacht* is a somewhat contested term in Germany. Many history books and government literature replace it with the term *Reichspogromnacht* which unambiguously implies crime by using the term *pogrom* (Jacobs 2008).
3 Here I pay homage to the writer Paul Auster's evocative account of an aural experience when visiting Bergen-Belsen in the 1970s. Writing in the second person: 'You heard the bones of the dead howl in anguish, howl in pain, howl in a roaring cascade of full-throated, ear-splitting torment' (2012, p. 148).

References

Aschauer, W, Weichbold, M, Foidl, M & Drecoll, A 2017, 'Obersalzberg as a realm of experience on the quality of visitors' experiences at National Socialist places of remembrance', *Worldwide Hospitality and Tourism Themes*, vol. 9, no. 2, pp. 158–174.

Auster, P 2012, *Winter journal*, Faber & Faber, London.

Brown, L 2015, 'Memorials to the victims of Nazism: the impact on tourists in Berlin', *Journal of Tourism and Cultural Change*, vol. 13, no. 3, pp. 244–260.

Curry, A 2017, 'Remaking a onetime Nazi resort', *The Journal of the American Institute of Architects*, 21 November, www.architectmagazine.com/design/remaking-a-one-time-nazi-resort_o, viewed 29 May 2019.

Czaplicka, J 1995 'History, aesthetics, and contemporary commemorative practice in Berlin', *New German Critique*, no. 65, pp. 155–187.

Dalton, D 2015, *Dark tourism and crime*, Routledge, London.

Dekel, I 2013, *Mediation at the Holocaust memorial in Berlin*, Palgrave Macmillan, London.

Deutsche Welle 2016, 'Exhibit replica of Hitler's bunker opens in Berlin', *Deutsche Welle, 27 October*, www.dw.com/en/exhibit-replica-of-hitlers-bunker-opens-in-berlin/a-36178824, viewed 29 May 2019.

Flanagan, P 2015, 'Hitler Hotel: see inside the Fuhrer's 10,000 room "Butlins" resort after 70 empty years', *Mirror*, 19 July, www.mirror.co.uk/news/world-news/hitler-hotel-see-inside-fuhrers-6096616, viewed 29 May 2019.

Gross, AS 2006, 'Holocaust tourism in Berlin: global memory, trauma and the "negative sublime"', *Journeys*, vol. 7 no. 2, pp. 73–100.

Hagen, J & Ostergren, R 2006, 'Spectacle, architecture and place at the Nuremberg party rallies: projecting a Nazi vision of past, present and future', *Cultural Geographies*, vol. 13, no. 2, pp. 157–181.

Huyssen, A 2003, *Present pasts: urban palimpsests and the politics of memory*, Stanford University Press, Stanford.

Jacobs, J 2008, 'Memorializing the sacred: Kristallnacht in German national memory', *Journal for the Scientific Study of Religion*, vol. 47, no. 3, pp. 485–498.

Jordan, JA 2006, *Structures of memory: understanding urban change in Berlin and beyond*, Stanford University Press, Stanford.

Kaplan, BA 2007, 'Masking Nazi violence in the beautiful landscape of the Obersalzberg', *Comparative Literature*, vol. 59, no. 3, pp. 241–268.

Kirschbaum, E 2016, 'A controversial replica of Adolf Hitler's bunker now on display in Germany', *Chicago Tribune*, 12 November, www.chicagotribune.com/news/nation-world/ct-hitler-bunker-german-20161112-story.html, viewed 29 May 2019.

Knudsen, BT 2011, 'Deportation day: live history lesson', *Museum International*, vol. 63, no. 1–2, pp. 109–118.

Ladd, A 1997, *The ghosts of Berlin: confronting German history in the urban landscape*, Chicago University Press, Chicago.

Landsman, M 2004, 'Balancing past and present', *Jewish Quarterly*, vol. 51, no. 1, pp. 59–66.

Lehrer, E & Milton, C 2011, 'Introduction: witnesses to witnessing', in E Lehrer, C Milton & E Patterson (eds), *Curating difficult knowledge*, Palgrave Macmillan, London, pp. 1–19.

Liyanage, S, Coca-Stefaniak, JA & Powell, R 2015, 'Dark destinations – visitor reflections from a Holocaust memorial site', *International Journal of Tourism Cities*, vol. 1, no. 4, pp. 282–298.

Niven, B, 2001, *Facing the Nazi past: united Germany and the legacy of the Third Reich*, Routledge, London.

Neumann, C 2010, 'The twisted legacy of Hitler's mountain retreat', *Spiegel Online*, 1 April, www.spiegel.de/international/germany/the-fuehrer-s-flagstones-the-twisted-legacy-of-hitler-s-mountain-retreat-a-686221.html, viewed 29 May 2019.

O'Donoghue, K 2008, 'Gottfried Helnwein: memorialising the Holocaust', unpublished dissertation, http://gottfried-helnwein-essays.com/Dissertation.htm, viewed 29 May 2019.

Pollock, G 2003, 'Holocaust tourism: being there, looking back and the ethics of spatial memory', in *Visual culture and tourism*, Berg, Oxford, pp. 175–189.

Popescu, DI 2016, 'Post-witnessing the concentration camps: Paul Auster's and Angela Morgan Cutler's investigative and imaginative encounters with sites of mass murder', *Holocaust Studies*, vol. 22, no. 2–3, pp. 274–288.

Reynolds, D 2016, 'Consumers or witnesses? Holocaust tourists and the problem of authenticity', *Journal of Consumer Culture*, vol. 16, no. 2, pp. 334–353.

Reynolds, D 2018, *Postcards from Auschwitz: Holocaust tourism and the meaning of remembrance*, New York University Press, New York.

Rohr, S 2010, '"Genocide pop": the Holocaust as media event', in S Komor & S Rohr (eds), *The Holocaust, art, and taboo*, Universitätsverlag, Heidelberg, pp. 155–178.

Scally, D 2015, 'Site of Hitler's death still a tourist attraction 70 years on', *Irish Times*, 30 April, www.irishtimes.com/news/world/europe/site-of-hitler-s-death-still-a-tourist-attraction-70-years-on-1.2194156, viewed 29 May 2019.

Walden, G 2014, *Hitler's Berchtesgaden: a guide to Third Reich sites in the Berchtesgaden area*, Fonthill Media, Stroud.

Worldwide Universities Network 2018, *Using digital technology to preserve Holocaust memory and place*, Worldwide Universities Network, https://wun.ac.uk/article/using-digital-technology-to-preserve-holocaust-memory-and-places, viewed 29 May 2019.

Young, A 2005, *Judging the image: art, value, law*, Routledge, London.

Index